Freedom and Responsibility in Broadcasting

SPEAKERS

LeRoy Collins
Newton N. Minow
Louis L. Jaffe
Roscoe L. Barrow

DISCUSSANTS

Warren K. Agee
Fairfax M. Cone
John E. Coons
   Conference Director
Peter Goelet
John W. Guider
Charles H. King
Clair R. McCollough
Ralph McGill
Sig Mickelson
Nathaniel L. Nathanson
Morris S. Novik
W. Theodore Pierson
Ward L. Quaal
J. Leonard Reinsch
   Conference Chairman
Sol Taishoff
John Taylor

Freedom and Responsibility in Broadcasting

EDITED BY
John E. Coons

NORTHWESTERN UNIVERSITY PRESS/1961

Preface

by John E. Coons

The first message on Mr. Morse's telegraph was a self-effacing, "What hath God wrought." Whether television's first message gave credit to such a transcendental source is unrecorded, but by 1960 in many quarters radically different origins for television were being suggested.

Each morning's newspaper recorded assaults on the television industry from cultural leaders, churchmen, and educators who laid at the doorstep of the unhappy medium calamities ranging from juvenile delinquency to the divorce rate. Even some spokesmen of the industry itself were critical of television's performance. Nevertheless, television had its defenders, the shows went on, and the broadcasters' profits climbed higher than ever. Thus the controversy remained in essence a paper war until, in 1961, the advent of a new national administration gave to the problem an entirely different dimension. Criticism of the industry from a high official and the acceleration of government investigations made it clear that, whatever the need for reform, if any, broadcasters now faced the real possibility of more vigorous governmental control.

Wide disagreement existed concerning the proper role of government as one among many institutions and forces which influence program content. It was argued forcefully by some that the market alone must determine content and that free competition in the long run would purge the undesirable from the air waves or at least provide acceptable alternatives for the viewing and listening public. At the opposite end of the ideological spectrum, others argued from a public-utility analogy based on the limited number of frequencies; they urged firm governmental controls, sometimes adding partial public ownership. In between there appeared a multitude of schemes for reform.

The Northwestern University School of Law considered it appropriate at this stage of the debate to invite leaders of opinion in the communications field to meet in an informal and "neutral" atmosphere to consider the state of the broadcasting industry and the divergent proposals for its repair. Twenty conferees came to the School from government, broadcasting, law, education, and the newspaper industry. On August 3 and 4, 1961, they met in what was probably the first such conference under academic auspices. This book comprises the entire proceedings of that conference, including addresses made to the public session of the conference by LeRoy Collins, President of the National Association of Broadcasters, and Newton N. Minow, Chairman of the Federal Communications Commission. Also printed in full are the papers delivered at the two seminar sessions of the conference by Professor Louis L. Jaffe and Dean Roscoe L. Barrow and the comments on these papers by former Commissioner Charles H. King and Mr. W. Theodore Pierson. Toward the end of the book will be found the edited transcript of the seminar conversations of the conferees and an extensive monograph by Mr. Joel Rosenbloom of the Federal Communications Commission, who explores the basis and extent of the Commission's power with regard to program content.

As conference director I have already expressed the thanks of the University and the Linthicum Foundation to Leonard Reinsch, whose persuasive talent brought to the conference a splendid galaxy of industry and newspaper representatives. Now in the role of editor I wish to thank him for his judicious chairmanship of the seminar conferences, which produced a readable and often exciting transcript. In addition thanks go to my colleagues Nathaniel Nathanson for his invaluable counsels in planning the conference and Willard Pedrick for the germinal idea that was our starting point. Finally, of course, the University and Foundation are grateful to the speakers and conferees whose contributions now appear in enduring form in this book, and to the Westinghouse Broadcasting Company whose generous aid has made its printing possible.

This book achieves in some measure three ends. First it reveals in more than a superficial way some of the relevant facts about broadcasting life which must be taken into account in assessing the wisdom of proposed changes. Second, in these pages most of the presently conceivable solutions to the problems of programming are subjected to analysis—some in detail, others in at least suggestive fashion. Third, and equally significant, the conference and this book stand as a uniquely revealing record of the reaction of the communications world to the real or supposed threat of governmental restraints.

Contents

Freedom and Responsibility in Broadcasting

FREEDOM THROUGH RESPONSIBILITY
by LeRoy Collins

Nothing could be more timely than the theme "Freedom and Responsibility in Broadcasting," for these are testing times not only for broadcasting but for our whole nation. Nor could anything be more pertinent, for in a real sense freedom and responsibility are inseparable. We can have no real freedom without responsibility, just as responsibility needs a free soil to nourish its fulfillment.

The degree of freedom which American broadcasting—indeed, America itself—is to enjoy will be determined by how broadcasters and other Americans measure up in the exercise of responsibility. To interpret this correctly, we must consider responsibility in the context of current circumstances. What is the proper meaning of freedom and responsibility in this day—in this nation, in this world which encircles us—fashioned by the constant and startling challenges of change? These changes have brought upon America countless new political, economic, and social demands, which can no more be solved in terms of the thinking of 30 years ago than the needs of 30 years ago could be met with the thinking of 300 years ago.

I start from the premise that broadcasting in America today is an essential component of our national purpose. It has a great responsibility to spark free enterprise, but it also has a great moral responsibility which goes beyond a profit-and-loss statement and the marketing of goods—a responsibility to contribute constructively to the enhancement of the character, enlightenment, citizenship, and stature of the American people. This latter is not a cross to bear; it is broadcasting's glory. It is a responsibility which most broadcasters, through magnificent efforts, are attempting to discharge. And this is a far better nation because of them.

We would be foolish, of course, to consider the responsibilities of broadcasting without understanding that, in order to be in a position to serve at all, broadcasting under our system must first exist as a successful business. And it is perhaps America's most complex business.

First of all, it is a big business. Ninety-nine per cent of Americans are within the sound of radio and 90 per cent in sight of television. We now have four radio sets per family in America. And broadcasting has become so accepted as an essential item that today there are fewer American homes without radio and television sets than there are without indoor plumbing.

Since the advent of radio, more than $1 billion has been invested in broadcasting facilities in this country. The American people have a still larger investment in broadcasting, for during the same period they invested more than $24 billion in radio and television receiving equipment. And last year alone, advertisers spent more than $2¼ billion for radio and television messages moving American goods to market.

Yet, broadcasting is also small business. Out of the nearly 5,000 radio stations and more than 500 television stations, the biggest portion by far are small, individually operated facilities serving our smaller communities.

Broadcasting is a variegated business. For example, it includes the giant networks—three for television and four for radio—as well as group and individually-owned stations, network-affiliated as well as independent stations, FM and AM radio, daytime broadcasters and clear-channel operators, stations which specialize in classical music and some which broadcast almost wholly in foreign languages. These various elements of broadcasting are keenly competitive with one another; yet they all share many common problems and interests.

Yes, conducting a mass-communications medium like broadcasting is no simple accomplishment.

If ours were a static, uniform society, it would be easier. But it is not. America is a dynamic nation composed of many composite cultures, all of them in constant change. If ours were a society in which the state controlled the means of communication as an instrument of its own policy, it would be easier. But it is not. If ours were an economy in which the production and distribution of goods were planned and carried out by the state, it would be easier to conduct a mass-communications medium. Then it would be a question of what those who fixed the policies of government decided the people should receive. There would be no pressure of the market place. But in America the basic means of communication, including the most powerful of them all, broadcasting, is run by free, highly competitive enterprise.

Complicating the picture further is the fact that broadcasting, because of the technical nature of its means of communication, must receive its license from the government. It therefore becomes a free enterprise under permit subject to grant and renewal by the government, but with neither the advantages nor the disadvantages of a utility franchise monopoly.

Thus, broadcasting must earn its own economic support and at the same time live up to its social and moral and legal responsibility to operate in the public interest. There is nothing else like it on the American scene or in the world.

Within this setting, then, where does the proper role of government lie?

I begin with the conviction that broadcasting—more than any other means of communication and especially because it is the most powerful and effective means of communication—must be creative. Therefore broadcasting must be free—free in the full meaning of the word—because only those who truly are free can have the range of vision and action necessary to create.

Sometimes we tend to get tangled up in Fourth-of-July semantics when discussing concepts such as "freedom" and "liberty," so perhaps I should define these terms as I am using them here. I think there is a valuable lesson to be learned from the ancient distinction between the two words "liberty" and "freedom." Often now they are incorrectly used interchangeably.

Originally, the word for "liberty" was used in the sense that one may be "at liberty" to do as he pleases. It implied total absence of restraints, whether imposed by others or by one's self.

Originally the word for "freedom," on the other hand, had a more refined connotation. It implied understanding of the world about us, achievement of proper relationships with it, and, thereby, release from and ascendancy above what otherwise would be the restrictive and limiting forces which operate in life. In fact, the word for "freedom" bore a close kinship with the word for "truth," almost as if it were a precursor of the later Christian concept that "ye shall know the truth, and the truth shall make you free."

In a democratic society such as ours, we as individuals are at liberty to do many things which, because of their injurious effects on the rest of society, may cause us to lose some of our larger freedoms. And, by the same token, we are able to expand our larger freedoms through the responsible application of restraints and discipline in the exercise of liberties.

America was founded upon the relatively new concept, so far as the history of nations goes, that the people are capable of deciding their own destinies and that the government is their instrument, not the other way around. The corollary to this is the concept that if, indeed, the people are to be allowed to make decisions, then the means of communication—the one ingredient which is essential to the free exchange of ideas—must remain independent of any governmental thought-control.

No doubt government could destroy freedom of broadcasting by laying the heavy hand of dictation on broadcasters. But I am not afraid of government, for I have found by some direct experience that government is the instrument through which the people administer democracy and make it work. In fact, government is the only agency through which all the people can work together to advance their common interests.

We are fortunate in having freedom of speech guaranteed to broadcasters as to all of us by the First Amendment to the Constitution and further safeguarded by express anti-censorship provisions in the Federal Communications Act. Thus the people have laid out important basic safeguards. The people in this country are the strongest allies broadcasters have, and we rightfully expect government, as their representative, to be equally the ally of broadcasters.

Because there is a limit to the broadcast spectrum—not room for everyone who might want to broadcast to do so whenever and wherever he pleases—the government has prescribed a set of engineering ground rules. These are administered by the Federal Communications Commission, which is the agency established by law for the technical regulation of broadcasting.

No one questions the need for ground rules. The big argument centers over the degree of regulation—indeed, whether there should be any regulation beyond the purely technical. Some assert that the FCC has no proper or lawful concern with programming. I shall be quite candid and say I disagree with this position.

The FCC may not substitute its taste and judgment of programming for that of a licensee. But, at the same time, we should not expect the FCC to close its eyes to abuses in programming reflecting a gross lack of qualifications to enjoy the license privileges. Furthermore, the FCC should be expected to hold every licensee accountable for sincere efforts to serve the public interest in accordance with the representations which he made in his application for original or renewal license.

This has long been the position of the National Association of Broadcasters. It is a position which our legal staff continues to find completely sound, based upon statutory requirements and judicial interpretations. I believe that the vast majority of broadcasters concur in this view, and I stand with them.

Every member of the FCC knows that I am dedicated to the proposition of free broadcasting. At the first sign of governmental abuse of the broadcasters' constitutional rights I am prepared to carry the fight not only to the FCC and the Congress but to every home in America, beginning with the one on Pennsylvania Avenue.

I believe broadcasters' best interests, and the public interest, can be served most effectively and intelligently by calm, candid, and sincere appraisals. A recent decision of the FCC denying a new license application for FM service in Elizabeth, New Jersey, has been assailed by some trade-press editorialists as constituting "censorship." I cannot accept this view. The applicant in his filing simply duplicated a form used for Alameda, California, and for Berwyn, Illinois. The Commission found that he made no effort whatever to determine the needs to be served in Elizabeth, nor were his program proposals designed to serve those needs. For the FCC to hold this showing to be inadequate was not "censorship." It was, in my judgment, merely an effort to assure responsibility in the public interest in line with duty imposed by law.

Most broadcasters I have talked with approve this decision. Actually, it strongly supports the professional posture of broadcasting we are working to achieve. It elevates the expected stature of a broadcaster above mere technical and financial competence. Perhaps it portends the application of some brakes on the debilitating policy of putting more and more broadcasters in the radio field. And, of further great importance, it places emphasis upon the proposition that the needs for service in a given community are individual to that community—that what may be good in Alaska may not be good in Florida; that what works in California should not be presumed to fit New Jersey.

In urging broadcasters to improve their product, Chairman Minow is not speaking just for himself or just for the commission he heads. He is speaking for the President of the United States. He is speaking for the people as he interprets their best interests and needs under law. I am convinced that the attitude of the federal government is one of high respect and admiration for broadcasting. But I also know that broadcasters are expected to make greater efforts to meet the broad needs of the people this year and in those to follow.

I disagree with those in our ranks who would view the actions of the FCC as dealing death blows to freedom. By draping the honorable flags of free speech and free enterprise around the shaky shoulders of those who abuse liberties in their own selfish interests, we will succeed not in protecting but in jeopardizing the good name and welfare and freedom of the overwhelming number of broadcasters who are acting responsibly. It is not fair to those broadcasters who are doing such a splendid job in so many important ways, often at considerable financial sacrifice, to be lumped together with the few fast-buck and public-be-damned operators.

Now, I certainly do not feel that broadcasting is without its dangers. There is even serious danger of losing freedom through influences not specifically associated with government. The loss of freedom can be by self-imposed or self-indulged limitations, and against this the Constitution affords little or no protection as it does in the area of free speech.

The other day I saw on the back page of a paper a little item describing how a man who built a new county jail became its first prisoner. It seems that, as soon as the building was completed, this workman went out on the town, got drunk, and had the distinction of being the first person to be locked in.

I frankly worry about broadcasters becoming locked up in jails they build for themselves. Creativity, for example, is now being curtailed by slavish addiction in some quarters to audience measurements or ratings of questionable validity and administered outside any qualitative control of broadcasters. There are broadcasters also who pull down the shade and refuse to benefit from constructive criticism, blandly attributing it to calculated competitive efforts of others in the advertising business or to "crackpots" or to small groups of "eggheads" with limited tastes. The advertising cost-per-thousand concept, rigidly embraced, encourages mediocrity, just as program-copying makes for dull conformity and serious curtailment of the diversity distinctive to a free society.

Actually, there would be something wrong with the American people if they were not complaining about broadcasting's shortcomings. If they were ready to accept broadcasting "as is"—if they were willing to accept the bad in programming because of the good in it—this would be an indication either of weakness in their own aspirations or of their resignation to the false idea that broadcasting is incapable of improvement.

But the American people are not weak. Nor are broadcasters. And broadcasters are not marking time, content in a posture of defensiveness. We are pushing forward, to improve; we are applying the best minds and resources in broadcasting, to become better. We do not want improvement forced upon us by the government or by our critics.

Our NAB board of directors recently approved the development of a plan for the establishment of a Research and Training Center, in association with one of our leading universities, where we can explore the myriad problems broadcasters encounter from day to day and find intelligent, dependable answers. This will be a place for advanced research on the basic issues of broadcasting and a place for training broadcasters in a wide variety of fields.

To maintain high standards, NAB is expanding greatly the scope and effectiveness of its radio and television codes. We are developing a unified Code Authority, under a director of outstanding competence, who will give leadership and strength to advancing further the profession's standards of good practice.

These are giant new steps to advance freedom through responsibility.

I knew a university once, with a great football team that drew capacity crowds to the stadium every Saturday and brought national sporting fame to its campus. But something happened. A scandal developed over recruitment practices, and as a result the spotlight was turned upon the school's whole program of education. It looked so bad that accreditation was summarily withdrawn.

The president met the challenge head-on and called upon the alumni to do the same. The result was a decision to put first things first and build a great university. They started with the liberal-arts college and settled for nothing short of excellence. Then they similarly upgraded their other colleges and the graduate school. This university now ranks high academically on any national grading scale. It is doing a magnificent job of building young men and women of character, intelligence, and leadership. Its students, its alumni, its state are all far prouder of it than ever before. And it still has a fine football team, one whose players are recruited according to all the rules.

Is there not a parallel here in the recent story of broadcasting?

The industry has been jolted by some scandals in recent years. And broadcasting, too, has come face-to-face with the question of where it shall go, not in the narrow sense of merely meeting the immediate problem, but in the achievement of its broad purpose. I believe broadcasters, like that university, want to build greatness—something that will do more than fill the stadium on Saturdays. Broadcasters, too, are accepting the larger challenge of excellence.

There are serious problems in broadcasting, especially radio, which call for understanding and help through cooperative efforts of radio licensees and the FCC. Most of these spring from economics. In many areas of the nation, the FCC has licensed entirely too many operators—far more than the available advertising revenue can with reason adequately support. Under the abnormally heavy competitive pressure, the charges for advertising go down to ridiculously low rates. This means that each station scrambles with all its might to sell enough extra spots to offset the low rate and produce enough gross revenue to keep the station going. Such a situation almost invariably reduces the public-affairs programming which the FCC so keenly desires. In short, the licensee who builds up his commercial volume finds that he is running afoul of the FCC. Thus many conscientious small radio operators, through the pressure of competition, find themselves in the position of being damned if they do and broke if they don't.

The way many radio broadcasters get hit coming and going brings to mind the World War II letter the sailor wrote to his commanding officer to explain his AWOL status. It went something like this:

SIR:

I am writing this letter to explain why I have been detained and will not be able to get back to duty from my home in Cobble Rock, Arkansas, on time. It all started while I was helping my brother, who stayed home to run our farm, repair the brick silo which was struck by lightning and badly damaged at the top.

We had rigged a hoist to get the bricks up where the repair work was needed, and when we finished, we had quite a few bricks left over which we needed to get back down to the ground. We decided to use the same pulley hoist, and I went down to the ground to hold the rope while my brother, who stayed at the top, loaded the bricks on the hoist platform.

Well, my brother loaded so many bricks on that they were heavier than I was, and when they started down, I couldn't turn loose and let them fall, so I started up.

As we passed, the load of bricks hit me aside the head, scraping a lot of skin—but I held on.

By the time I reached the top of the silo, I was going at a pretty good speed, and my hand got jammed in the pulley.

At the same time, the bricks hit the ground hard, and about half of them fell off the platform.

Then, you see, I was heavier than the bricks, and so I started back down, and they began to come back up. When we passed this time, the skin came off the other side of my head.

I hit the ground very hard and got so dazed I turned loose the rope.

Of course, then the platform and bricks that had got back to the top came tearing back down right on top of me sprawling there.

The next thing I remember, I woke up here in the hospital.

I hope you feel that this calamity explains why I will be a little late getting back.

I think many radio broadcasters and some television broadcasters find themselves in the same fix as the sailor with the hoist—they cannot turn loose, and the tighter they hold on, the more they get hit coming and going. In the case of radio, I feel the responsibility for the overpopulation of licensees is that of the FCC.

I could not be in more disagreement with Chairman Minow, who has said he feels the road to better programming in broadcasting lies through additional stations on the air and additional competition. If he will check, I believe he will find that where there is a reasonable number of radio licenses in a market, the services generally are superior. The reason is that good operators can earn enough with a reasonable amount of advertising at reasonable rates to allow for reasonable public-service efforts. Increasing competition beyond the reasonable-support potential in any community does not produce better programming or better broadcasting. In fact, experience shows the very opposite to be true.

I hope that this lesson so painfully learned too late in radio will be heeded in television while there is time. Television needs to be fully competitive, but not to the extent that in order for the broadcaster to survive every corner must be cut, every possible dollar earned. When this happens, the dollars are not there to finance the special efforts required to produce the highest-quality operation.

There is great merit in the development of a serious study by the FCC seeking answers to the complex economic questions now plaguing so many of our radio broadcasters as they try to operate within the regulations. In this, NAB would be glad to join. It might well be in order, while such a study is under way, for the FCC to declare a moratorium on the issuance of additional AM grants, as suggested by Commissioner Lee at the 1961 NAB convention.

Another concern facing broadcasters, especially radio broadcasters, and one which bears directly on their ability to perform with maximum responsibility, is the matter of the FCC's proposed new license application and renewal forms. I have made it clear that I can find no legal objection to the FCC requesting information from licensees about their programming. But I do object—and very strongly—to the almost impossible amount of detailed paperwork broadcasters, especially the smaller radio broadcasters, will be required to perform to respond to some of the questions in the proposed forms. In many of the smaller stations this will place an intolerable burden on already overloaded personnel. And these stations simply cannot afford to increase their staffs.

I have seen first hand the mountains of paperwork the forms entail in terms of the day-to-day operation of the smaller stations. I recommend that every member of the FCC take the time to make such an examination if he has not already done so. I am certain that it is not the desire of the Commission to keep a station from doing a proper job by imposing an unfair and unreasonable administrative burden on it, and yet this will be the result in many cases unless modifications are effected.

While we are on the subject of the proposed forms, as they apply to programming in radio, I would like to oppose the concept that each station in a multiple-station market should broadcast what might be called a "balanced" or "diversified" schedule of programming. I do not know that this is the intent of the FCC. But I do feel strongly that it would be foolish to expect each station to carry such a "balanced" program diet. This would produce not real diversification of programming but rather insidious conformity, in which every station would be sounding much the same as any other.

What I hope the FCC has in mind—and it seems to make very good sense, from the standpoint of the broadcasters as well as the public—is to encourage specialization among stations where there is a large number in a given market, so that a person might be able to tune in on one station for the best in good music, another station for needed foreign-language programming, another for special teen-age programming, and so on across the scale of diversified interests. If the FCC will spell out that it has this in mind in asking the questions about programming on the new forms, it will prove extremely helpful.

One of the most frequently expressed concerns of broadcasters is that the FCC and its staff have little appreciation of the administrative complications—the burdensome details—facing licensees in their day-to-day operations. The FCC, on the other hand, I am sure, feels that the industry does not appreciate the Commission's burdens, problems, and goals.

I propose, therefore, that we hold a meeting to be attended by the commissioners and appropriate staff members and by a representative group of radio broadcasters. The purpose of the meeting would be to exchange freely and frankly the views of all participants regarding current radio broadcasting problems in a very informal conference atmosphere. I would not contemplate this meeting taking on the aspects of a formal, recorded hearing, but I believe it should involve the proposal of the Commission to modify its application form and logging requirements. This would be entirely in order, procedurally; for the Commission has expressly stated that it would not be limited to comments of record but would further take into account any relevant information obtained in any manner from informal sources. I feel that such a meeting would help all around, and we offer the services of NAB in making appropriate arrangements therefor.

This nation of ours is in trouble. History has called broadcasters and all Americans to do more than get by. We are challenged to build more than tall towers, to teach Americans more than how to rock and roll.

We must build a nation and save a world. America simply does not have the time any more to accept anything less than the best from broadcasting. As a nation we cannot afford to indulge in the luxury of allowing a few shortsighted spokesmen for the status quo to symbolize broadcasting—or any other aspect of the national life.

Long before I had any idea I would be associated with broadcasting, I developed an admiration for General David Sarnoff. He had some very sage comments to make in his article for the "National Purpose" series last year.

"Why," he wanted to know, should America engage in "the shrinking from lofty goals for all mankind in favor of the safe, the compromising, or mere survival?"

General Sarnoff said that "the time when America could serve passively as an example or inspiration to other nations has run out. Today," he said, "professions of principle have serious consequences: they must be implemented in policy and action. To say it in slang, the time has come to put up or shut up."

He is so right. Prating about freedom as if it were a franchise to do as one pleases, uttering pious phrases about the sanctity of the broadcast license as if it were a vested, untouchable personal-property right once obtained, guarding the status quo as if it were the ultimate rather than a steppingstone to still further greatness—these things will get us nowhere.

The time has come—the urgencies of the hour demand it—for broadcasting to demonstrate that it can do even better, can act still more responsibly. This is the surest defense against tyranny. This is the real road to greater freedom. This is the course I am convinced most broadcasters want to pursue.

It is the course the President has called us to follow.

It is the course the American people expect of us.

And it is the course I have no intention of abandoning.

THE PUBLIC INTEREST
by Newton N. Minow

Before I was sworn in for my job as chairman of the Federal
Communications Commission, I was invited to participate in this
symposium on "Freedom and Responsibility in Broadcasting."
Since taking the job and now joining in the symposium, I have
seen a number of things happen. A speech which I made in May,
1961, received a very low rating with some broadcasters. The
Commission has taken a series of actions which some broadcasters regard as intrusions into their private affairs. Conversely,
many citizens have agreed with me that it was about time to inquire whether the public interest has been adequately served.

Perhaps the most controversial news was announced just recently. A television station dropped "The Untouchables" from its
schedule in favor of a better program balance, replacing it with
the Chicago Symphony Orchestra. We can only speculate about
the reaction of the television audience when they discover what
comes out of those violin cases!

So you see, things have changed since I accepted the invitation. *Broadcasting Magazine* had this to say about our conference
in its July 24, 1961, issue:

> From a standing start a few weeks ago [*sic*] unusual interest sud-
> denly is being manifested in the symposium on broadcasting at
> Northwestern U. School of Law in Chicago next month.
> The reason isn't difficult to discern. Broadcasting has been sub-
> jected to unprecedented criticism and the regulatory vise has tight-
> ened in the intervening weeks. The symposium, which first had the
> aspect of a prosaic, legalistic study of communications history, now
> is being built up as a historic debate on freedom and responsibility
> of broadcasting—mainly television.

Perhaps this may be a historic debate, but I assure you I have
not come here to create sensations or to seek headlines. My own
views and philosophy about broadcasting have received wide ex-

15

posure. This position has been attacked as censorship—despite my specific statement in that May speech as follows: "I am unalterably opposed to governmental censorship. There will be no suppression of programming which does not meet with bureaucratic tastes. Censorship strikes at the taproot of our free society."

Nevertheless, the censorship alarm has been sounded, or shouted, or whispered, or printed, and so I want to take this opportunity to discuss it in depth. For many years, the word "censorship" has smothered and obscured analysis about the relationship between government and broadcasting. Instead of beginning a thoughtful debate, the word "censorship" has inhibited discussion because nobody—least of all me—wants to be put in the role of censor. For that reason, let us calmly discuss censorship: what it is and what it is not.

The dictionary says a "censor" is a "person whose task is to examine literature, motion pictures, etc., and to remove or prohibit anything considered unsuitable." The Supreme Court says that the term censorship, "as commonly understood, denotes *any* examination of thought or expression in order to prevent publication of objectionable material." * We see that censorship is *"previous* restraint" of communications or publications. Even as early as 1644, when John Milton attacked censorship in his "Appeal for the Liberty of Unlicensed Printing," he "vigorously defended the right of every man to make public his honest views 'without *previous* censure.' "

Naturally, our concern here is with two special limitations on censorship: the First Amendment, which prohibits abridgement by the government of freedom of speech, and Section 326 of the Communications Act, which very wisely proscribes any censorship by the Federal Communications Commission.

I am going to explore these at length, but first I want to make an admission against somebody else's interest. There *is* much censorship. Even as it is defined here, there is much censorship in broadcasting today. It is as much to be examined, spotlighted, and at times deplored as any form of censorship by a government agency. And since it is done by our own governmental licensees every broadcast day, it violates the spirit of the First Amendment

---

* For a summary of the legislative acts and judicial decisions bearing on regulation of broadcasting, see Appendix I.

and Section 326 of the Act just as surely as if we had done it ourselves.

The censorship I speak of here takes two forms.

First, there is the censorship connected with "ratings" and the almost desperate compulsion of some of our licensees to work and to plan and to live by the numbers—always striving to reach the largest possible audience, in order to attract and hold the mass advertising dollar. At best, only the majority interest can be served here. Therefore the interests even of massive minorities will be poorly served, and in a broad sense the public interest is not served at all.

The First Amendment embodies the fundamental idea that minority views will and must find their place in a free market of ideas and communications. When the broadcaster ignores minority tastes and serves only the majority which the advertiser seeks (and this sometimes means rejecting a program which many millions of people want to see), he is unconsciously rejecting one of the fundamental concepts upon which our society is based and upon which, to quote Judge Learned Hand, "we have staked our all." And in so doing, he is using *public* property as a trustee for the public.

Let me give you an example. The networks produce some magnificent informative programming. The need for this kind of programming is both urgent and obvious in view of the many critical subjects in our troubled times—such as Berlin, Colonialism, Space, Cuba, Medical Care, Education. Yet often over half the networks' affiliates won't carry these programs. Instead, they substitute a commercial program designed to get a better rating. You can be sure that their schedules aren't overbalanced with public-service programming. It's simply that too often when presented with public service of a high caliber, these "trustees" choose to reject their opportunity to serve that smaller audience numbering sometimes in the millions.

The other form of censorship I speak of is what Clare Booth Luce has called "dollar censorship." Here, the broadcast licensee simply abdicates his own judgment and turns programming decisions over to an advertiser or his agency. The advertiser is not licensed or required to serve the public interest. His interest is directed almost entirely to increasing the sale of his product. This is a perfectly legitimate private interest, true; but when a broadcaster defers to the advertiser in permitting the private interest to have priority over the public interest, the result is censorship—and in a most pernicious form.

Sometimes the results can be as serious as in the "rating races" I have talked about. And sometimes, they can be downright silly. Take a look at the testimony elicited at our recent hearings in New York City. An electric company wanted a different title for Kipling's "The Light that Failed." And the Civil War drama, "The Andersonville Trial," came up on camera as "The Trial of Captain Wirtz" because the advertising agency "wanted to disguise the fact in the South that this was going to be Andersonville." What's more, the agency nudged out President Lincoln's name because Chrysler sponsored the program. As for Edith Wharton's bleak tragedy, "Ethan Frome," the agency inquiry was: "Couldn't you brighten it up a little?"

Now these examples are amusing, but they are also frightening; for it is obvious that the public interest has simply been conveniently forgotten and that the public's taste and knowledge has been treated with contempt. I hope that you will keep these forms of private censorship in mind while we examine just what the Commission does that brings its critics to cry "censorship."

First of all, I believe that the Commission clearly does *not* censor anything. We don't censor rock-and-roll, or Westerns, or quiz shows, or even overdoses of brutality. Nor do we say: "Put on this program. Do not broadcast that program." Even in such matters as obscenity, lotteries, and political broadcasts under Section 315, we are concerned only after the broadcast, not before. We never view a program in advance of broadcast and prevent its being seen by the public.

You surely know that the Commission looks to the applicant's over-all—and I stress the word *over-all*—programming proposal to determine whether granting him a license would serve the public interest. At first we look at his proposals. Later, when the station asks for a renewal, we also examine over-all performance during the license period, and when more than one applicant wants the same facility, we compare their programming proposals to determine which one would best serve the public interest. It is this that is called "censorship." It is this, they tell us, that violates the First Amendment and the Communications Act.

Let us review their arguments at some length.

First, the analogy to newspapers. The First Amendment, the

argument runs, prohibits governmental concern with the content of a newspaper; ergo, the government is similarly barred from concern with a broadcaster's programming. Some of you will say that I have erected a straw man, that this is not a serious argument in 1961. I hasten to assure you that I have not. I have heard this argument from persons in the highest positions in broadcasting. To again quote the July 24, 1961, issue of *Broadcasting Magazine:*

The nation's press is interested too. Although most editors and publishers have gloated over the broadcaster's plight because of competitive instincts, the more discerning ones know that if censorship through program control strikes broadcasting, the press is only one step removed.

Thomas Jefferson once said, "Were it left to me to decide whether we should have a government without newspapers, or newspapers without a government, I should not hesitate a moment to prefer the latter." I'd like to paraphrase that. Were it *possible* to have broadcasting without any governmental regulation, I should not hesitate a moment to abolish the FCC. No one who believes in democratic ideals would hesitate—if it were possible. But it is *not* possible, and broadcasters, especially old-timers, know this better than anyone else.

In the mid-1920's, broadcasters operated under little more than token regulation, since a series of court decisions had limited the scope of the Radio Act of 1912. The result was complete chaos. Stations "jumped" frequencies—interfered with each other at will—and stepped up power to the destruction of other stations' service. Broadcasters petitioned, cajoled, and literally begged Congress to restore order. Congress responded with the regulatory pattern we now have.

Government assumed control over the airwaves. Congress set up a regulatory agency—the Federal Radio Commission between 1927 and 1934 and since then the Federal Communications Commission—to give out temporary, not permanent, licenses to use frequencies. It directed that licenses be granted or renewed only where it was found that the public interest would be served. It specified that the license vests no ownership right or any right to operate the station or use the frequency beyond its term, which was not to exceed three years. In effect, it authorized the granting of a renewable, limited privilege.

The Supreme Court has succinctly stated the basis of government regulation—namely, that radio "facilities are limited; they are not available to all who may wish to use them; the radio spectrum simply is not large enough to accommodate everybody. . . . In enacting the Radio Act of 1927 . . . Congress acted upon the knowledge that if the potentialities of radio were not to be wasted, regulation was essential."

Here the analogy to newspapers becomes nonsense. The government does not, cannot, and will never license newspapers. There is no physical limit on their number; anyone who has the means is free to publish a newspaper. But the government must license radio stations, because in radio there is far too little room. In short, the First Amendment requires the government to keep its hands off newspapers. There is no censorship, no "prior restraint." But the Amendment necessarily works out differently for broadcasting simply because broadcasting *is* different. There is a "prior restraint"—because it is necessary—but this restraint is against getting into the business in the first place unless you have a license.

Is this a denial of free speech? The Supreme Court in the *NBC* case squarely addressed itself to this point. The networks there argued that the Commission's Chain Broadcasting Regulations must fail because they abridged the networks' right of free speech. Here is what the Supreme Court said:

If that be so, it would follow that every person whose application for a license to operate a station is denied by the Commission is thereby denied his constitutional right of free speech. Freedom of utterance is abridged of many who wish to use the limited facilities of radio. Unlike other modes of expression, radio inherently is not available to all. That is its unique characteristic, and that is why, unlike other modes of expression, it is subject to governmental regulation. Because it cannot be used by all, some who wish to use it must be denied. But Congress did not authorize the Commission to choose among applicants upon the basis of their political, economic or social views, or upon any other capricious basis. If it did, or if the Commission by these Regulations proposed a choice among applicants upon some such basis, the issue before us would be wholly different. The question here is simply whether the Commission, by announcing that it will refuse licenses to persons who engage in specified network practices (a basis for choice which we hold is comprehended within the statutory criterion of "public interest"), is thereby denying such persons the constitutional right of free speech. The right of free speech does not include, however, the right to use the facilities of radio without a license. The licensing system established by Congress in the Communications Act of 1934 was a proper exercise of its power over commerce. The standard it provided for the licensing of stations was the "public interest, convenience, or necessity." Denial of a station license on that ground, if valid under the Act, is not a denial of free speech.

I have read the entire holding because it is the only *ruling* of the Supreme Court directed to this First Amendment argument. It flatly says that the denial of a station license, if valid under the Act, is not a denial of free speech.

And so we must resolve another question. Under the Act, may the Commission validly consider, in making its public-interest finding, the station's over-all programming?

Let's first look at the Act itself. Not only does the Act employ the broad public-interest standard; it contains several other explicit references to programming. It gives the Commission authority to "prescribe the nature of the service to be rendered by each class of licensed stations and each station within any "class" (303b). It bestows power to make regulations "requiring stations to keep such records of programs . . . as [the Commission] may deem desirable" (303j). "Records of programs?" What for, if the Commission has no concern with programming? In 1934 Sections 325b and 325c were added for the specific purpose of sustaining the Commission's authority over the programming of stations whose transmitters were located just across the American border but who used American studios. This was to get at border-jumping by persons whose licenses had been terminated by the Commission for programming reasons. Are we to believe that the Commission has such authority over programming from foreign transmitters but no authority to consider the over-all programming of American licensees?

The legislative history of the Radio Act of 1927 is important here. None of the men prominent in the hearings or legislative debates showed any doubt as to the power of the Commission to consider programming as one facet of the public interest in the classification of stations and the assignment of frequencies and the renewal of licenses. Section 29, the "censorship" provision of that Act, was intended as a reference to the First Amendment and not as a separate limitation upon the authority of the Commission. It was thought to exclude certain arbitrary judgments by the Commission in considering program content, as, for example, partisan interference with political opinions broadcast on the station. Still, the Radio Commission felt from the very beginning that it was barred from interfering—prior to broadcast—with any specific program. Nevertheless, also from the outset, the Radio Commission considered program content when it developed general standards for the evaluation of programming in renewal and in comparative proceedings. Renewal proceedings were held for 164 stations whose past operations raised questions as to whether they were serving the public interest. Eighty-one licenses were renewed, 26 were denied (and the stations were deleted), and the other 57 stations surrendered their licenses. Moreover, the character of programs broadcast was a key factor in deciding which of these stations should be deleted.

Support for this procedure came quickly from both the Court of Appeals for the District of Columbia and the Supreme Court. In the *Nelson Brothers* case, the Supreme Court stated that the "character and quality of services" were relevant elements of the public-interest standard. And in the *KFKB* and *Trinity Methodist* cases, where the Commission had denied renewal applications, the Court of Appeals squarely upheld, not only the Commission's authority to consider past programming on a renewal application, but also its construction that the prohibition of censorship related only to previous restraint of specific programs.

The *KFKB* case was memorable. A station had been licensed to one Dr. Brinkley, who advertised his hospital and prescribed for patients—sight unseen—over the air. One script ran: "Probably he has gall stones. No, I don't mean that, I mean kidney stones. My advice to you is to put him on Prescription No. 80 and 50 for men, also 64. I think he will be a whole lot better. Also, drink a lot of water."

The Commission's remedy: no license. The Court agreed, saying:

It is apparent, we think, that the business is impressed with a public interest and that, because the number of available broadcasting frequencies is limited, the commission is necessarily called upon to consider the character and quality of the service to be rendered. In considering an application for a renewal of the license, an important consideration is the past conduct of the applicant, for "by their fruits ye shall know them." Matt. VII:20.

The appellant contended: "Censorship!" The Court answered:

There has been no attempt on the part of the commission to subject any part of appellant's broadcasting matter to scrutiny prior to its release. In considering the question whether the public interest, convenience, or necessity will be served by a renewal of appellant's license, the commission has merely exercised its undoubted right to take note of appellant's past conduct, which is not censorship.

When Dr. Brinkley moved his practice to Texas, with a Texas studio and a transmitter located in Mexico, Congress countered with section 325b. It countered expressly, as I have said, to give the Commission control over such programming.

In the *Trinity Methodist* case, the station had been used to attack religious organizations, obstruct the orderly administration of justice, defame certain groups, and indulge in similar highly personal attacks. The Court held that it was the Commission's *duty* to consider these actions of the appellant in deciding whether to renew its license and that a refusal to renew on the basis of this record was "neither censorship nor previous restraint, nor is it a whittling away of the rights guaranteed by the First Amendment, or an impairment of their free exercise."

Now with full knowledge of these early developments, Congress extended the life of the Radio Commission three times between 1927 and 1934, and in that time it considered many amendments. Here are the words of a chairman of the F.R.C., testifying at a Congressional hearing in 1934:

Our licenses to broadcasting stations last for 6 months. The law says that they must operate in the public interest, convenience and necessity. When the time for a renewal of those station licenses comes up, it is the duty of the Commission, in passing on whether or not that station should be relicensed for another licensing period, to say whether or not their past performance during the last license period has been in the public interest.

Still Congress carried over the identical provisions affecting programming into the Communications Act of 1934, and in so doing it can only have ratified this interpretation.

What did the industry think in 1934? The National Association of Broadcasters in 1934 told a House Committee considering one Communications Act proposal:

It is the manifest duty of the licensing authority, in passing upon applications for licenses or the renewal thereof, to determine whether or not the applicant is rendering or can render an adequate public service. Such service necessarily includes the broadcasting of a considerable proportion of programs devoted to education, religion, labor, agriculture, and similar activities concerned with human betterment.

In actual practice, over a period of 7 years, as the records of the Federal Radio Commission amply prove, this has been the principal test which the Commission has applied in dealing with broadcasting applications.

And on January 15, 1934, *Broadcasting Magazine*, under the same editorship as today, commented:

Under the radio law [the Radio Commission] cannot censor programs. But it can consider the merit of programs in passing upon applications of stations for renewals of their licenses, just as it did in deleting the stations formerly operated by Brinkley, Baker and Shuler.

There is much to indicate that, far from being critical of the Radio Commission's examination of over-all programming, Congress thought it wasn't enough. The debates in 1934 indicate a strong dissatisfaction with the Radio Commission in failing "to take the steps that it ought to take to see to it that a larger use is made of radio facilities for education and religious purposes." And so the new Commission was required in the new Act to study this question and report its recommendations to Congress. This was done, and the FCC reported on January 22, 1935, that there was "no need for a change in the existing law" and that "in order for a non-profit organization to obtain the maximum service possible, cooperation in good faith by the broadcasters is required. *Such cooperation should, therefore, be under the direction and supervision of the Commission*" (emphasis supplied).

The Federal Communications Commission, like the Radio Commission, from the beginning accepted the importance of program service in its public-interest determinations, and this view has, of course, continued down to the present time, and has been consistently sustained in the courts. I am going to review these cases briefly.

In the *NBC* case the Supreme Court rejected the notion that the Commission should be little more than an electronic traffic officer with no duty but to prevent stations from interfering with one another. The Court pointed out that the Act does not limit the Commission merely to engineering or technical supervision but puts upon it "the burden of determining the composition of [the] traffic." Congress, it said, gave the Commission a very large grant of authority—the public interest, convenience, and necessity.

The same Court in the *Carroll* case flatly stated that "the qualifications of the licensee and the character of its broadcasts may be weighed in determining whether or not to grant a license." In the *Simmons* case the Commission had denied a license to an applicant who proposed to broadcast all the programs of a national network, irrespective of their quality or the need of the community for other programs. The Court of Appeals affirmed. And in the *Noe* case the Court, citing *Trinity Methodist,* pointed out that if the winning applicant in the comparative case should "in the future fall short of the rules and regulations of the Commission in regard to proper programming, the Commission may always review the matter in a renewal proceeding or otherwise."

There are many other decisions to the same effect, and they all boil down to a summation by Attorney-General Rogers in his 1959 report to President Eisenhower (pp. 30–31), that "in every case in which the question has been presented, the courts have upheld the Commission's authority to concern itself with a licensee's program policies and practices. *No action by the Commission has ever been held by the courts to constitute censorship or to violate constitutional protections of freedom of speech or of the press"* (emphasis supplied).

And to those of you who think that all the present debate started with the New Frontier, let me read Attorney-General Rogers' Fourth Recommendation to the FCC in the same report:

Adopt a program of more intensive scrutiny of licensees' past performances in connection with renewals. It might be appropriate for the Commission to adopt a system similar to that followed by the Internal Revenue Service, which chooses a certain number of returns at random for a spot check in depth. The Commission might follow the same course by requiring narrative and detailed accounts of past operations, and, in addition to acting on specific complaints, choose a certain number of renewal applications or all the licensees in a particular community for close examination, requiring more detailed information where necessary, and setting questionable cases for hearing. The procedure would include consideration of advertising practices, material which has been advertised, and action taken on complaints by the Federal Trade Commission. The procedure should emphasize a comparison of the licensee's actual performance with the promises he made as to his programs and operations when his license was originally granted or last renewed. The licensees would thus be put on notice that from time to time they might have to give a detailed accounting as to their operation in the public interest.

There is one other aspect of the judicial history which I believe must stump the critics, and that is the Commission's practice in comparative hearings. The Commission has always compared the programming proposals of competing applicants to determine which applicant will best serve the public interest. And the courts have approved this in every case where the issue has been raised. The Court of Appeals has said, "Such a comparison of proposals is not a form of *censorship* within the meaning of the statute."

This power of the Commission to compare the programming proposals of mutually exclusive applicants is virtually conceded. Yet the critics balk at the same exercise of authority in noncomparative cases. Is there any real difference? I think not. Service to the listening public is still the vital element of the public interest, and programs are still the essence of that service. The public interest exists whether there are competitors for the channel or not.

Finally, some more recent legislative history. In 1952, Congress revised Section 307d so as to simplify the procedure which governs the granting of renewal applications. But in doing this, the Senate Report stated:

It should be emphasized that while the recommended amendment does eliminate the necessity for the type of involved and searching examination which the Commission must make in granting an original license, it does not in any way impair the Commission's right and duty to consider, in the case of a station which has been in operation and is applying for renewal, the over-all performance of that station against the broad standard of public interest, convenience, and necessity. This authority of the Commission is made explicit by specifying that such renewal grants are subject to findings by the Commission that the "public interest, convenience, or necessity would be served thereby."

To conclude, in amending Section 315 in 1959, Congress explicitly incorporated one of the Commission's existing programming requirements—namely, "the obligation imposed upon [broadcasters] to afford reasonable opportunity for the discussion of conflicting views on issues of public importance."

There ends my summary of the authorities. I am sorry to have gone on at such length, but I don't consider it a very tortuous trail. The cases, the history of regulation, and the legislative history are consistent, and I think they establish two things: first, that the no-censorship provision refers to previous restraints, in the sense that the Commission may not *enjoin* stations from broadcasting any particular program or type of program; and, second, that the Commission has the authority and the duty to consider a station's programming in determining whether grants of construction permits or license renewals are in the public interest.

Well, then—how do the critics answer all this? Simple. They ignore it. They argue each time as if the slate were completely clean. Don't study the law books, they imply. A station is like a newspaper. Getting into programming must inevitably lead to bureaucratic judgment of what constitutes good programming. Tastes will obviously be imposed. There is simply no way to draw a proper line between permissible review and censorship. Freedom of speech cannot be qualified without being destroyed. Therefore, other than in such areas as obscenity or lotteries, the Commission, they conclude, cannot concern itself *at all* with programming content. Their argument to the Commission—the very agency charged by law with the protection of the public interest— is often the same as their answer to dissatisfied listeners: "If you don't like it, turn your set off."

As you may have gathered, I cannot accept these arguments in the face of the law and the Commission's lawful duty. If they are serious arguments, however, then such arguments should be addressed to Congress.

They were addressed to Congress in 1947. After the issuance of the Blue Book, the NAB urged Congress to amend the Act so as to give radio the same degree of freedom from governmental regulation of content as newspapers. In the hearings before the Senate Interstate and Foreign Commerce Committee on the matter (80th Cong., 1st sess., S. 1333), Senator Wallace White, the committee chairman and one of the "fathers" of the Communications Act, said that "there is a vast difference in principle between the absolute right of anyone who wants to go into the newspaper business and the necessarily limited right to operate a broadcasting station" (p. 120). He stated (p. 126): "I do not accept in any degree that there is no difference between the power of Government with respect to newspapers and the power of Government with respect to radio communications. . . . If you [radio people] are placing your feet on that foundation, [you] are just indulging in dreams. Because Congress will not stand, in the long run, for any such interpretation." Other senators were equally critical. Senator Edwin Johnson declared that the notion that "radio presents a direct analogy to the press" is "as far-fetched as comparing an elephant to a flea."

Still, I would like to meet this argument head on—the argument that "you can't draw a line." It seems to me that just because it is difficult to delineate the exact limits of a law does not mean that the law should not be enforced at all. I wonder what would have been the history of the Sherman Act and similar "broad" statutes if that standard had been applied to them. If the Commission ever oversteps its permissible province in the area of programming, the doors of the courtroom are open. Any case the Commission decides must be on a public record. Any arbitrary action will meet rejection by the judiciary. The courts will give the full measure of protection to anyone who has a legitimate claim to any intrusion on his freedom. But those broadcasters who would clothe themselves with the arguments of John Milton should also be prepared to serve the public interest.

Think what these advocates are urging when they say that the Commission cannot concern itself at all with programming content. What if a radio station proposes to play a record of "The Old Gray Mare, She Ain't What She Used to Be," all day long, every day, for a three-year license period. Or, a TV station comes up for initial license or renewal and proposes to broadcast only the adventures of "private eyes." Under the hear-no-evil, see-no-evil view I have described, the Commission is helpless—it must find that a grant of these applications is in the public interest. The Dr. Brinkleys and the Reverend Shulers of *KFKB* and *Trinity Methodist* could be welcomed back. It was all a mistake: their operation *is* in the public interest, and maybe their ratings were high enough to "justify" their continued use of the public airwaves. I would reply to this proposition as did Senator White at the 1947 hearings I referred to:

But so long as we have in the law that basic conception that an applicant has no absolute right to a license but must establish to the satisfaction of the Commission that he is serving a public interest or meeting a public necessity or a public convenience, something which seems to me to be basic in our law, I just do not see how there can be any judgment as to whether a station is serving a public interest or not unless there is a chance to view and review the programs which a station has been passing out to the listening ear of the American public.

You will say that I am posing facetious examples. So I am, because they show the utter fallacy of the proposition. Now let's take a more typical example. A TV station, say, proposes to present no or almost no educational, religious, or public-affairs programming and very little local live programming. I submit that the Commission is free—and indeed obliged—to require such a station to show, in a hearing, how such a proposal can be said to meet the public-interest needs of its service area. This requirement is not censorship. The Commission is not prescribing the specific programs to be presented. It has a right to ask why that applicant should have a piece of a precious resource.

"Well, all right," say the critics. "Maybe the Commission isn't censoring by prior restraint, but it's using a device just as awesome—fear of subsequent punishment. Maybe the broadcaster *is* free to air what he chooses, but then the Commission warns us, 'If you do not measure up to our public-interest standard, you may end up without any license.' You have us groping."

They certainly would be groping, if it were so. But it's not. The Commission requires applicants to set out their programming proposals. We take those proposals seriously whenever we grant a license. If the applicant did what he said he would do, there obviously can be no controversy between him and the Commission at the time of renewal. But if he fails to honor his own application for reasons of business expediency, then this constitutes bad faith on the part of the applicant. Then there *is* going to be a controversy, and the issue between him and the Commission will not be programming—it will be his character or fitness to be a licensee.

Finally, I would say to those who argue about "subsequent punishment": "Your quarrel is not with the Commission it is with the Act itself. For the Act says that you get only a temporary license and that at least once every three years you must come back to the Commission and establish that your over-all operation meets the public interest. If Congress wanted to eliminate this fear of a subsequent accounting of your public trust, it would have given you a *permanent* license. But Congress decided upon exactly the opposite course, and we intend to follow it. It wanted an accounting to make sure that those using this valuable portion of the public domain were not getting rich on their promises by shortchanging the public on fulfillment. Frankly, Congress invited an even greater threat—a competing application at your renewal time and then a comparative hearing where you must prove your ability to better serve the public interest than this new applicant."

I submit that a broadcaster making an effort in good faith to serve the public interest can have no real fear of "subsequent punishment" by the Commission. There need be no triennial flirtation with a new flame. The licensee necessarily has very wide leeway as to programming. If he makes a bona fide effort to meet what he deems to be the needs of his area, there is little chance of controversy between him and the Commission.

Then, why so much controversy? Now I believe we are down to the nub. What's behind the outcry?

The trouble, in my opinion, is that far too many licensees do not regard themselves as trustees for the public. The frequency is regarded as theirs, not the public's; and the license is not one to operate in the public interest but rather to get the greatest financial return possible out of their investment. When the Commission, in discharging public-interest responsibilities, challenges such operations, the first, almost reflex reaction is the cry of "censorship."

What shall we do? Surrender to the men who "want provocative programs that don't provoke anybody"? Or to the advertising agencies who reportedly "want a strong, hard-hitting, noncontroversial show that won't offend anybody—and above all, no 'gloom.' " What is the future of a medium under such influence?

Let's think, for example, what would have been the fate of the world's greatest dramatists if they were solely dependent on television for performance of their plays. Under the advertiser's code of censorship, would any of them have made the grade . . . Ibsen, Shakespeare, Shaw? ("Sorry, Henrik, but just too provocative for us." "Willy, how many times do I have to tell you? You can't have a couple of sweet, lovesick kids killed off at the end.") I am informed that good writers today *are* turning out TV shows—under pseudonyms.

At the same time, the amount of violence, murder, mayhem, and sadism on TV shows increases, because in somebody's opinion—sponsor, agency, network—the ratings need a boost. If this is the public interest, I can only echo the words of Mark Twain: "The more you explain it, the less I understand it."

To answer my own question: "No—we are not going to surrender in our efforts." In fact, we've done a few things recently that should make our purpose clear. Some of you will recall first that in its July, 1960, Programming Statement, the Commission stressed that licensees must make a good faith effort to find and fulfill the programming needs of their service areas. We mean just that. On June 28, 1961, we denied an application for a new FM station by a party who had made no effort to ascertain his area's needs but instead had submitted a "standard" programming proposal.

And, in doing so, I am sure we will have the support of almost all the broadcasters. Governor LeRoy Collins honorably exemplifies the best in broadcasting. Most broadcasters take pride in their service. They know that broadcasting is more than a business, that it constitutes vital public service to their community. They are *proud* of this. And proud people resent those whose only interest in broadcasting is the dollar sign—those fast-buck operators, many of them new to the industry and lacking in a traditional dedication to serving the public interest. Thus the Commission, in discharging *its* responsibilities, is serving not only the public but the responsible *broadcaster* also.

On July 13, 1961, we informed every broadcaster of a change in the Commission's renewal policy. In the past, we granted renewals even though there had been a substantial failure to live up to the programming representations, where the applicant upgraded his proposals and gave reliable assurances that these new proposals would be carried out. This will no longer be the case. We have put our licensees on notice that "proposals *vs.* actual operation" is of vital concern to the Commission, that licensees are not entitled to any license period in which they do not in good faith make an effort to deliver on their public-service proposals, and that if they have not been endeavoring in good faith to discharge their representations, they should take *immediate* steps to do so.

Finally, we have issued a proposed revision of the programming sections of our application forms, in order to obtain greater information as to the applicant's programming efforts, both proposed and in actual operation. We are seeking more information about the opportunities afforded for local expression, about the presentation of controversial issues, and about program categories, with special reference to education, politics, local news, and programs for children. We have also taken a first step in dealing with the failure of the network affiliate to carry the network public-affairs programming. We propose to require the applicant to set out the amount of such programming which it carried. Unfortunately, as I made clear in a concurring statement, this gives us only half the facts. I propose to add another question calling, first, for the number of hours and time slots of network public-affairs programs which were made available to a station but were not accepted and, second, for a statement on the general type and source of programs which it did broadcast instead. Surely the public is entitled to know which licensees consistently reject network public-affairs programs and whether they were rejected for reasons having to do with ratings and dollars. The valuable grant to use a scarce public channel should go to those who provide more public service in preference to those who provide less.

I submit that this pattern of activities is not censorship. It is the very reverse of censorship. We are not seeking government prescription of programming. On the contrary, we are seeking diversity of programming by the licensee as a result of his good faith and diligent efforts to discover and meet his area's needs. Surely, to quote from the *Simmons* case, censorship is "a curious term" to apply to a requirement that licensees make such efforts in living up to their responsibilities.

I think broadcasters were given a very apt reminder of those responsibilities by the Court of Appeals recently in the *Television Corporation of Michigan* case:

All too often in cases like the present the broadcasters involved appear to be chiefly interested in the revenues to be derived from operating their stations in the most profitable manner. It seems clear in the present case that WOOD-TV will make more money in its new location than in the old: it is moving to a more prosperous and more highly populated area, and its advertising revenues will no doubt increase. But such considerations, though legitimate, cannot be controlling. Television and radio are affected with a public interest: the Nation allows its air waves to be used as a matter of privilege rather than of right. The interests which today are profiting so handsomely from radio and television may in the end find it in their own best interest to treat their businesses primarily as a public trust.

This important teaching of the Appeals Court should be studied by all of us. And while we are studying, let us heed the conclusions contained in the Report of the President's Commission on National Goals which was submitted to President Eisenhower on November 16, 1960:

The American system of broadcasting is deeply entrenched and is founded on the rock of freedom from government interference. It is not, however, beyond critical examination in the light of its performance. It is too easy to say that the people are getting what they want. The fact that large audiences can be attracted by fourth-rate material does not acquit the broadcasting companies or the government which has an ultimate responsibility for use of this valuable and scarce resource, from asking whether the public interest is being adequately served. . . . Thus far, television has failed to use its facilities adequately for educational and cultural purposes, and reform in its performance is urgent.

I would add that programming responsibility is most urgently needed in these critical days. To those few broadcasters and their professional associates who would evade the nation's needs by crying, "Censorship! Oh, where will it end?" I ask, "Responsibility! When will it begin?"

THE ROLE OF GOVERNMENT
by Louis L. Jaffe

We ask ourselves the question: what is the role, what is the responsibility of government for the end product of TV? It will help us if we attempt to identify that product. That it is multifarious is one of the facts that complicates our question. TV is education, education in the sense of formal instruction and in the broader sense of intellectual interchange; TV is news, public affairs, political controversy; TV is entertainment, both simple delight and spiritual refreshment. TV functions as schoolroom, lecture hall, town meeting; theatre, cinema, concert hall, sports arena. All this adds up to that big bundle of goods which we call culture. If this is so, can there then be any question that government has a responsibility for the end product of TV? Is there anything more important to government than the good husbandry of its people's culture? But lest the implication of these rhetorical questions disturb some of you and excessively encourage others, I hasten to assure you that I do *not* envisage government as the Great Cultural Father and Mother regulating all spheres by universal decree. That is not our way. We do, it is true, sometimes proceed by direct prescription, and this is relevant to our inquiry. Within the last century government has undertaken to run schools and colleges. Even here we leaven officialdom by boards of citizens, and we encourage competing private schools and colleges. In music and the arts subsidies are necessary, but so far the bulk of subsidy and the direction of the enterprises have been nongovernmental, though mightily encouraged by tax exemption. To my mind there can be no question that were such methods to fail, government should maintain all of these enterprises directly.

My argument thus stands as follows. Government has a basic responsibility for the maintenance and advancement of our culture. In a few areas—education is one—this responsibility is di-

35

rectly discharged by government prescription. In the remaining spheres it is currently discharged by the creation of favorable conditions, by financial and moral encouragement. It would not violate fundamental principle for the government here and there to enter these spheres directly, but it is our philosophy—the philosophy of the Western world—that official direction of culture tends toward the academic, the safe, the thrice tried, the inoffensive, the mediocre; that it is the herald and the certificate of sterility.

In the current TV controversy madly and magnificently raging, it is surprising how much agreement there is—at least in principle. No one appears to deny that TV licensees have a public responsibility to provide good, well-balanced programs. The concept of balance developed over the years by the joint action of the FCC, the networks, and the stations, is designed to insure that TV will perform the various prime functions which it is distinctively able to perform. Perhaps the chains and the licensees have been chivvied and maneuvered into agreement. Over the years they have decried the Blue Book and have denied its statutory warrant. But the once angry cry has diminished to a whimper. Apparently apprehensive that the FCC, if too completely flouted, might be forced to test and perchance make good its claims in the courts, the industry does now profess to follow the necessarily loosely defined precepts of the Book. Congress all these years has maintained a resounding silence, but the echo is probably adequate to demonstrate Congressional ratification of the principle of responsibility for balanced programs, even though it leaves unclear the powers of the FCC to police the obligation.

Why should TV have such an obligation when its cultural siblings—the theatre, the cinema, the newspaper, the magazine— are free? It is often said that because TV is given a license to use public property—the air waves—it can and should be required to serve the public. I do not find this convincing. In my opinion the responsibility of the licensees rests on the present limited number of frequencies. Were it possible for anyone to broadcast, I can see no reason for imposing any responsibility on the broadcaster different from that which it would be appropriate and constitutional to impose on the other communication media. There is no assurance, by the way, that TV, unlimited, would be any better than it is today. But though it might even be a great deal worse, we would have no warrant for doing anything about it unless we were similarly prepared to control the other media. As matters stand, we cannot put competition to the test, and so we are warranted in insisting that TV serve all those uses of which it is potentially capable and which at least might be served under competition. Thus the condition of scarcity is an opportunity as well as a handicap, since it provides us with a legitimate basis for demanding something more responsible than competition might provide.

How shall we implement this responsibility? What at least shall government do to see that this end is achieved? There are two aspects to the problem—a negative, the control of the deleterious, and a positive, the promotion of the good. In dealing with both we must face up to the fact that taken as a whole the culture of TV cannot be very different from our total culture. In one or another department we may be able to make it better or not be able to keep it from being worse, but by and large the general culture is a limiting factor.

Now as to the negative: the control of excessive sex, violence, and intimations of immorality. The general condition of our communication media is relevant. Whether we look to popular or highbrow drama, motion pictures, or literature, we find an unprecedented and increasing exploitation of sex and violence. Our newspapers batten on it. We debate whether this corrupts children or adults, or both, or neither. Recently the broadcasting industry proposed an investigation of the question. Such an investigation would appear to be futile. How can the influence of TV be divorced from the massive general tendencies of our society? It should be enough, as far at least as children are concerned, that the effects may be bad. Even if it cannot be demonstrated that orgies of sex and violence have harmful effects—and I doubt whether any procedure could isolate the influences of TV and measure them—I fail to see what would be lost by eliminating them. Whatever its effect on morals, it is clear to me that there is taking place a substitution of sensationalism for decent workmanship. When the writer is no longer able to produce his effects honestly, he soups up his script with bare flesh. The current sexual exhibitionism of our media is the strip tease made respectable by its pretensions to enlightenment and high art. But what is to be done about it? Shall government measure out the quantity of sex and sadism that will be tolerated? To police programs directly would be impractical because the standards would be either vague or arbitrary. And the Supreme Court, except in cases of so-called hard-core obscenity, might hold that the Constitution forbade censorship, though it is at least possible that censorship of the hours when children are ordinarily viewing might get by. There remains the possibility which we shall discuss subsequently that the FCC might in its standards for license renewals control flagrant and persistent sensationalism. I am inclined to believe, however, that a determined and continuing effort by the organized citizenry brought to bear on advertisers and licensees will bring about some amelioration. Given our prevailing culture, not much more can be expected.

Our greater concern is with ways and means to increase the positive achievements of TV. We must break down the problem: first, education; second, news and public affairs; third, entertainment. Educational TV can embrace formal educational projects and can be a valuable supplement to TV on all of its higher cultural levels. Education is, after all, a high specialty, and if it can be put under the supervision of specialists, they should be our chief reliance. This, it is to be hoped, will be without prejudice to educational programming by the industry, some of which has been very valuable. The proposed bill for subsidies to educational TV should be enacted. There is a large potential here, and since a good deal of solid, serious educational TV can be transmitted and received over UHF, the problem at that point becomes not so much a TV problem as an educational one.

This brings us finally to the heart of our problem: the two complexes of news and public enlightenment and of entertainment, low, medium, and high. My discussion will assume certain postulates and derive from them certain axioms. I assume at the outset the present organization of broadcasting. There are ever so many other possible organizations which have been suggested as capable of eliminating the defects of the present system without any loss of conceded virtues. I am not enough of an economist, business analyst, or seer to assay the worth of these proposals or these prophecies. The present system is essentially semi-monopolistic —in the double sense of the basic TV monopoly and of a limited number of closed organizations controlling the major share of the business. A chain and its affiliates constitute an association which in effect, if not strictly, pools capital and provides common direction. This kind of organization may lead to the usual evils of monopolistic associations: the loss of initiative, freedom of action and innovation. It is one way, however, of mobilizing sufficient capital to underwrite the costs of a balanced program. In return for permission to operate this double-barreled monopoly, the public can demand that the monopoly devote part of its profits to expensive, high-level programs. This may be a virtue of monopoly, since it might not be possible to finance such programs under a system of perfect competition. The continuance of the present organization then is the first premise of my discussion. The second premise is the one to which I have already referred: namely, that TV is limited by our cultural standards and resources, plus the rather special distortion introduced by advertising.

Perhaps we do not for the moment have an acute problem in the news and public-affairs area. Mr. Sarnoff stated recently that 30 per cent of NBC's prime time was devoted—in February, 1961—to news, public affairs, or education. (This, by the way, is NBC's rather than any particular licensee's percentage.) George Rosen, writing in the June, 1961, issue of the NAB Newsletter, believes that the chains are showing increasing imagination and enterprise in this area. This may be not so much virtue as an intensification of audience interest in imaginative news presentations which in turn is bringing greater commercial sponsorship. Nevertheless many good news and public-affairs programs are rejected by the licensees for programs with an assumed greater mass appeal. The potential here is considerable; the question remains as to the role of the government, if any, in its ultimate realization.

Finally, entertainment. Let's face it: there are a vast number of programs which by cultivated standards are bores. But surely part of the problem is just that there are a vast number of programs. Mr. Minow seems to think that there are thousands of clever people ready and willing to civilize his "vast wasteland" with an infinity of pleasant prospects. Look at the other media. There are only a few good movies each year, three or four good plays, and a handful of good musicals. Surely there has never before been anything comparable to TV's enormous maw, hungering for entertainment. How is it possible running on a timetable week in and week out to avoid the stereotype? Anyone who sits supinely before TV waiting to be constantly amused deserves no better than he gets. The most alarming thing about TV is not its undeniable dullness but the apparent fact that so many people have nothing better to do than to sit constantly before it. I insist that these sponges are so completely bereft of culture that for them the quality of programs is immaterial.

The busy, active-minded citizen neither spends his whole evening in entertainment, nor does he find it only in TV. If in addition to his occasional live drama, movie, novel, magazine article, his Saturday afternoon radio opera, his weekly radio symphony, he could from time to time seek out and find—let us put it high at, say, three times a week—a rewarding TV program, the medium would be justified! But the demand is not just for number; scope and variety are also needed. For remember our premise: given the monopoly situation, TV is under responsibility to approximate the variety that could conceivably emerge from pure competition, and so must include something for all tastes. Many of the present popular programs do in fact satisfy a wide range of tastes. Even the most cultivated person relishes an occasional thriller, a good Western, a ball game, a bit of comedy or music; but he—and as many more as can be brought to like it—is entitled once in a while to an adult drama, be it an original (could we have six a year?) or Shakespeare, Shaw, O'Neill, Hellman. Yet if this is not too much to ask, it is nevertheless asserted that this decent minimum is not achieved. We are told that the writers of original drama have been almost completely squeezed out, discarded or discouraged. I do not know which of the reasons given for this are the true ones—whether pressure of advertisers, slavish reliance on ratings, or what. It makes no difference. The chains and the licensees are obliged to deliver. It was recently reported that CBS has sought original scripts by top writers, and while some have responded, others have refused. Perhaps the failure of TV to produce their work come-hell-or-high-water has alienated them. Perhaps the basic conditions of the medium, both technological and economic, are unattractive to writers who can choose. Perhaps TV must encourage and rely upon new talent. One practice which enormously and artificially increases the quantity demand is the single showing of programs no matter how distinguished. This is incredible and incomprehensible waste. Could Broadway or Hollywood conceivably function on such a basis? The practice is pecularily hurtful to just those discriminating and occasional viewers who are not automatically on tap night after night and cannot always spare the time or may not know of the program. One of the most important functions of the program critic is lost when the audience cannot respond to a favorable review. If the reason for this practice comes back to advertising, ratings, etc., I say once more, those reasons are not good enough. They do not justify this wanton waste of the only resources available to discharge TV's responsibility.

This then is TV's responsibility: to provide programs designed to fulfill all TV functions and to satisfy all legitimate tastes. What is government's role in assuring the objective? Least debatably, to encourage and subsidize educational TV; most debatably, to police program balance. This, of course, is the question which gives us all so much trouble.

I have not been very much impressed with the premise—at least as the basic premise of control—that the FCC is doing no more than enforce the promises made by the licensees in their applications. This seems to me to be something of a bootstrap argument. These proposals have been more or less extorted in the competition for the license—a competition which is played under rules which are obscure and inchoate. Insofar as these rules are in terms of percentages, they are arbitrary to begin with and may become more so with the passage of time. Though the contrary is arguable, it seems doubtful to me that the public responsibility of licensees should differ depending on what each saw fit to propose, or, put in another way, that each licensee should determine his own measure of responsibility. I will say, however, that though the licensee's proposals may not be the prime measure of performance, a radical departure from them may be relevant to a total judgment of performance.

The question remains whether policing is feasible or desirable. I conclude that it is, but primarily through enforced publicity and reporting. There is an opinion abroad which is critical of investigation and exposure by public officials who may be without the power or perhaps the intention to pass laws, make regulations, or prosecute. Supreme Court judges have condemned, as exposure for exposure's sake, Congressional investigations intended merely to publicize rather than to lay the groundwork for legislation. I do not mean here to endorse the conduct of the Un-American Activities Committee. Nor am I speaking to the issue of compelling witnesses to become the instruments of their own obloquy. But the view which condemns exposure for exposure's sake (as it is called) is, I think, unsound. In areas of opinion—and it is with such an area that we are concerned—it is precisely flat legal prescription which we should avoid. Law in this area is likely to be inept or arbitrary; it may even trench on the Constitution. But I can see no reason why government should not enter the arena of opinion-making, should not hold up for public scrutiny ideas, performances, associations, which it regards as dangerous, unsound, or deleterious. This is part of the very process of free discussion. The public may be without the resources to give content, depth, reality to its consideration. To enable the non-official forces of the community to do the community's business is a healthy exercise of governmental power. Accordingly, I envisage government as a Grand Court of Inquiry. It can assemble, digest, and bring into focus the totality of opinion concerning the role and performance of TV. I applaud the proposed moves of the FCC to increase the scope and the precision of licensee-reporting and to compel the licensee to make studies relevant to the discharge of responsibility. I approve, too, the proposal to subject renewal applications to occasional public hearings—or informal investigations—in which the licensee will be called upon to defend programs, to account for spates of lust and violence, to explain persistent refusal to carry meritorious chain programs whether sustaining or of low audience appeal, to justify niggardly budgets. The chains, too, must report, since their programming is the key to licensee programming. I do not know whether it is necessary to give the FCC additional powers over the chains. This is simply a matter of legal mechanics. The chains may already provide the Commission with all the relevant information. But if there is any doubt about it, powers to compel adequate reporting could be easily devised.

Will the obligation to account, will the glare of publicity suffice to enforce public responsibility? Most of us would hope so. If the record of the past does not seem to support this hope, it may be said that investigation and reporting has not been systematic. But even if publicity would not suffice, there will be many disinterested persons to whom sanctions *beyond* publicity—license forfeiture being the ultimate—would be distasteful. They would argue that strict sanctions end in arbitrary administration and official control of expression. Though we can get agreement on the abstract desideratum of the balanced program and even a loose consensus on the general categories that make it up, there is an infinite and very wide range of reasonable judgments as to proper proportions and worthy ingredients. This is true both of the kinds and the qualities of programs. It is not clear that balance should be entirely in terms of the single licensee. Would it offend the demand for responsible programming if one of the seven New York City stations offered only caviar and ignored the claims of the general? Where the standard for judging legal compliance is thus difficult to formulate, enforcement may be arbitrary, capricious, and tyrannical. And even if such supervision of programs were held not quite to offend the Constitution—a question which I shall reserve for the moment—such supervision could come close enough to be thought a greater evil than, to put the alternative at its worst, low-grade TV.

There is a contrary position. It starts, of course, from the premise that publicity, however useful, will not suffice without a sanction hovering in the background; and it holds that such a sanction would not violate the canons of good government. Though, as we have argued, it may not be possible to agree on a formula for desirable program balance, it probably is possible to get a fair measure of agreement that a particular performance falls substantially short. Such a showing would be most convincing if made not primarily in terms of percentages but in gross failures to do the key jobs—news, public discussion, some good entertainment combined—as would so often be the case with excessive advertising and insufficient budgets. In making this judgment a marked departure from key proposals would be a relevant factor. It might be countered that so low a standard is worse than none at all; that, in effect, it legitimates the mediocre; and that it does not avoid the risks of arbitrary administration and censorship. Let us address ourselves first to the latter point. Would it infringe the constitutional protection of the freedom of communication? Though the question is too difficult to explore comprehensively at this time, I incline to the view that it would not. My conclusion rests on the premise that TV is a basic medium of expression, access to which is a right of the people and for the people. Since TV channels are limited, this right cannot be assured unless access is rationed, and, as I have tried to demonstrate, the balanced program is an effort to effect this rationing. Rationing need not reach to the censorship of concrete opinion other than an opinion as to what in a particular case is a balanced program. Indeed, this principle, though it has not been put to a formal test, has already been accepted by the industry with respect to equal time for major political candidates and political opinion. To require a licensee as a condition of presenting its opinion to offer an opportunity for rebuttal is surely as direct a regulation as any presently implied in the concept of a balanced program.

But is not this sort of power—ill-defined, threatening, but seldom if ever put to the test by the authorities (government by the raised eyebrow, it was called some time ago)—is not such power contrary to a regime of law? As a lawyer, I am no lover of it. Yet it is more or less just what TV has been living with for some years. It is an example of the blend of private and public power which is typical in the United States, which is perhaps inherent in any complex, sophisticated, diverse, democratic society. Neither side wishes to run the risk of clarification. Each derives from the situation some positive power; each must adjust itself to, must manipulate, the margin of doubt. Whether, as some may fear, it simply perpetuates dead-center mediocrity or whether, as I suspect, it be useful as a prod and a reminder, is hardly demonstrable. To date we have not been able to work out anything better, and I see little prospect for clarification. I conclude first, that government has a prime responsibility for the end product of TV; second, that responsibility can best be discharged by the official formulation of standards, by unrelenting publicity, and by an obligation on the industry to study the programmatic needs of its constituencies, to report on and to defend its performance.

Reply
by Charles H. King

In discussing the responsibilities of broadcasting, especially television broadcasting, Professor Jaffe remarked: "It is surprising how much agreement there is." I can document this by specifying a number of points on which, if I interpret his remarks correctly, he and I are in complete agreement.

He said that "Congress has left the powers of the FCC unclear." He said the proposition that television owes a duty to serve the public because it's using public property, namely, the air waves, is unconvincing. He said that for the government to police programs directly would be "impractical." Standards would be difficult to formulate, enforcement would tend to be tyrannical, and the whole business might be held unconstitutional by the Supreme Court.

Professor Jaffe said that much of television is a "bore," and he blamed a good deal of this on its tremendous appetite for material. He said that many of the popular programs presently on the air do in fact satisfy a wide range of tastes. He said that public opinion will bring about some amelioration and that not much more than this can be expected. I'm not sure just what he meant, but I gathered that he thought intervention by the government would be largely ineffectual.

He said he was unimpressed by the proposition so frequently advanced: that the performance of licensees should be measured vis-à-vis their promises. He said that many people would find sanctions beyond publicity—license forfeiture being the ultimate—distasteful, that they would regard this as leading toward official control of expression. As a lawyer, he said he had no love for "government by the lifted eyebrow."

On all these points I simply couldn't agree more! With those out of the way, let me turn to points that for lack of complete knowledge I can't disagree with positively but against which I would enter some "caveats."

One is Professor Jaffe's fundamental proposition that "the

45

government has a basic responsibility for the maintenance and advancement of our culture." I'm not a political scientist, and so I can't argue the point. But I'm reasonably sure that it would have come as a distinct surprise to the gentlemen who were assembled in Philadelphia back in 1787 to draft our Constitution.

He made a further point when he said nobody seems to deny that licensees have a public responsibility to provide good, well-balanced programs. If by "public responsibility" he means "an obligation to be enforced by governmental sanctions," I think I could make up quite readily a long list of dissenters to that proposition.

He said that the proposed bill for subsidies to educational TV should be enacted. Maybe so. But just why this should be done by the Federal Government, instead of by the states where the educating is going to be done, is a little unclear to me! Why should the people of Michigan, to use my own state as an example, be taxed to support education in some other states where the people apparently aren't willing to tax themselves enough to supply an education for their own children, particularly where they hold out tax incentives for business to move out of our state into theirs?

To come to outright disagreement, Professor Jaffe said that the responsibility of licensees to serve the public rests on the limited number of available frequencies. The limitation precludes competition and therefore serves as a legitimate basis for demanding what competition would otherwise provide. "The public can demand," he said, "that the monopoly devote a part of its profits to expensive, high-level programs."

To this, all I can say is, I'm sure that Messrs. Goldenson, Sarnoff and Stanton would be extremely surprised to learn that they are no longer in competition with each other, that between them they're just a happy family with a great big fat monopoly! They're just about as much a monopoly as Ford, Chrysler, and General Motors! The four television stations in Detroit, too, I think will be equally pleased to learn that they don't have to compete with each other any more as the *News* and *Free press* do.

Professor Jaffe says he applauds the changes which the FCC proposes to make in the part of its application form which deals with programming. I'd like to comment on this, because I had something to do with it and because I think it throws an interesting and revealing sidelight on the administrative process.

The main part of the application, the program part of the application form which the FCC has been using for many years, is the so-called "Composite Week." The licensee reports in terms of percentage how much entertainment he broadcast during the week, how much religion, how much news, how much education, and so on through a half-dozen or more categories. He also reports the percentages he proposes to broadcast during his next license period. If what he reports for the past corresponds pretty much to what he proposed the last time he applied, and if what he proposes for the next period doesn't depart too much from the past, he gets his license! Assuming, of course, that everything else is in order.

The idea behind this, I suppose, was to promote and encourage what's been referred to as "balanced programming." But the "balance" which we all assume to be so desirable is not, in my opinion, a balance between so much entertainment, so much religion, or so much news and so much agriculture, and so on. The balance we want is a balance in "taste," a balance in quality, a balance in appeal, not merely a balance in quantity.

Disparity between the balance reported and this ideal balance led to dissatisfaction with the "Composite Week." As a result of the FCC's program inquiry some time ago, instead of asking the licensee how much of this and how much of that he broadcast, the FCC began to ask him first what he had done to ascertain the needs, interests, and desires of his listening community. Secondly, it began to ask what he had done, or proposed to do, to satisfy these interests, needs, and desires of his own community. All this was to be in narrative form, the original idea being that these narratives would take the place of the traditional composite week.

I had some reservations, some expressed and some not. First, I thought it very likely that these narratives would inevitably end up as being pretty much standardized. The Washington lawyers, I was sure, would soon know what sort of narratives would satisfy the commission, and they would advise their clients accordingly. This isn't intended as any criticism of the lawyers. Quite the contrary. Any communications lawyer who failed to do it ought to be disbarred immediately for incompetence. I even notice that there's a service available now from which you can hire this examination of your community done for you.

Second, I couldn't help but feel that these narratives would soon turn out to be another batch of quantitative statistics. It seemed to me that programming could not be described any other way. The licensee would say that he went out and talked to the ministers in his town, and they all thought that there ought to be X hours of religion. So he was going to broadcast X hours of religion. The mayor would say that there should be X hours of discussion of public issues. And so he was going to broadcast X hours of that. The police chief would say X hours of traffic safety . . . and so on.

Third, I wondered who was going to read all these narratives? Remember that there would be more than 1500 narratives a year. The work would have to be passed around as they used to do with girls who gave the weather and time over the telephone —they couldn't leave them on it for very long, or they'd go crazy.

Now for my interesting sidelight. Somebody on the staff raised this question. They asked: "What guide lines are we going to have, to check these narratives against? You've told us the percentages that you'll allow in a composite week." (I remember I had a little slip in my desk that said, "Such a percentage of this and such a percentage of that." If that's what the form stated, why the staff was to O.K. it. "But," they said, "we don't have any such thing to check these narratives. And we need something specific." What happened? An equivalent of the composite week, stated, I will admit, in terms of hours and minutes instead of percentages, went right back into the form!

So the proposed form now has both the narratives, and a modified composite week. The result as I see it is that the broadcaster's work is going to be at least doubled, to no useful purpose. My guess is that after the first bloom of novelty has worn off, not one in a hundred of these narratives is ever going to get read, at least thoroughly.

I would hate to say that this is typical of the administrative process. And I would hate to have to deny it.

Professor Jaffe also applauds the FCC's proposal to designate renewal applications for occasions of public hearings. By this I assume he means local hearings rather than hearings held in Washington. Again, I have some reservations.

To devote very much of its manpower to that type of hearing is going to put the FCC even further behind in its work than it is now, unless of course the agency gets more money and more staff. That a reasonably representative cross-section of the community will show up at such a hearing I think is highly unlikely. Most of those who attend will be spokesmen for special groups with special axes to grind; and I'm sure the television stations would drum up quite a few people to speak in their behalf too. If the hearing gets beyond the usual generalities about too much violence and not enough culture, if it gets down to specifics, my guess would be that there will be as many conflicting opinions as there are people present.

Professor Jaffe spoke at some length about the value of "publicity" in respect to the shortcomings of television, with the government acting as a sort of "focusing agent." When it comes to programming, I have my doubts. Would people stop watching a show they like because it was publicly denounced by or through the government? If so, how can you explain that in Detroit, for example, which I assume is typical, "The Untouchables" draws a larger audience than the three competing shows put together?

Professor Jaffe himself said that "the culture of TV cannot be very different from our total culture." I agree. The American people have a very effective mechanism for keeping television within the limits of their total culture. When it gets too far above or below these limits, they can and they do turn it off. I doubt very much that any publicity, focused by government or otherwise, will prove nearly as effective as the power to turn the knob!

Perhaps, and we can concede this, the level of our culture should be higher. But the only way that television can help to raise that level of culture is to move only a little ahead of the crowd, not too far. All the high-quality television in the world isn't going to raise the cultural level of John Q. Public if he turns it off!

In his remarks Professor Jaffe postulated the existing organization of broadcasting. Many years ago when radio first came on the scene, the American people had a choice to make. One choice was a broadcasting system operated by private enterprise, with competition relied on to produce the best end result and with the cost to be borne by advertising. The other choice was a system which we can label as the British system, where the government itself does the broadcasting and pays the cost out of tax revenue. Through their Congress the American people chose the former type of system; and many years later they made the same choice again in respect to television.

To put it as simply as possible, I don't think we can have our cake and eat it too. I don't think we can have an effective system of broadcasting by private enterprise and at the same time have the government telling the industry what they must or must not put out over the air. What makes private enterprise tick is profits. Only by making a profit can television render the public service that it does. And surely no one would deny that the total of such service is very considerable. On the other hand, profit is not a goal of government. Quite the contrary. When the government steps in to tell the broadcaster what he must or must not broadcast, both the opportunity for profit and the incentive that goes along with it are bound to be affected adversely. Once started, this sort of thing tends to expand rather than to diminish.

By this I don't mean that the industry should be completely free of program regulations by the government. I concede that under its police power the government can establish certain minimum standards of program content. It was Justice Holmes, I think, who said: "The right of free speech does not extend to yelling 'Fire!' in a crowded theater." There is no question that the government can, could, and does in some instances prohibit the broadcasting of obscenity, profanity, material that would be subversive or incite to riot, and anything else that could be defined as clearly offensive to public health, safety, or morals.

If excessive violence on TV could be established as clearly detrimental to public morals, and if the government could formulate a standard about it which would keep the "Untouchables" off the air, for example, but leave "Macbeth" on, I might even concede the validity of such a standard. Fortunately for ABC, no such standard has been developed, nor do I think it likely to be in the foreseeable future.

But getting beyond the area which might be embraced within such minimum standards, assuming them to be formulated, the application of governmental sanctions against the broadcaster, either directly or by the "lifted eyebrow" on account of what he does or does not broadcast, is simply putting the government into the business of determining the program content of broad-casting. And that's the British system, not ours.

Take, for example, the illustration Chairman Minow used in his "Vast Wasteland" speech. He said that at license-renewal time the Commission would consider carefully the fact that the licensee had shown an old movie instead of a network public-service program. I note that his fellow commissioners did not go along—at least the last I read—but assume that they did. Wouldn't this be simply the government determining that available public programs should be shown in favor of old movies? Yet the ratings show that a substantial majority of the people prefer the movies!

I don't think the American people want their government making this sort of determination in respect to their television. And I don't think that this is what the American people ought to have.

PRIVATE INTERESTS
by Roscoe L. Barrow

INTRODUCTION

The free society is dedicated to promoting the maximum development of the individual. Television, of all mass media, offers the greatest potential for stimulating the individual's social and cultural development. The combination of sight, sound, motion, and simultaneous broadcast to substantially all Americans renders television a medium with unique impact. A single broadcast of "Oedipus Rex" is viewed by more persons than have seen the play in theatres since the days of Sophocles. A complex political issue can be placed before the people in a short time. Children spend as much time viewing television as they spend in school, which causes concern regarding television's effect on the young and impressionable. Through television the best that genius, art, and learning creates can be made available to all people, and thus there is an opportunity to raise the level of culture of our society.

In the free society, decision-making processes are rooted in informed mass opinion and judgment. Communications media have the challenging task of interesting and informing the mass of our people. Television offers a potential "Forum of Democracy" of great value in making social and political progress. This is of even greater importance when the Free World is in ideological conflict with totalitarian concepts around the globe. World-wide live television broadcasts, which will be made possible by the satellite system of transmission, will contribute to the image which people in other lands have of the American. The television spectrum is a publicly owned resource which, the Congress has declared, shall be used in the public interest. All engaged in television have a responsibility to make it a vital communications medium. The FCC, of course, shares this responsibility. In terms of social, cultural, and political development of our people, the responsibility of no governmental department or agency is greater.

Television also has the greatest sales impact of all the advertising media. Advertisers have been quick to take advantage of television's mass sales power. As the advertising dollar turns the wheels of the television industry, commercial motives loom large in the program-selection process. The merchandiser seeks a national market, and the networks seek a national audience for the merchandiser. Thus programming is offered which will ensure the maximum number of viewers. Action-adventure programs achieve the highest audience ratings. Gresham's Law operates in television to drive out programming of interest to substantial minority audiences, such as serious drama. Television programming, unlike radio programming, is costly, and most television stations must depend upon a program source, such as a network or syndicator, for the bulk of programming. Broadcasters have placed a practical reliance on networks to provide programming, and networks, in turn, use programming which serves commercial purposes. Thus commercial motives influence programming and tend to shape television as an advertising medium at the expense of television's potential development as a communications medium.

The essence of broadcasting is, of course, programming. Evaluation of the television service must be made from the armchair of the viewer in the intimate setting of the home. If the radio spectrum is public property to be used in the public interest, it follows that the communications function of television should be primary and that the commercial function should be secondary.

From the beginning of broadcasting, influence by government on programming has been indirect and minimal. The free society is wisely cautious of measures which might involve censorship or thought control. The regulatory approach in broadcasting has been to select and license a qualified broadcaster at the "grass roots" level and impose upon him the non-delegable duty of fulfilling the tastes, needs, and desires of the community he is licensed to serve.[1] However, no application for renewal of a

1. The FCC's licensing function and the responsibility of broadcast licensees are analyzed in *Network Broadcasting*, the report of the FCC Network Study Staff (85th Cong., 2d sess., H.R. No. 1297), pp. 124–56, 160–70. The report is cited hereafter as *Network Broadcasting*.

television license has been denied on the ground of inadequate program service, and during the period from 1952 through 1957 only three applications for renewal were set for formal hearing.[2] In this atmosphere, the license-renewal process has not served its purpose of insuring that broadcasters serve in an appropriate degree the tastes, needs, and desires of the community, and broadcasters have permitted their programming to be influenced by commercial considerations. Recent actions by the FCC, denying an original application for radio license on the ground that the proposed programming was not suited to needs of the community, limiting an application for renewal of a radio license to a term of one year, portend a greater use of the license-renewal process to improve television programming.[3] However, the role of the FCC in influencing programming must be, in view of free speech and anti-censorship principles, a limited one.

Since the balancing of freedom and responsibility restrains the hand of government, it behooves the broadcasting industry to use social imagination and creativeness in developing program service in the public interest. The President's Commission on National Goals has observed that, quite the contrary, the industry has permitted the level of culture and ideas in television programming to fall below that in any popular art field. The Commission reports: "Thus far, television has failed to use its facilities adequately for educational and cultural purposes, and reform in its performance is urgent."[4]

The principal influence on the character of television programming is the utilization of the television medium as a marketing instrument. As the structure of the industry has been built around the advertising role, the program-selection function at the national level has passed, by and large, into the hands of the advertisers, advertising agencies, and networks. It has become unfeasible for the licensed broadcaster to exercise, in an appropriate degree, his non-delegable responsibility to select programming.

A few other private interests influence the character of television programming. These include the National Association of

2. *Network Broadcasting*, pp. 163–64.
3. These actions are reviewed *infra*.
4. *Report of the President's Commission on National Goals* (Prentice-Hall, 1960), pp. 9, 132.

Broadcasters, which promotes industry self-regulation; the talent agencies, which exercise a degree of control over programming; and racial, religious, and other pressure groups.

The purpose of this paper is to describe the way in which television programming is effected by non-governmental influences and to review the numerous proposals which have been made for improving the variety, quality, and cultural level of television programming. In view of the writer's relationship as consultant to the FCC, no solution has been proposed.

THE INFLUENCE OF THE ADVERTISING FUNCTION

The structure of television is designed to market products. In national television, the networks serve a major programming function. For a composite week in 1955–56, network programs were on the air 51.4 per cent of the broadcasting time of all stations, affiliated or unaffiliated. During evening prime time, network programs occupied 91 per cent of the time on CBS and NBC basic affiliated stations, and these stations covered 80 per cent of all television hours.[5] In terms of "viewer hours," television is largely a nation-wide network medium serving national advertisers. Understandably, marketing motives are a major factor in the network program-selection process.[6] This is the strongest influence in the character of television programming today.

The Advertiser and Agency

The advertiser's motive in sponsoring television programming is, of course, to sell products. A program is sponsored because it is deemed a good vehicle to carry the advertising message. With rare exception, a program does not stay on the air unless it sells the product. "Omnibus," a show of great cultural and educational quality could not survive the hot sun of commercial analysis. The advertiser pays the bill for "free" television. This bill is high. Alternate-week sponsorship of a national network half-hour program for a season costs approximately $2,750,000 for time, program, and commercial.[7] Management is answerable

5. *Network Broadcasting*, p. 188.
6. See Bryant, Ashbrook, "Responsibility for Broadcast Matter," *Journal of Broadcasting* (Winter, 1960–61), p. 3.
7. *In the matter of Study of Radio and Television Network Broadcasting*, FCC, Docket No. 12782, Interim Report, p. 138. The Interim Report of the Office of Network Study Staff is cited hereafter as *Interim Report*.

to stockholders, and, to justify such high expenditure, the television program must reach a large audience and achieve a favorable sales result. Heavy reliance is placed on audience ratings.

A few advertisers on national television sell products used by a limited audience, such as high-priced automobiles and cameras. Some of these advertisers have sponsored high-quality, cultural and entertainment programs, including drama and public-affairs programs. However, even where the purposes of the sponsor are served by reaching a limited "target" audience, considerations of competition between networks and the importance of audience flow in this competition may prevent acceptance of the program. Thus a large insurance company, which had developed a drama series built around the contributions of universities to American life, recently found that there was no available network prime time for this type of show.[8] Advertisers of products used by a limited group usually sponsor special features rather than a regular weekly series. The number of these advertisers is too small to assure an adequate measure of high-quality programs.

The greater part of advertisers on national television sell products which the mass of the population uses, such as soap, cigarettes, food, and pharmaceuticals. These sponsors require a program vehicle which will carry the advertising message to the largest possible audience. Surveys by rating services show that the highest audience ratings are attained by shows which feature strong physical action and violence, such as "Westerns," "Private Eyes," and other action-adventure types. High ratings are attained also by situation comedy, quiz shows, and variety shows. If a Western will attract thirty million viewers and a serious drama only fifteen million, the economics of marketing dictates that serious drama go off the air and another Western be exhibited. Thus "Playhouse 90," which drew an audience of twenty million for four years gave way for "horsewhipping and heavy breathing."[9] The advertiser does not desire to control programming, as such, but his concern with programming as a

8. *Advertising Age*, July 3, 1961, p. 6.
9. *In the matter of the Study of Radio and Television Network Broadcasting,* FCC Docket No. 12782, Hearings, p. 5375. The hearings are cited hereafter as Transcript.

marketing implement requires that he choose a program capable of achieving maximum audience response.

As agent for the sponsor, the advertising agency has motives identical with those of the sponsor. Subject to the sponsor's approval, the agency develops a marketing plan, selects a line-up of markets, determines the network to be used, selects the program and network time to be sought, and develops the commercial theme of the campaign. The agency's program department may develop a program, in which case it, of course, controls the content. The agency may buy a program from an independent producer or use one produced by the network. Even so, the agency exercises numerous functions regarding the program. These include screening program ideas and pilots, approving talent and script, and integration of commercials.[10]

In the Commission's recent hearings on responsibility for broadcast matter, considerable testimony was taken regarding participation by the advertising agency in the creative aspects of programming. Though these hearings are not complete, the record contains information on the basis of which the functions of agencies can be described. The agency conducts extensive research to determine how it can create an "image" of the product. A program is then chosen which will, in the judgment of the advertiser and agency, be compatible with the product and assist in persuading prospective buyers to accept the advertising message.[11] The agency has a program department which protects the interest of the advertiser-client with respect to programs. Whether the idea and format are created in the agency's program department or the pilot is presented by outside interests, the agency participates in the creative aspects of production, and where the agency brings the program to the network, the network has little to do with the creative aspects.[12] The agencies' concern with maximum audience has led to dependence upon a few proved stereotypes, giving rise to imbalance in programming.[13]

A few examples, from the hearings on responsibility for programming, illustrate how the character of programming is shaped by the sponsor and agency. An advertiser turned down a

10. *Network Broadcasting*, p. 40.
11. *Interim Report*, pp. 140–41.
12. *Ibid.*, pp. 153–58.
13. *Ibid.*, pp. 163–64.

talented writer's script on the grounds that "I want happy shows for happy people with happy problems." [14] And another sponsor, after such plays as "Member of the Wedding" and "The Winslow Boy" had received low ratings, instructed the writer to prepare "happier vehicles." [15] Someone testified that today writers are told: "Write us a vehicle for a cowboy named X or a private eye named Y. It must follow our format." [16] A number of writers testified that they were instructed to work within a predetermined framework as to character, story, and mood.[17] A number of witnesses testified that violence is used by sponsor and agency for its audience response rather than for character delineation or development of theme.[18]

Instances were also cited of editorial changes to avoid reaction against the product or to render the story compatible with the product. Thus an agency official told how one cigarette company, which advertised filter cigarettes, required that the villain smoke non-filter cigarettes, while another cigarette company, which advertised non-filter cigarettes, required that the villain smoke filter cigarettes.[19] In a "Playhouse 90" script regarding the Nuremberg Trials, the word "gas," referring to the cyanide gas used in the execution chambers, had to be deleted throughout lest it be confused with the cooking gas sold by the sponsor.[20] A writer related how in a dramatization of the Andersonville Trial, the sponsor, an automobile concern, instructed that President Lincoln not be mentioned by name, since this was the name of a rival car, and, to avoid reaction by Southerners, the title was changed so as to disguise the fact that the story concerned events in a Confederate stockade for Northern prisoners.[21] Another writer was requested to change the character of the hero from a Negro boy to a Mexican boy.[22]

Editorial changes such as these, made to render the program compatible with the product or to avoid hostile reaction to the

14. Transcript, p. 5558.
15. Transcript, p. 5557.
16. Transcript, p. 5331.
17. Transcript, pp. 5421, 5428, 5693.
18. Transcript, pp. 5527, 5368, 5398, 5445, 5491.
19. *Interim Report*, p. 170.
20. *Ibid.*, p. 143.
21. *Cincinnati Enquirer*, June 30, 1961.
22. Transcript, p. 5426.

product, certainly constitute private censorship by sponsor and agency. They are not in themselves, however, highly significant in determining the character of television programming.

The significant result of advertiser and agency influence on television programming is that the character of programming is predetermined. Structurally and economically, national television is best suited to reaching a mass audience at great cost. The bulk of television programming, therefore, is designed to achieve the greatest mass response. Advertiser and agency consult the audience ratings. That oracle foretells the future of television programming. Programs which achieve the highest ratings become stereotypes for imitation. "Gunsmoke" was imitated by 26 programs and "I Love Lucy" by 16.[23] The network, the independent producer, and the writer know the types of programming which have a chance of acceptance by the sponsor. Thus before a script is written or a pilot made, the essential nature of television programming is predetermined by the commercial purpose of using a mass-marketing vehicle. The serious side of life, controversial issues, racial problems, information necessary to cope with the exigencies of the period are deemed too "downbeat" (sad and gloomy) to attract viewers and leave them with a happy, bright image of the sponsor and his product. The high cost of television programming discourages the risk of attempting new types. Hence, imagination, creativeness, and experimentation are stifled.[24]

The Network

The networks are the major source of programming for stations. Part of the network schedule is produced directly by the networks, part is supplied by other sources in which the network has an interest, and part is supplied by the advertisers subject to network agreement that the programs meet the network's standard of quality and are appropriate for the time segment.[25] Final determination as to whether a program is broadcast over the network is, of course, made by the network. However, because the network structure is designed to integrate a nationwide line-up of stations for the advertiser's desired market cov-

23. Transcript, p. 5524.
24. Roger Kennedy, "Programming Content and Quality," *Law and Contemporary Problems*, XXII, 541.
25. *Network Broadcasting*, p. 43.

erage, the network, of necessity, lends itself to the commercial motives of the advertiser and agency.

In the hearings on responsibility for programming, representatives of the three networks testified regarding the participation of sponsors and advertising agencies in the process of program production and selection. Included in the testimony of the representative of NBC are statements that the advertisers exercise a degree of influence on programming and that where the advertiser brings the program to the network, the network has little creative participation, although the continuity-acceptance department would determine whether the program conformed to NBC's program standards.[26] A witness for CBS stated that the network has exclusive control of public-affairs programs; that the objectives of the advertiser are taken into account; that in the creative phases of entertainment and serious drama, the advertiser or agency may participate with the network "at every step and as to every element of the process"; and that CBS has the ultimate responsibility for program selection.[27] A witness for ABC stated that the independent producers which ABC uses have creative control but that ABC sends the scripts to the advertiser and holds briefings between advertiser and producer regarding the program.[28] In short, except for news and public-affairs programming—in which the independence of the reporter is respected—the networks permit participation by the advertiser and agency in the creative processes of program production and selection.

The network continuity-acceptance departments of the networks enforce the NAB Code and the network standards. Sensitive areas, such as race, religion, sex, and treatment of animals are checked to insure that the programs are in good taste and that public dissatisfaction is not aroused. This process is an influence on programming. Involved is the problem of maintaining equipoise between realities of the world around us and due consideration for good taste and sensitivity of minority groups.

Usually the advertiser and network have a common interest insofar as the character of programming is concerned. However,

26. *Interim Report*, pp. 94–96.
27. *Ibid.*, pp. 96–98.
28. *Interim Report*, pp. 98–100.

there are instances in which a program satisfactory to the advertiser is not acceptable to the networks for reasons of network competition. The network desires to maintain audience flow. The advertiser is interested in having his program preceded and followed by popular programs because this adds audience that the program which he is using would not attract alone. The network must be able to compete with the rival networks in each time period.[29]

An example of this conflict of interest between advertiser and network is provided by the demise of the "Voice of Firestone." In 1954, NBC pre-empted the time period used by Firestone in order to include the "Sid Caesar Show." Firestone was unwilling to sponsor the "Sid Caesar Show" because it was not deemed to reflect the corporate image of Firestone. NBC was unwilling to continue the Firestone musical show because the show was not achieving audience ratings comparable to those of CBS's "Arthur Godfrey Show." The Firestone show then found a place on ABC, where it was subsequently replaced by "Adventures in Paradise." [30] Thus a high-quality show, attracting a substantial, but not the greatest possible, following, could not maintain a place in prime time although the advertiser desired to continue it.

The Broadcaster

The licensed broadcaster is under a non-delegable obligation to broadcast programming suited to the tastes, needs, and desires of his community. However, in television, as contrasted with radio, it is not economically feasible for the majority of stations to provide their own programming because of the high costs of production. Accordingly the broadcaster relies on networks and film syndicators for the bulk of his programming, and in the preferred viewing hours most of the programming is provided by the networks.

From the foregoing review of the control over programming exercised by the advertiser, advertising agency, and network, it is obvious that the broadcaster has little control of programming supplied by national services. The broadcaster places a practical reliance on the network to determine the character of programming provided by the network. The broadcaster has little ad-

29. Transcript, pp. 928–33.
30. Transcript, pp. 1120–77.

vance information as to the nature of network broadcasts, and
in most instances the station's viewers see the network program
at the same time that the broadcaster first sees it.[31] Also, it appears that the Network Affiliates Committees do not exercise
control over the service provided by the networks.[32] That the
broadcaster has been substantially insulated from the program-
selection process, insofar as network programs are concerned,
was indicated in the testimony of an advertising-agency executive, who stated: "I am afraid that [licensee responsibility to
select network programs] is an unrealistic situation. . . . Individual stations really do not have that authority, and if they
really exercised it, the economics of the situation is such that
they would not long be in business." [33]

Network-Affiliate Practices

The dependence of broadcasters upon networks for the program service and national advertising revenue gives the networks a superior position in bargaining with affiliates. This has
enabled networks to establish a number of industry practices
which affect the broadcaster's freedom to exercise his responsibility to select programming.

Under the "option time" practice, networks contract with
affiliates to pre-empt a portion of each of four segments of the
broadcast day. Recently the Commission reduced the time which
may be pre-empted from three to two and one-half hours in each
time segment and required that the broadcaster have greater
freedom to reject network programs. However, it is believed
that the network is still able to induce the station to take some
program fare which the broadcaster would not otherwise take.[34]
To this extent the freedom of the broadcaster to select programming is limited. Recently CBS has introduced a revised system
of compensating its affiliates which reduces their present compensation if the stations clear only at the present level; to increase compensation over the present rate, the affiliates must
clear for all network programs for which they are ordered.[35]
This would have the effect of persuading affiliates, even in one-

31. *Interim Report,* p. 101.
32. *Ibid.,* p. 102.
33. Transcript, p. 641.
34. *Network Broadcasting,* pp. 330–43.
35. *Broadcasting,* May 8, 1961, pp. 92, 96.

and two-station markets, to confine their network programming to one source. The FCC Network Study Staff recommended that the option time practice be prohibited as contravening the public interest and as constituting a possible violation of antitrust law on analogy to the blockbooking practice in *Paramount* and the tying device in *Times-Picayune*.[36]

The practice of networks in permitting advertisers to designate the line-up of stations results in some communities being denied the opportunity to view a network program which a broadcaster in the community desires to broadcast. The availability of some programs is thereby restricted. This raises a question as to whether, in the event the advertiser fails to order a market, the affiliate in that market, or, if the affiliate does not desire the program, any other station in the community, should not be given the opportunity to carry the program with the commercial deleted, upon reasonable payment by the station.[37]

Part Ownership by Networks of Independent Shows

Many programs are produced in a form of joint venture between networks and independent program producers. A common pattern is for the network to provide the risk capital for the pilot film in a proposed series and to acquire in return an interest in the program. The interest may consist of half profit from the program series exhibited on the network, from syndication, from merchandising rights, and from foreign sales, or some variation of this bundle of rights in the program. In instances in which a national advertiser desires to sponsor only half the program, the network may assume the unsponsored portion until a sponsor is found. In such instances, the network usually acquires an interest in the program, which may represent a percentage of profits "across the board." The coupling of network exhibition and acquisition by the network of an interest in the show raises a question as to whether programs are being selected on their merits.

THE INFLUENCE OF OTHER PRIVATE INTERESTS

There are a number of private interests, in addition to the commercial interests considered in the previous section, which have

36. *Network Broadcasting*, pp. 379–89.
37. This was a recommendation of the FCC Network Study Staff. *Network Broadcasting*, p. 657.

some influence on television programming. These include the National Association of Broadcasters, the talent agencies, and the minority groups and pressure groups.

National Association of Broadcasters

The National Association of Broadcasters, through the Television Code, exercises considerable influence on television programming and advertising. The preamble to the Code expresses the ideal which broadcasters should seek in programming in the public interest:

Television is seen and heard in every type of American home. These homes include children and adults of all ages, embrace all races and all varieties of religious faith, and reach those of every educational background. It is the responsibility of television to bear constantly in mind that the audience is primarily a home audience, and consequently that television's relationship to the viewers is that between guest and host.

. . . .

Television and all who participate in it are jointly accountable to the American public for respect for the special needs of children, for community responsibility, for the advancement of education and culture, for the acceptability of the program materials chosen, for decency and decorum in production, and for propriety in advertising. This responsibility cannot be discharged by any given group of programs, but can be discharged only through the highest standards of respect for the American home, applied to every moment of every program presented in television.

One reading the Code, while seated before his television set during a typical evening, may gain the impression that something was lost in the translation of this ideal into the programming viewed. However, it is well recognized that the NAB exercises a good and strong influence on programming and advertising. An example of industry self-regulation through the NAB Code is the prohibition of advertising of hard liquor, which has been uniformly followed by broadcasters. An example of an area in which self-regulation under the Code has not been as effective is programming for children. With respect to responsibility toward children the Code states:

The education of children involves giving them a sense of the world at large. However, such subjects as violence and sex shall not be presented with undue emphasis and only as required by plot development and delineation. . . .

It is not enough that only those programs which are intended for viewing by children shall be suitable to the young and immature. . . . Television is responsible for insuring that programs of all sorts which occur during the times of day when children may normally be expected to have the opportunity of viewing shall exercise care . . . in avoiding material which is excessively violent or would create morbid suspense, or other undesirable reactions in children.

The current hearings by the Senate Subcommittee to Investigate Juvenile Delinquency have pointed out the scarcity of programs designed especially for children, the early age at which children watch adult fare, and the excessive violence included in programs viewed by children.[38] Also, there was considerable testimony in the FCC hearings on responsibility for programming to the effect that violence is used to attract audience and not to delineate character or develop plot.[39] The President of the NAB has stated that "some crime and violence [on television] is unnecessary and undeserving of broadcast. . . . Such [programming] is offensive to good taste, seriously downgrades the television art, and should be eliminated."[40] He insisted, however, that improvement could come from industry self-regulation, that withdrawal of the Code's seal of good practice is an effective deterrent, and that governmental regulation is unnecessary.

It does not appear that administration of the NAB Code raises problems of private censorship which are harmful. To the extent that the code influences programming, it is for the purpose of insuring good taste. The prohibitions in the Code against use of profanity, obscenity, derisive references to race, attacks on religion, the use of horror for its own sake, and the like, while forms of private censorship, represent a desirable self-restraint and compliance with the law. Private regulation should seek a path between respect for the good taste and sensitivity of different ages and groups, on the one hand, and the painting of an unrealistic picture of the world around us, on the other.

It does not appear that the NAB code is administered with a

38. For example, see statements by Dr. Ralph J. Garry, Consultant to the Senate Subcommittee, and by James V. Bennett, Director of Federal Prisons.
39. See *supra*, n. 18.
40. Statement before Senate Subcommittee on Juvenile Delinquency.

view to insuring balance in programming. As has been shown above, the interest of the advertiser in obtaining maximum audience response and the ratings achieved by the violent action programs has resulted in sameness in television fare and the omission of high-quality programming desired by substantial, but less than maximum, audiences. President Collins, who has brought public-spirited leadership to the NAB, in commenting on the industry's reliance on ratings, has stated: "Broadcasting is, therefore, allowing an outsider to become its own master." He added that the industry must improve the quality of programming in prime time.[41]

The NAB is administered by the Television Code Review Board.[42] Utilizing an outside concern, the Board monitors commercial content on individual television stations and on the networks. Stations and networks are notified of violations, and corrective action is sought. However, it is recognized that the Board cannot substitute its judgment of programming for the judgment of the individual licensee. The Code is based on the assumption that broadcasters will voluntarily adopt the concepts for which the Code stands.[43] The Code Board has established an office in Hollywood to carry on liaison with producers of filmed programming for television. Approximately 40 per cent of all television programming is film originating in Hollywood, and in the case of network programs it is approximately 60 per cent.[44] In the event that a broadcaster persistently violates the code, he is denied the privilege of displaying the seal.

Self-regulation by industry under enlightened leadership is highly desirable. The NAB Code has contributed to good taste in television programming. However, even if it chose to encourage excellence and balance in programming, it is doubtful that it could overcome the commercial motives which have resulted in stereotyped mass-response programming.

Control of Talent

The FCC hearings on programming have included an inquiry into the effect on television programming of the activities of

41. *Broadcasting*, February 20, 1961, p. 50.
42. The functioning of the Board is described in *Interim Report*, pp. 201–6.
43. Transcript, pp. 1456–57.
44. Transcript, pp. 1460.

talent agencies. This inquiry is incomplete; however, sufficient information is available to describe generally the nature of the influences on programming.

The talent agencies represent the "Stars," for which a 10 per cent fee is received. The agency may "package" a show, i.e., supply all the personnel for a show, built around the Star which the agent represents. Where the agency packages a show, the agency receives a fee of 10 per cent on the selling price of the entire show. There may also be "across the board" participation in profits from use of the "property" on the network, in syndication, and in foreign sales. The tendency appears to be for the agency to place the more valuable talent in shows for which the agency is also the packager, since this enables the agency to exercise creative control, to protect the image of the Star, and to realize a greater profit. Two talent agencies, MCA, Inc., and William Morris, Inc., have the lion's share of the talent-agency business.[45]

The representation by two agencies of many talented performers and the agency's combination of the functions of talent agent and packager raise a question as to whether there exist anti-competitive practices affecting the character of programming available to television. There is an ancillary problem, of less bearing on programming, as to whether the talent agent has conflicting interests in representing the talent and dealing with the talent as packager-producer of the show. Talent is the necessary ingredient of excellent programming. Fluidity of talent and availability of it to prospective producers encourage experimentation and development of new program sources. Practices which limit availability of talent may have an adverse effect on television programming.

The House Anti-Trust Subcommittee in 1956 conducted hearings on network practices with respect to talent. The Subcommittee found that the networks at that time kept a substantial number of performers under long-term contracts. The contracts limited the artists' availability to other networks or producers. In some instances the contracts provided that the artists would be paid high salaries even though the network should not have a use for their services. The effect was to restrict access of com-

---

45. The activities of talent agencies are described in Transcript, pp. 4797–4888, and in *Broadcasting*, October 21, 1957, pp. 33–58.

peting networks to outstanding talent and, hence, to degrade
program quality.[46]

Group Pressures

The imperfect status in our society of some groups, who on
the basis of past discrimination are uncertain of their future
status, is one focal point of group pressure. These groups are
sensitive to adverse depiction of the group with which they are
identified because they fear that latent prejudice may become
patent. To say that a Yankee is a money-grubber does not produce the same reaction that one would expect from referring to
a Jew in the same way. Groups doubting the security of their
status react to an unfavorable image of the group. The reaction
to such a depiction on television may be stronger than a similar
depiction in other media because of the pervasiveness of television viewing and broadcast of the program to the entire country.

Familiar to all is the example of "The Untouchables," in which
gangster characters were depicted as being of Italian extraction.
Italians, fearful of an image of Italians as unworthy members
of society, took organized action. This resulted in an agreement
between the network and an Italian-group organization that the
program would not use fictional characters having Italian names
in gangster roles; that the characters representing law and order
and bearing an Italian name would be given a stronger role;
and that characters bearing Italian names would be featured in
roles of representative Italians who have advanced the American way of life.[47] Another example is the "Monitor South"
organization which monitors television and advises civic and
patriotic organizations of programs deemed to portray the white
Southerner in an unfavorable light.[48]

Television is sensitive to group pressure, not only because of
a desire to maintain good public relations, but also because the
advertiser wishes to avoid offending potential customers. There
is a need for balance in the handling of pressure-group problems.
On the one hand, due care should be given in handling the char-
acterization of groups whose history is such that sensitivity

46. *Report of the Anti-Trust Subcommittee on the Television Broadcasting
Industry*, March 13, 1957, pp. 55–61.
47. *New York Times*, March 26, 1961.
48. *Broadcasting*, January 2, 1961, p. 46.

would be anticipated. On the other hand, the network or broadcaster should not introduce changes which render the program unfaithful to the message which the program was intended to communicate.

Another pressure point which merits thought is the sensitivity of broadcasters to governmental policy, particularly in our international relations. Here again, possible adverse reaction to the advertised product by those persons who oppose the position taken in the broadcast is one of the factors in program selection. Familiar examples of this type of pressure are the CBS handling of "The Spy Next Door," the request by Murrow that the British not broadcast a film program on the migrant worker in America, and President Kennedy's request that the media exercise voluntary restraint in security matters.[49]

Not the least of the private pressures is the substantial lobby which the broadcasting industry is able to mount in the Congress. It has been widely stated that this was a factor in the defeat of the recent proposal for reorganization of the FCC.[50] The effectiveness of the industry's lobby has been attributed, in part, to the importance of television in political campaigns.[51]

REVIEW OF PROPOSED SOLUTIONS

During the hearings on responsibility for programming, numerous proposals were made for insuring greater freedom from commercial influence on programming and greater balance in programming. The following will be considered: (a) greater self-regulation by industry; (b) closer scrutiny of the performance of stations; (c) regulation of networks; and (d) establishment of advisory committees and independent analysis centers. These proposals will be reviewed for the purpose of delineating some values contributed and some problems raised by each.

Industry Self-Regulation.

A considerable body of testimony in the hearings favored industry self-regulation and advanced the opinion that no ad-

49. *Washington Post*, February 17, 1961, p. A14; *Broadcasting*, February 20, 1961, p. 56; *New York Times*, March 24, 1961; *Broadcasting*, May 8, 1961, p. 48.
50. *New York Times*, May 21, 1961 (editorial); *New York Times*, June 18, 1961, p. 6E; *Broadcasting*, June 19, 1961, p. 64.
51. *New York Times*, June 18, 1961, p. 6E.

ditional regulation at any level is necessary to insure that programming in the public interest is provided.

Industry self-regulation is the most desirable form of regulation, and it seems clear that more self-regulation in television can be accomplished. The hearings showed that advertisers, advertising agencies, and networks, relying upon audience ratings, select programs having maximum audience appeal and that programs which are desired by substantial, but not maximum, audiences are excluded from the schedule. If the spirit of the preamble of the NAB Television Code were observed by the industry, the imbalance in television programming would be corrected.

The existing character of television programs suggests, however, that industry self-regulation cannot be depended upon to fulfill the public interest in broadcasting. Competition in advertising products and in network service limit the extent to which public-spirited advertisers or networks can provide programming designed for the tastes and needs of substantial minority audiences. Each network has to compete with the rival networks, and it may not be feasible, for example, to exhibit a serious drama if this would result in loss of audience to more popular stereotypes on the other networks. It has been charged that the concentration upon Westerns and Mysteries by ABC was followed by a lowering of standards at CBS and NBC.[52] Each merchandiser is in competition with other merchandisers and commercial motives require that he reach as wide an audience as his competitors reach and with equal sales impact.

Television programming can be improved by greater competition in the industry. Increase in viable stations, new network entry, and the development of new program sources will increase competition in television and bring about more variety in programming. This would also result in programming for some substantial audiences not now served. However, it does not appear that reliance can be placed on competition alone. A combination of encouraging competition in the industry and of regulation to the extent that competition does not achieve programming in the public interest seems necessary.

The NAB Code has exerted good influence with respect to ad-

52. See *New York Times*, April 23, 1961, p. X17, and April 30, 1961; Transcript, p. 5526–27.

vertising in television and in treating matters of taste. However, it does not appear to have concerned itself with balance in program fare. Assuming that NAB should choose to make an effort in this direction, it is questionable that the commercial motives in program selection could be overcome. The available penalty, withdrawal of the seal of good practice, would be of questionable efficacy in achieving balance at the network level, and stations are able to operate without the seal. It is believed that the public has little awareness of the seal or its significance in television programming.

Enlightened leadership in all components of broadcasting can go far towards providing television programming which meets the tastes, needs, and desires of all substantial segments of the population. Television has the opportunity to provide our people with information which will enable them to cope with the exigencies of their period and to make the decisions which are necessary in their time. It can give the people a taste of culture, represent the constituent elements of society, and clarify goals and values of society. Those who serve the publicly-owned airways should not be satisfied with less.

Scrutiny of the Stations

Numerous witnesses in the hearings recommended that the FCC scrutinize more closely the performance of television stations. In the past the Commission has not made an extensive use of the license-renewal process to influence the quality of program service.[53] Recently, the Commission has taken actions which portend a greater use of the license-renewal process to improve program service. These actions were heralded by Chairman Minow's so-called "Wasteland" speech before the NAB, in which he expressed well-based and serious concern over the character of much television programming. Applicants are more and more being asked to base their programming proposals on the needs of their community.[54] The application form affords a better basis for comparing performance with promised performance. In the recent *Suburban Broadcasters* case, the Commission denied a construction permit for a new FM station on the ground that the program proposal was not designed to meet the needs of the community to

53. See *supra*, n. 2.
54. FCC Docket No. 13961, document FCC 61-863, 6692, adopted July 6, 1961.

be served.[55] In the recent *KORD* case, involving application for renewal of a radio license, the Commission, finding substantial deviation of performance from promised performance, limited the renewal to one year and served notice that performance of the licensee in that term would be scrutinized with care.[56] In its opinion, the Commission had these words for broadcasters generally:

. . . by issuing this opinion, we immediately make clear to broadcasters the seriousness of the proposals made by them in the application form. The Commission relies upon these proposals in making the statutory finding that a grant of the application would be in the public interest. The proposals, we stress, cannot be disregarded by the licensee, without adequate and appropriate representations as to change in the needs of the community. In short, a licensee cannot disregard his proposals in the hope that he will simply be permitted to "upgrade" when called to account. He does not have the right to one or any license period where he does not have to make a good faith effort to deliver on his public service proposals.

The application of the *Suburban* and *KORD* doctrines to television would have a salutary effect on programming. It may be noted that the high cost of television programming and the practical reliance of television stations on networks and other program sources raises a factor which no longer exists in radio.

The public-interest standard and the balanced-program doctrine have been applied by the Commission to stations since the beginning of commercial broadcasting, particularly in the contexts of comparative hearings on original grants and in license-renewal proceedings.[57] Thus the public-interest standard and balanced-program doctrine have been given quite definite meaning. The broadcaster is obligated by these concepts to make an effort in good faith to ascertain the tastes, needs, and desires of all substantial groups in the community served and to meet these needs in appropriate proportion by a well-rounded program service. In a society dedicated to promoting the maximum development of the individual, diversity of programming is the *sine qua non* of broadcasting service. At the local level, balanced program service includes: (*a*) opportunity for local self-expression; (*b*)

55. *In re application of Suburban Broadcasters*, FCC Docket No. 13332, released July 5, 1961.
56. *In re application of KORD, Inc.*, FCC Docket No. 14003, released July 12, 1961.
57. *Network Broadcasting*, p. 129. More generally, see pp. 54–64; 127–41.

opportunity for development of local talent, artistic and otherwise; (c) programs adapted to tastes and needs of children, (d) religious programs; (e) educational programs; (f) public-affairs programs; (g) editorial comment by licensees; (h) political broadcasts; (i) news; (j) agricultural and other local economic group-interest programs; (k) weather and market reports; (l) sports; (m) service to minority groups; and (n) entertainment.[58] In all communities it may be presumed that balanced programming in the public interest includes opportunity for local self-expression, religious programs, news and public-affairs programs, political broadcasts, and educational programs.[59]

Some authorities have expressed the view that the Commission is precluded from considering programming because this would constitute an unreasonable restraint on free speech.[60] The Attorney-General and the Commission have taken the position that the Commission can consider programming at least in the licensing and renewal contexts.[61] It is not a purpose of this paper to analyze the conflicting views as to whether the free-speech and censorship provisions preclude action by the FCC with respect to programming. The essence of broadcasting service is programming. Broadcasters are licensed to serve in the public interest, and the Commission applies the public-interest standard and balanced-program doctrine in the comparative-hearing and license-renewal contexts.[62] In every instance in which a question has been presented, the courts have upheld the Commission's concern with the licensee's program policies and practices. It would

58. For a discussion of these elements, see *Interim Report*, pp. A5–A10. In the case of radio, where there are a number of stations serving the same community, it may fit the over-all needs of the community to permit one or more stations to render a specialized service.

59. *Ibid.*, p. A10. Each community has characteristics which give rise to a presumption that, in its case, balanced programming would include additional types of programming. For example, an agricultural community should receive some programming regarding agriculture.

60. For example, see statement of W. Theodore Pierson, submitted in FCC Docket No. 12782 and memorandum of Whitney North Seymour, Special Counsel, NAB, submitted in FCC Docket No. 12782.

61. *Report to the President by the Attorney-General on Deceptive Practices in the Broadcast Media; Report and Statement of Policy re: Commission En Banc Programming Inquiry*, FCC 60–970, dated July 29, 1960.

62. For a review of the Commission's decisions in which evaluation of program service was involved, see *Network Broadcasting*, pp. 145–56, and *Interim Report*, pp. 39–57.

seem that programming should be the most vital concern of the FCC. It seems likely that reasonable regulations designed to achieve broadcasting in the public interest would be regarded by the courts as regulation of a condition in broadcasting calling for regulation and not as an unreasonable restraint on free speech. Clarification by the courts of doubt as to the Constitutional limit on the Commission's power to consider programming would aid the Commission in the administration of the Act.

A more vigorous use of the license-renewal process should achieve substantial improvement of the station's program service. However, television stations place practical reliance on networks for programming, particularly in the prime evening hours. Hence regulation of stations alone, the Commission has recognized, will not insure use of the airways in the public interest.[63]

Regulation of Networks

A number of witnesses recommended that networks be licensed and regulated as an approach to the improvement of television programming. As has been seen, the commercial motive of the advertiser and network in reaching a national market dictates that program fare achieve mass response, and it results in displacement of high-quality programming and imbalance in programming at the national level. The stations place practical reliance on the networks to choose programming supplied by the network. Thus the character of program service provided by integrated networks of licensed stations has a heavy bearing upon the exercise by the stations of their responsibility to broadcast in the public interest.

The FCC has informed committees of the Congress that it is in accord with the objectives of bills to permit regulation of network policies, practices, and activities which directly affect the ability of station licensees to operate their stations in the public interest.[64] The statutory framework proposed by the Commission is that the Commission be given authority as follows: (*a*) to classify networks; (*b*) to require networks to file with the Commission statements regarding network policies and practices; and (*c*) to

63. Comments of the FCC on H.R. 11340 (86th Cong., Doc. 88411), adopted May 4, 1960, p. 11.
64. *Ibid.* The Report of the Network Study Staff recommended that the FCC be authorized to apply its rules directly to networks. See *Network Broadcasting*, chap. XIV.

regulate policies, practices, and activities of networks which adversely affect the ability of broadcast licensees to operate their stations in the public interest. However, the Commission has cautioned that control of programming should remain the primary responsibility of the licensed broadcasters and that any responsibility for programming which may be placed on networks should be complementary to the responsibility of stations.[65]

The Commission's proposal contemplates regulation of networks without licensing. The Special Committee on Legislative Oversight has proposed that networks be licensed.[66] It is believed that a feasible regulatory system could be devised through either approach. Of greater significance would be the nature and efficacy of any such rules. The objective of any such regulation should be to reduce the weight of commercial factors in the selection of programming for national television to the extent necessary to enable the broadcaster to exercise his responsibility to serve the needs, tastes, and desires of his community. The problem is to devise a framework which promotes diversity and improves quality without impairing the function of networks as a national program service. Accommodation of an advertiser-supported system of broadcasting to a society made up of persons having diverse tastes, needs, and backgrounds is a complex process. Any actions taken should allow for the complexity of the industry and the factors necessary to a creative, viable national television system.

Advisory Committee and Independent Analysis Centers

Some witnesses recommended the appointment of an advisory committee to evaluate television programming and to advise the Commission of indicated changes in programming. Others suggested that the Commission utilize independent analysis centers to evaluate programming.

The function of the advisory committee and independent analysis center woud be to conduct periodic review of network programming in terms of the balanced-program doctrine. Through the committee's work, the Commission would be provided with conceptual tools and empirical data for the appraisal of program service. The "public interest" is not a static concept but is an evolving one, sensitive to changing national and community tastes, needs, and desires. An advisory committee composed of

65. *Ibid.*
66. Committee Report (86th Cong., 2d sess., H.R. 1258).

eminent Americans in business, labor, the arts, professions, education, religion, government, broadcasting, etc. would be in a position to sense and appraise the national tastes, needs, and aspirations and the degree to which the over-all broadcast structure is performing in this respect.

Such an advisory committee, being an *ad hoc* body, might well be aided by continuing, scholarly, conceptual analysis in defining public-interest criteria and collecting and evaluating information about program performance. This assistance might be provided by independent analysis centers. Such centers would be able to keep abreast of the changing concept of the public interest. It is possible that non-partisan foundations interested in contributing to the appraisal of the quality of the arts, the reassessment of entertainment values, and the improvement of communications media would give financial support to such centers if it were known that the Commission deemed their contribution of value in furthering the public interest in television.

Advisory bodies such as those suggested in the hearings may well have the merit of stimulating the broadcasting industry to make voluntary improvements in program service. Thus the area for regulation might be limited.

CONCLUSION

The national advertiser seeks a national market and the network seeks to deliver a national audience. Audience ratings show that a few stereotypes, such as Westerns, Mysteries, Quiz and Variety Shows, achieve the highest ratings. Gresham's Law operates in television to drive out high-quality shows, such as serious drama, which attract a substantial, but not a maximum, audience. Broadcasters place a practical reliance on networks to select programming transmitted via the network. In this way the licensed broadcaster's responsibility to serve the tastes, needs, and desires of his community is impinged.

In this paper various proposals for rendering television more responsive to the needs of our time and the tastes of substantial segments of our population not now served have been reviewed.

The Report of the President's Commission on National Goals speaks of a "time of trial" for the democratic process. It notes that our success in advancing technology has led to complexity of urbanized living, standardization of tastes and attitudes, and centralization of communications and that the cumulative tendency of these factors is to isolate the individual from the centers of control, to flood him with over-simplified knowledge, and thereby to discourage his responsible participation. A serious problem arises as to the capacity of the democratic system to maintain its forward motion. The character of our social-political problems make them difficult to decide, and many of them by requiring rapid decision increase the chances for error.

The adequacy of our public decision-making machinery, the quality of the decisions, and the confidence of the public in them are being tested. With this challenge in mind, it is pertinent to pose this question: Is broadcasting contributing to the resolution of fundamental issues, or does the content to which we are exposed lead only to superficial knowledge and a sense of well-being? What is television doing to stimulate and extract excellence in this time of conflict with totalitarian ideology? Is not the ultimate question one of the degree to which this great public resource—television—is furthering a strong, confident democratic spirit or the degree to which its use as a marketing implement impedes television's service in the public interest?

Reply
by W. Theodore Pierson

I commend Dean Barrow on his review of television programming, the alleged causes, and the postulated cures. I will not cavil over the criticisms and causes, not only because I believe them to be substantially correct, but because my principal disagreement is with the cures he postulated. Indeed, I believe that the greatest threat to television's achievement of its proper role in our free society comes in the form of the restrictions and restraints that the censors and controllers have placed and would place upon the medium, most of whom appear to have the complete support of Dean Barrow.

Perhaps my disagreement with Dean Barrow is really a disagreement over the role that mass media can properly play in a free society, which in turn may stem from lack of agreement on the principles upon which our society was built. To avoid needless capering in the leaves and branches of the controversy, perhaps I should state my understanding of the roots and trunk of the matter.

The principle of freedom upon which our society was built, as I understand it, starts with the premise that man is imperfect, whatever his station in life, and holds that he will become a more perfect moral and social creature through liberty and that attempts to coerce cultural or political perfection through governmental or other concentrated power merely conforms the subject to the imperfections of the central power. Such conformity destroys new ideas at gestation, prevents re-examination of the standards and rules by which we live, perpetuates the mistakes of those in power, reduces political intelligence, and degrades human dignity. Media of communication, being manned by imperfect beings, are bound to be imperfect, but in a free society the value of their service is proportional to the degree to which they can resist conformity to centralized control.

Contrast this to the Marxist-Leninist ideology with which we are now locked in a deadly combat. Our antagonist starts as we do with the premise that man is imperfect but, contrary to our

79

beliefs, holds that man cannot be allowed freedom until he has been recast, remolded, and reconditioned by the Communist apparatus, which is presumed to be perfect, to the end that the individual has no will to do anything other than what the state requires. Under Marxism-Leninism, media of communication are presumed to be perfect because they are dictated by a perfect authority. New ideas, re-examination of standards, correction of mistakes, political intelligence, and the dignity allowable to individuals can originate only at the top of this monolithic society. Under this ideological concept, mass media are valued in proportion to their conformity to centralized control.

If this layman's analysis of one important part of the ideological conflict between ourselves and the Communist world is substantially wrong, in Dean Barrow's view, then argument between us on the efficacy of the various proposals to improve television would avail little, since we are headed in opposite directions. But I will assume substantial agreement by him, if for no other reason than that a lawyer—and I am a lawyer—rarely stops when he is given the opportunity to continue.

Dean Barrow's paper, in summary, pointed out what's wrong and why and what to do about it. He emphasized throughout the great capacity of television for good or evil, with which I agree.

He alleged that television as now practiced is an imperfect instrument for the political, cultural, and educational improvement of our American society. With this, also, I agree. I will go farther than he. It will *always* be unless we develop a perfect machine that requires no imperfect human being to perform tasks or make judgments. The pall of imperfection that is cast on commercial television shrouds all human activity, including, above all, governmental action. We are constantly deluged with exposures by our intellectual elite of imperfections in education, politics, economics, government, the arts, and the sciences.

Where Dean Barrow and I disagree is that he seems to believe that we will come nearer to perfection if we centralize program control in a rather closely knit combination of seven members of the FCC, the Board of Directors of NAB, and a small select advisory group of outstanding citizens. He heads toward more centralization of control over programming. I would go the other way. He seeks conformity of television program schedules to centralized ideas of balance. I would seek balance in the total output of the industry through maximizing the diversified imbalance of individual licensees. I believe that a balanced fare from the industry as a whole can ultimately be accomplished, without the censorship or centralized control that Dean Barrow postulates, by the proliferation of television stations under conditions that permit any station to unbalance the types of programs they broadcast at will and with abandon. The sum of such specialized program formats would result in over-all balance in the industry output.

I cannot disagree with Dean Barrow's assignment of the principal cause for the present caliber of television fare. Since, except for the non-commercial or educational stations, we have a free-enterprise television system, which by definition is motivated by profit, it ought to, and does, follow that considerations of profit will substantially influence the programs broadcast. To expect otherwise is to ignore the natural and inevitable consequences of our choice of a system. Every medium of communication that operates under a free-enterprise system is influenced in over-whelming degree by the profit motive. That the objective of profit substantially influences its product can be demonstrated conclusively with respect to any commercial medium one desires to name—newspapers, magazines, books, motion pictures, or theatre. And those media have their Anthony Comstocks too—Comstocks who are every bit as critical as any that television has.

Wherever free enterprise operates, its product or service is substantially influenced by the profit motive. The styling of clothes, automobiles, and household appliances are thus governed. The architecture and construction of homes, factories, and office buildings show the ever-present influence of the profit motive. Indeed, it is not unusual for the eggheads and intellectuals to seek opportunity to conform their output to the necessities of the profit potential. If the profit motive is evil, it is a virulent and contagious one, because it infects many of its loudest and most snobbish critics.

While I appreciate that, in Washington, to investigate is the thing, I really do not think we needed the costly Barrow investigation to establish that the profit motive influences television programming. This was and is one of the most open and notorious facts within my knowledge.

The investigation went farther than this, however. It sought to determine where the control of programming lay. It found no single or concentrated repository. Rather, as Dean Barrow has just pointed out, it found that control was dispersed among many advertisers and their agents, three competing networks and their hundreds of competing affiliates, and a few talent agencies. Compared to centralized control in the Commission, the NAB, and an elite advisory council, as Dean Barrow postulates, this is a tremendous fragmentation of control.

But it does not seem to be a principal Barrow complaint that too few private enterprisers are involved. It is that they are all possessed by the same motive—to earn a profit—and that all too frequently the profit goal is better served by catering to mass audiences. It is this parallelism among enterprisers that seems to gall him most. Could he have been surprised to learn that a mass medium supported by the suppliers of mass consumption seeks a mass audience a great deal of the time?

What did he postulate as means of curtailing this appeal to mass tastes? First, greater self-regulation through the NAB, which he did not believe would suffice because, being an industry organization, in spite of the enlightened leadership of Governor Collins, it might be quite contaminated with the profit motive. Second, more extensive and intensive program policing by the Commission, which solution he seems to adore most. Third, an advisory committee "composed of eminent Americans" to advise the Commission in its police work. This would nationalize in a truly effective fashion the method used by Comstocks in many communities to employ the police power to restrain books, periodicals, and motion pictures in unabashed cultural censorship.

Whatever success these measures might have in reforming television to meet the tastes of Dean Barrow, Chairman Minow, Governor Collins, and their admirers, I care not to argue. I would pray they would fail, because it is a complete formula for centralized cultural censorship and control.

Dean Barrow said that it was not his purpose to discuss the censorship issue raised by his paper. He professed no real concern with the problem. Well, I do feel concern, and I am constrained to discuss it.

In the past Commission efforts at program control and censorship have been quite submerged, and, while always lurking in the deep, they have been hard to surface and catch. To change the metaphor, Chairman Minow's program of action, announced first before the NAB and publicly many times since, offers a rare opportunity to grapple with more than a ghost. To demonstrate the nature of Dean Barrow's proposals, I wish to turn to the program of Chairman Minow.

Chairman Minow in his NAB speech bluntly told the broadcasting licensees that he had no confidence in their product (this, of course, after observing the amenities expected of a guest by telling them that they were nice chaps). He was very specific about the types of programs that he thought *should not* be broadcast or should be broadcast less frequently. He said, "The old complacent, unbalanced fare of Action-Adventure & Situation-Comedies is simply not good enough." He further observed that next season will be little better because "of 73½ hours of prime evening time, the networks have tentatively scheduled 59 hours to categories of action-adventure, situation-comedy, variety, quiz and movies."

He also was specific in certain areas as to the types of programs that *should* be broadcast. He declared quite specifically the proper format and purpose of children's shows and implied the time that they should be broadcast. He named his favorite shows by specific title. Chairman Minow exhibited impatience with the imperfect tastes of the masses and the broadcaster's imperfect response to public tastes.

His description of what he approves and disapproves was sufficiently explicit to enable any normally intelligent broadcaster to choose and select programs that will satisfy Chairman Minow's standards. The message was loud and clear. The broadcaster can throw out some programs completely, change the formats of others, and get some new ones that fit the specifications. No problem.

Thus far, on the basis of my summation, Chairman Minow's NAB speech could be characterized as just an example of clarity in the exercise of freedom of speech, albeit somewhat less restrained than normal for regulatory officials. It, after all, is nothing more than has been said by many television columnists, critics, and viewers.

But Chairman Minow went further. He said:

1. That the broadcaster owes to the public the type of programming that *he*, Minow, specified.
2. That he intends in his official capacity to see that the broadcaster pays the debts *he* stated.
3. And that he intends to accomplish this through the licensing power of the Commission.

Here he is playing the role not of citizen Minow but of the dispenser of the privilege to live or die as a broadcaster.

Now it seems to me that, considering these vigorous words, the Chairman simply said to the broadcaster, "Unless you broadcast or propose to broadcast what I favor and have specified, you will not be permitted by our Commission to broadcast anything." This, in my opinion, is a prior restraint upon broadcast communications, it is censorship, and it violates the First Amendment.

In the same speech that he said the things I have just described, he disavowed censorship in these words: "I am unalterably opposed to governmental censorship. There will be no suppression of programming which does not meet with bureaucratic tastes. Censorship strikes at the tap roots of our free society." He has been reported as having repeated this disclaimer many times since. But, in the speech, what did he say he would do but suppress programming which does not meet with bureaucratic tastes? If you are a bureaucrat and you tell a broadcaster that he may operate if he broadcasts what you favor and may not operate unless he suppresses what you disfavor, what are you doing but requiring broadcasters to conform to your taste?

Did Chairman Minow mean that refusing to permit applicants to broadcast is not a suppression of what they propose to broadcast? Did he mean that in his few months as Chairman he had been able to discern what no one else has ever known or been able to define—public interest in programming? Or is this some kind of exotic philosophy that reconciles logical irreconcilables by the mere assertion that they are reconcilable?

Perhaps it could be said that the Chairman did not intend to cause broadcasters to conform to his taste. But his speech had no professed or discernible purpose but to reform television programming after his pattern. I understand he has received several thousand letters commending him on his efforts in this regard, i.e., the use of his powers as a government dispenser of licenses to suppress some programs that he and his correspondents dislike and to engender others that he and they like. The widespread changes in television programming that will result from his efforts must surely have been intended by him. His perspicacity is demonstrably too great to conclude otherwise.

I am proceeding, therefore, not only on the basis that he intended to use governmental power to change television programming but that he will—the other members of the Commission and the courts willing—be eminently successful in obtaining wide-spread conformity with his expressed ideas on programming. The trade press, since his speech, has depicted frantic activity among producers, networks, syndicators, and station licensees to conform as quickly as possible to his program format. Make no mistake about it. If you tell any businessman that you can and will put him out of business unless he conforms his product to your standards, few will commit business suicide.

I submit that, if the Commission pursues the Minow plan for program reform, it will be the direct cause of the suppression of many programs and the release of many others that would not otherwise have reached your television screen, all tending to be stereotyped after the Minow pattern. Whether each of us would like the Minow format better than what we now have is a matter of personal taste for each individual. I personally would like it better than present fare. But what price do I pay for receiving the Minow format for the period that he holds sway?

It seems to me that the price is my concession that the Chairman and his fellow members at any time have the right and the power to set and enforce the format and structure of television program schedules—what they do to please me today can be undone tomorrow. They can prohibit violence today and editorials tomorrow—and editorials have been prohibited in the past.

More bluntly, the price I pay is acceptance of a high degree of centralized governmental control of television fare. Still more bluntly, it is censorship.

Constitutionally, it must violate the First Amendment; otherwise, that supposed protection against control over speech and press by government is inapplicable to the most effective means of communication yet devised by man. It would mean that free speech and press are only for the less efficient and most ineffective modes—books, newspapers, magazines, handbills, and movies. It would mean admitting that technological advance inevitably and progressively takes its price in loss of liberty.

Would it not be better to prohibit radio and television absolutely than to embrace it at the cost of liberty? If not, should we not be more honest with ourselves and cast off the façade of freedom and accept the governmental control of communications that has been so effectively and efficiently used by the ideology which we despise but the power and success of which we cannot gainsay?

I say that Mr. Minow cannot have it both ways. Brilliant, articulate, and sincere person that he is, he cannot free us from our own imperfect tastes by binding us to his imperfect tastes without denying the principle of freedom upon which our society was built, that is, diversity and liberty instead of conformity and restraint.

Any real and impending danger that lies in present television programming, much as I personally dislike much of it, is, of insufficient magnitude to justify Chairman Minow in substituting his imperfect personal tastes through governmental coercion for the imperfect tastes of the public or the imperfect responses of the broadcaster. The success of his endeavors would bring governmentally-induced conformity, not the diversity which is the intended goal of liberty and competitive enterprise. There are glaring imperfections in our present efforts, but to substitute governmentally-induced conformity (to borrow a phrase from Mr. Justice Frankfurter) "is to burn the house to roast the pig." Hence, I believe the course upon which he has embarked is illegal, unconstitutional, and violates basic principles upon which our American society has been built.

I wish to be very precise about the area in which I believe Chairman Minow's proposed course of conduct offends against liberty of speech and press. In many other areas, I not only agree with the Chairman but have nothing but admiration for his intelligent and vigorous approach.

I believe freedom is abridged whenever a licensee broadcasts a program or a series of programs, or fails to broadcast a program or a series of programs, not because in his judgment his public is thus served, but because unless he does so, the Commission can and will put him out of business. Congress took great care to lodge program control in the only place it can be lodged in a really free society—outside of government. Control was to be dispersed among the large number of licensees competing for public patronage. The natural forces of the market place—not government— were to determine the program fare, just as in every other medium of communication. Congress could not have hoped that its efforts would uniformly yield a perfect product any more than freedom and competition had done so in the other media. No perfect human institution or system exists, but the free system was chosen as the best of the alternatives.

Congress sought to insure service to the public by limiting licenses to those whom the Commission found qualified and of good character. The Commission can deny licensees when the licensee lacks the qualifications of a public trustee, and a determination of those qualifications does not require the Commission to review or restrict his judgment as to programs. It can require the trustee to be financed, equipped, organized, and disposed to make an informed judgment of the public's needs and desires. I have no quarrel with the Commission refusing a license where the licensee does not demonstrate that he will make reasonable efforts to inform himself on the needs and tastes of his public, in order that his judgment *is* an informed one. But I do quarrel with the Commission's attempt to substitute its judgment for that of the licensee. It was the wide variety of judgments by competing licensees, not stereotyped formats from government, that was to determine program fare. It is precisely because Chairman Minow seeks to impose his judgment as to program structure upon the licensees that I doubt the legality of his course—however subtly this is done and no matter how many times he denies that he is doing it.

There have been numerous justifications and excuses offered for Commission intrusions into broadcast programming. They range from denials that what the Commission does constitutes program interference to implied admissions that it does interfere but that the interference necessarily results from the Commission's performance of its statutory functions. Chairman Minow did not invent these contentions; most of them are old and hackneyed. But he has resurrected and repeated most of them at one time or another during the short period that he has been Chairman. In spite of his added endorsement, I am still convinced that they are nothing more than euphemisms for censorship.

It is contended that the Commission in its program investigations and review does not censor because it only examines and weighs "over-all programming." This is one of those phrases, the utterance of which seems to invoke some mystical power that changes restraint to liberty. An official accused of censoring needs only to utter these words, and the evil spirit of censorship is supposedly exorcised. An otherwise impure act by this incantation becomes pure and holy. Mysticism to one side, how in logic can one consider total programming without considering its parts? This is an esoteric rite that I have always wanted to witness but never have been so privileged.

Chairman Minow's talk before the NAB was no revelation of the secret. He dealt with specific types of programs of which he approved and disapproved. With his speech as a guide, one could examine the whole program spectrum and easily classify the favored and unfavored—which I believe was his intention. For him to have classified all programs by title would have been redundant and wholly unnecessary to his purpose of reforming television programming.

Moreover, I defy anyone to find a meaningful discussion of "over-all programming" in any Commission decision that did not deal with specific programs or specific categories of programs. If the Commission restrains or requires a whole category, is that acceptable, whereas to condemn or approve only one in a category is unacceptable? I cannot understand why it is censorship to require a station to broadcast a single educational program, for example, but it is not censorship to require several. Or why it would be censorship to interdict one program of violence but not censorship to silence many. Nor, in weighing a station's "over-all programming," have I ever understood how small are the parts into which it can be broken before it ceases to be mere consideration of "over-all programming" and becomes consideration of particular programming. What is the location and size of the barrier erected by Section 326 and the First Amendment? I cannot believe that the barrier against infringement of speech and press is a small corral for a single program that disappears as if by witchcraft when it is joined with one or several others. I refuse to believe that our sacred rights to liberty can be destroyed by such sorcery.

I submit that the area of Commission consideration of over-all programming is but a vast wasteland of withered liberties that should not be preferred over the "vast wasteland" Chairman Minow found in one long boring day and night before his television screen.

Closely associated with the "over-all programming" alibi for Commission interference with programming is the term "balanced programming." Balance would seem, on the surface, to refer to some proper mixture of program types—entertainment, religious, educational, agriculture, public affairs, discussion, live, etc. In actual practice it has been used to coerce licensees into carrying types of programs the Commission favors at the expense of programs that it disfavors or favors less. For example, I have never heard of a station being challenged for having too much educational, public-affairs, or discussion programs and too little entertainment, even though its "performance" of the favored shows exceeded its "promise." If the mixture is the thing, then imbalance in one category should be as bad as any other. A "performance" of 10 per cent educational against a "promise" of 5 per cent would seem as much a broken promise as a similar variance in entertainment.

The fact is that the balanced-programming concept, where it has been applied, has generally been used to coerce stations into carrying relatively unpopular programs at the expense of the relatively popular ones. It has been used to protect so-called minority tastes, never majority tastes.

Now I am willing to concede that broadcasting fails as an effective democratic instrument if it serves only majority tastes. The question is: Can a wide variety of program types be obtained only by the Commission requiring conformity to its stereotyped formats? If so, perhaps it is better that television remain ineffectual than make this concession to censorship and conformity. Moreover, if station formats are going to be stereotyped through conformance to Commission formulas, why do we need a great multiplicity of stations merely to repeat the same formulated fare on a variety of channels? Frequencies are too scarce for this waste.

There is a way established and intended by the Act that tends to diversity rather than conformity and does so without endangering our liberties. With a multiplicity of stations competing with each other, each must constantly search out unsatisfied wants. The more stations there are, the more assiduously each must search. With relatively few stations competing, the majority tastes constitute a large and rewarding market that tends to satisfy the few competitors. As stations increase, the majority audience must be shared by more stations, and the point is ultimately reached where a station's small share of a majority audience can be less rewarding than a large share of a minority audience. Hence some competitors forsake mass tastes and specialize in some unrequited minority desire. As more stations specialize, more special tastes are satisfied. This is not mere theory—it is demonstrated by a glance at the radio fare in many of our markets, which has resulted wholly from the proliferation of radio stations in the last decade and a half.

I submit that the balanced-programming guideline is but an instrument of conformity and censorship; freedom to specialize as competition in the market dictates is the opposite. The choice is between conformity through censorship and diversity through liberty.

Of course, we have not as yet in most television markets reached the point in television growth where stations are forced by economic imperatives to look far beyond the majority tastes. But television is farther advanced on this road now than radio was at the same age. We will arrive at this goal of diversity and total accommodation of tastes if the Commission and the industry work together to increase the economic support, the program sources, and the available channels for television. However tough some of these problems may be, the hope of success is not so dismal that we should accept censorship and conformity as a substitute.

Perhaps the most false and yet high-sounding excuse that the Commission has given for interference in programming has been that it is only seeking to require the licensee to perform what he has promised. The supporting contention that makes this sound so fair and proper to the uninitiated is that, if a licensee voluntarily promises something to get his license, he ought not to complain when the Commission exacts performance. There are two things wrong with this contention: first, the applicant has not made and cannot make a promise; second, his program representations were not in any real sense voluntary.

The form that requests him to submit a breakdown of his expected programming as to type and source states as follows: "It is not expected that licensee will or can adhere inflexibly in day-to-day operation to the representation here made." It goes on to state that an application should "reflect accurately applicant's responsible judgment of his proposed program policy." Program representations under this caveat simply do not rise to the dignity of a promise to specifically perform as represented. And the caveat was not just soft-heartedness on the part of the Commission; it was rather a recognition of the reality that it is beyond human prescience to predict program performance three years in advance without casting the licensee in an inflexible mold that itself would prevent him from serving his public.

The type of programs one broadcasts results from a judgment of the public needs and tastes *at the moment* and an attempt to implement that judgment from the programs available *at that moment*. The only predictable certainty about public needs and tastes is that they are eternally and constantly changing. Program sources, likewise, are constantly opening and closing.

A commitment over three years to an inflexible mixture of types and sources of programs is not only a commitment that would be impossible to perform, but, if it were possible, it would cause the licensee to ignore the changing needs and tastes of his public. Thus, the promise-*vs.*-performance dictum places the licensee in the hopeless dilemma of embracing inflexibility which, per se, should disqualify him as a licensee.

In view of Chairman Minow's threats to deny applications where the program structures do not conform to his specifications, it can hardly be said that the program representations in an application are uncoerced and voluntary. A quixotic few might propose program structures that Chairman Minow has said he will suppress by denying the license, but most will take the expedient and practical approach and conform to his format. Thus the Commission coerces a "promise" and then demands performance of the "promise" it has coerced. This mode of getting the programming the Commission wants is not sufficiently devious, under analysis, to conceal its true nature—it is an instrument of censorship.

I do not wish to imply that under all circumstances it would be improper for the Commission to weigh program representations *vs.* performance. Where the Commission seeks to determine whether the licensee willfully and fraudulently misrepresented his intentions and therefore has character defects, I believe the Commission can properly consider his performance as evidence of an intent not to perform what he represented at the time he filed the application. This has nothing to do with whether his programs were good or bad or what programs he proposes for the future; the only question is whether he intentionally deceived the Commission. If the evidence establishes that he did, then the Commission must weigh this along with other evidence on character, to determine whether he is a qualified licensee. In considering the character issue, it is irrelevant that he is now willing to make a new representation or to "upgrade" his programs. If his character is found to be bad, what good are new "promises"? If his character is found to be good, in spite of the misrepresentation to the Commission, that ends the inquiry, for it adds nothing to his character for him to make a new "promise" or to say that he will "upgrade" his programs.

But the Commission has not used the promise-*vs.*-performance standard as a mere test of character; it has been used principally to force a licensee to change his program proposals. The recent *KORD* case is an example.[1]

In 1960 KORD filed an application for renewal of license and proposed a program structure that contained no educational, discussion, or local live programs. The application disclosed that this was essentially its past performance. The Commission wrote a so-called McFarland letter indicating that a hearing would be required because a 1957 application had proposed a program structure that included programs in the categories that were not carried. KORD amended its application to propose programs in the favored categories and reduce its entertainment and recorded programs. The Commission designated the application for hearing but, upon petition for reconsideration, granted the application without a hearing.

The decision contains no real discussion of the character issue and relies heavily upon KORD's new "promises" to "upgrade" its programs by adding the favored categories. That the Commission is directly responsible for many programs that KORD will broadcast in the next three years and for the absence of others that, but for the Commission restraint, it would have broadcast cannot be in doubt. *KORD* is merely an example; many similar cases can be found. In fact, in the *KORD* decision the Commission boasted that it had been doing this since 1946.

Other supposed justifications for Commission interference with programming are that it must interfere because broadcasters use the public domain and operate pursuant to a license. These justifications stand up under neither analysis nor analogy.

I had always understood that one of the primary purposes of public facilities was to promote commerce and communication among our people. I had never understood that our liberties depended upon our avoiding use of the public domain.

If use of public domain deprives a communication medium of its right to be free from government censorship, then what medium today has the right to be free? All use the publicly owned postal system; many besides broadcasting use radio frequencies; all to a greater or lesser degree use public highways, streets, and airways; all do this under government regulation and many pur-

1. *KORD, Inc.*, Docket 140003, July 12, 1961.

suant to licenses. With the explosion of electronic and space-satellite developments, it is not too far-fetched to suggest that in a few years no substantial communications medium will be able to function without using the public's radio frequencies to a substantial degree.

I cannot see that, where government uses the licensing mode as its instrument of regulation, its power in areas circumscribed by the Constitution is increased. The printed media operate in large measure pursuant to a *permit* to use second-class mails. City streets, parks, and halls in many cities cannot be used for meetings or speeches without licenses from the city authorities. In a number of states and cities, motion pictures cannot be exhibited except pursuant to government license. Under no precedent that I can find has the fact that they were licensed been used as a justification to whittle away their rights under the First Amendment. As a matter of fact, in nearly all the cases, the very fact that the licensing mode of regulation was used, which by definition is a prior restraint, has caused the courts to be extraordinarily diligent in making certain that the instrument was not used to abridge liberty of press, speech, or religion. If communication media cannot use the public domain pursuant to a license and still maintain their freedom from government dictation of the things they communicate, then we have to say that the First Amendment died at the beginning of the radio and space age; that these liberties were intended only for the days when communication was infrequent, difficult, and relatively ineffective; that such liberties cannot be indulged in this modern world of technology. If we believe these things to be true, it seems to me that we have accepted a major element of the philosophy of Marx and Lenin.

The Commission claims that it has judicial approval for what it has done and is doing. I have to concede that the Commission enjoys the better of it in precedents. The Federal Radio Commission's power to deny renewals of licenses because it disapproved of past program performance was approved by the Court of Appeals in two cases, now thirty years old.[2]

In one case a Dr. Brinkley used his radio as a business adjunct and to prescribe for his patients. In the other case a Reverend

2. *KFKB Broadcasting Assn., Inc.* v. *F.R.C.*, 47 F.2d 670 (1931) ; *Trinity Methodist Church South* v. *F.R.C.*, 62 F.2d 850 (1932).

Shuler used the facilities to obstruct justice and make defamatory attacks. Mr. Shuler had a newspaper counterpart, by the name of Near, who had been doing about the same thing at about the same time in Minnesota, but through a newspaper instead of a radio station. A year before the *Shuler* case was decided by the Court of Appeals, the Supreme Court denied, as unconstitutional, an injunction against Near's continued publication of the newspaper, and this decision was cited in the *Shuler* briefs and cited in the Court's decision.[3] What Minnesota did was held by the Supreme Court to be a prior restraint, but what the Commission did was held by the Court of Appeals not to be a prior restraint.

I cannot reconcile *Near* and *Shuler* except on the grounds that the First Amendment applied to newspapers but not to broadcasting. At that time this belief was quite generally held. Not until 1948 did the Supreme Court unequivocally state that broadcasting was within the protection of the First Amendment.[4] (The applications of Brinkley and Shuler, incidentally, could have been denied on grounds that would have raised no question of censorship.)

In other Court of Appeals cases, the Court has upheld the Commission's right to use its evaluation of programming proposed in comparative applications as one of the deciding factors.[5] But the questions have never been squarely presented to the Supreme Court, although there is dictum to support my contention and other Court expressions which can be interpreted contrary to my position.

I do not believe that, in the light of the First Amendment cases decided in the last score of years, the precedents upon which my opponents rely are trustworthy. That is to say that, if broadcasting is protected by the First Amendment, as the Supreme Court says it is, then by analogy to cases in other media, the Commission cannot use its licensing power to previously restrain broadcast communications in the manner that the Commission has been doing and proposes to do. I believe the Court would so hold in a case squarely presenting the issue upon a complete record.

Moreover, I believe that attempts to achieve standardization of public tastes and broadcaster's response through centralized

3. *Near* v. *State of Minnesota,* 283 U.S. 697 (1931).
4. *U.S.* v. *Paramount Pictures, Inc.,* 68 S.Ct. 915, 933 (1948).
5. *Johnston Broadcasting Co.* v. *FCC,* 175 F.2d 351 (1949).

control by the NAB is only somewhat better than censorship by the Commission. Each seeks the concentration of control over programming and the standardization of tastes that is anathema to diversity and liberty. NAB is more acceptable because it lacks the coercive power of government, and there is always the probability that there will be some non-conformists in the industry.

It should be apparent to all at this point that I am not speaking for the industry. Indeed, many in the industry probably find censorship and control a more comfortable way of life than being constantly confronted with competitors who just do not conform to the standard pattern.

These are only my opinions—ill-qualified ones at that, compared to the qualifications of some of those who hold contrary views. But, at a time when we are locked in a life-and-death struggle with the Communist world, when that external threat is going to require many sacrifices, including the loss of many of our peacetime liberties, should we concede that the enemy's creed of cultural censorship and control must at long last replace our historic and yet to be perfected liberties of speech and press? If these American liberties are thus blithely to be discarded, what is there left to fight for except narrow, selfish, materialistic, and nationalistic ambitions?

Appendix I
by Joel Rosenbloom

AUTHORITY OF THE FEDERAL COMMUNICA-
TIONS COMMISSION

I. INTRODUCTION

This memorandum establishes that the following propositions are, for all practical purposes, settled law:

1 The Communications Act of 1934, as amended, authorizes the Federal Communications Commission to classify broadcasting stations on the basis of the general types of programs such stations transmit, to make reasonable judgments as to the public interest served by the programs offered by each class of stations, and to assign radio frequencies to each class on the basis of those judgments.

2 The Communications Act authorizes the Commission to consider the nature and content of the programs proposed to be broadcast by individual applicants in deciding whether to grant construction permits or station licenses; similarly, it authorizes the Commission to consider the general nature and content of the programs which have been broadcast or which are proposed to be broadcast in deciding whether to renew, modify or revoke broadcasting station permits or licenses, whether to consent to the assignment of the same or to consent to the transfer of control of broadcasting permittees or licensees.

3 The Communications Act forbids the Commission to censor, *i.e.,* to prevent the broadcasting of any individual program on the ground that its content is objectionable. It also forbids the Commission to select broadcasting licensees on the basis of the social, political, or economic views embodied in their programs, or on any other arbitrary basis. However, the Act both permits and requires the Commission to make reasonable judgments as to the nature of the broadcasting program service which serves the public interest and to carry out its licensing functions on the basis of such judgments.

4 These provisions of the Communications Act are fully compatible with the guarantees of the freedom of speech and of the press contained in the First Amendment to the Constitution.

II. STATUTORY AND CONSTITUTIONAL MATERIALS

The statutory standard prescribed for the exercise of the Commission's licensing and general rule-making functions is "the public interest, convenience or necessity." [Communications Act, Sections 303, 307, 308, 309, 310(b), 312(a)(2), 316, 319(a); 47 U.S.C. §§ 303, 307, 308, 309, 310(b), 312(a)(2), 316, 319(a).] The basic question is whether this standard authorizes the Commission to consider the content of broadcasting programs in the performance of those functions.

There are, however, certain specific provisions of the Act which, either on their face or in view of their legislative or judicial history, bear a special relationship to the Commission's authority in the programming field. From the point of view of authority which is granted, these are:

1 Subsections (a), (b), (c) and (d) of Section 303, which grant to the Commission authority to "Classify radio stations," to "Prescribe the nature of the service to be rendered by each class of licensed stations and each station within any class," to "Assign bands of frequencies to the various classes of stations," to "Assign frequencies for each individual station and determine the power which each station shall use and the time during which it may operate," and to "Determine the location of classes of stations or individual stations;"

2 Section 303(i), which provides that the Commission shall "Have authority to make special regulations applicable to radio stations engaged in chain broadcasting;"

3 Section 303(j), which provides that the Commission shall "Have authority to make general rules and regulations requiring stations to keep such records of programs, . . . as it may deem desirable;"

4 Section 307(c), which provides that "The Commission shall study the proposal that Congress by statute allocate fixed percentages of radio broadcasting facilities to particular types or kinds of non-profit radio programs or to persons identified with particular types or kinds of non-profit activities, and shall report to Congress, not later than February 1, 1935, its recommendations together with the reasons for the same."

5 Sections 308(b) and 319(a), which provide that applications for station licenses, construction permits, or modifications or renewals thereof, shall set forth such facts as to ". . . character, . . . and other qualifications of the applicant to operate the station," and as to "the purposes for which the station is to be used," as the Commission "by regulation may prescribe."

6 Section 315, which requires that, if the licensee of a broadcasting station permits a legally qualified candidate for any public office to use his station, he shall afford "equal opportunities to all other such candidates for that office in the use of such broadcasting station." The section exempts appearances by legally qualified candidates on certain types of news programs from its requirement. It states, however, that nothing in the exemption "shall be construed as relieving broadcasters, in connection with the presentation of newscasts, news interviews, news documentaries, and on-the-spot coverage of news events, from the obligation imposed upon them under this chapter to operate in the public interest and to afford reasonable opportunity for the discussion of conflicting views on issues of public importance." It also states that "The Commission shall prescribe appropriate rules and regulations to carry out the provisions of this section."

7 Section 317, which requires that "All matter broadcast by any radio station for which any money, service or other valuable consideration is directly or indirectly paid, or promised to or charged or accepted by, the station so broadcasting, from any person, shall, at the time the same is so broadcast, be announced as paid for, or furnished, as the case may be, by such person." The section grants the Commission authority to waive the requirement of an announcement in any case or class of cases "with respect to which it determines that the public interest, convenience or necessity does not require the broadcasting of such announcement." It also states that "The Commission shall prescribe appropriate rules and regulations to carry out the provisions of this section."

8 Section 325(b), which provides that "No person shall be permitted to locate, use, or maintain a radio broadcast studio or other place or apparatus from which or whereby sound waves are converted into electrical energy, or mechanical or physical reproducion of sound waves produced, and caused to be transmitted or delivered to a radio station in a foreign country for the purpose of being broadcast from any radio station there having a power output of sufficient intensity and/or being so located geographically that its emissions may be reached consistently in the United States, without first obtaining a permit from the Commission upon proper application therefor."

Two provisions of the Act, on the other hand, must be considered from the point of view of limitations which the statute may impose upon the Commission's authority over programming. Section 3(h) defines the term "common carrier" for purposes of the Act. It states that ". . . a person engaged in radio broadcasting shall not, insofar as such person is so engaged, be deemed a common carrier." And Section 326 states that:

Nothing in this Act shall be understood or construed to give the Commission the power of censorship over the radio communications or signals transmitted by any radio station, and no regulation or condition shall be promulgated or fixed by the Commission which shall interfere with the right of free speech by radio communication.

Finally, of course, any authority which the Commission might exercise in the field of radio and television programming is limited by the provisions of the Constitution, and particularly by the First Amendment's requirement that "Congress shall make no law . . . abridging the freedom of speech, or of the press."

These, then, are the basic materials which determine the scope and limits of the Commission's authority in the programming field, for the Commission is a creature of the statute, and the statute is a creature of the Constitution. It is evident that the bare words which are quoted do not, of themselves, provide answers to the critical questions concerning the Commission's authority over programming. The remainder of this memorandum establishes that the words have been given meaning and that the critical questions have been answered by Congress and the Courts.

III. THE HISTORY OF THE ACT

The relevant legislative history of the Communications Act falls roughly into three chapters: (A) The advent of radio broadcasting and the enactment of the Radio Act of 1927; (B) The legislative, administrative and judicial history of the Radio Act from 1927 to 1934; and (C) The legislative history of the revision and re-enactment of the Radio Act as Title III of the Communications Act of 1934. The basic substantive provisions of the Act have not changed since 1934. Indeed, "the objectives of the legislation have remained substantially unaltered since 1927." [*FCC* v. *Pottsville Broadcasting Co.*, 309 U.S. 134, 137.] Legislative and administrative developments since 1934 are significant primarily as they cast light upon the earlier history.

A. The Radio Act of 1927

1. Regulation of Broadcasting Under the Radio Act of 1912
When Congress enacted the Radio Act of 1912, 37 Stat. 302,

forbidding the operation of radio apparatus without a license from the Secretary of Commerce and Labor, radio broadcasting was nonexistent. The first broadcasting stations went on the air late in 1920. [See Archer, *History of Radio to 1926*, pp. 190–208 (1938).] The first license for a radio broadcasting station as such was issued in September, 1921. [*Hearings Before the Committee on the Merchant Marine and Fisheries, House of Representatives*, on H.R. 11964, 67th Cong., 4th Sess., p. 29 (1923).] The growth of the industry thereafter was little short of phenomenal. By July 1, 1922, 382 broadcasting stations had been licensed; by December 27, 1922, the number of licensed stations had risen to 569. [*Ibid.*]

The powers which the Secretary of Commerce possessed with which to meet this unprecedented situation were subject to doubt. On November 22, 1912, the Attorney General had issued an opinion to the effect that, under the Radio Act of 1912, the Secretary had no discretionary power to refuse a license. but must grant the same unless an application was specifically barred by the Act. [29 Ops. Atty. Gen. 579.] This ruling was affirmed in 1923 by a holding of the Court of Appeals for the District of Columbia that a writ of mandamus to compel the granting of a license would lie. [*Hoover* v. *Intercity Radio Company*, 52 App. D.C. 339, 286 Fed. 1003, *writ of error dismissed as moot*, 266 U.S. 636 (1924).]

On the other hand, the license to be granted under Section 1 of the Act was to be "revocable for cause." Moreover, Section 2 of the 1912 Act provided:

That every such license shall be in such form as the Secretary of Commerce and Labor shall determine and shall contain the restrictions, pursuant to this Act, on and subject to which the license is granted; . . . shall specify the ownership and location of the station in which said apparatus shall be used . . . ; shall state the purpose of the station . . . ; shall state the wave-length or the wave-lengths authorized for use by the station for the prevention of interference and the hours for which the station is licensed for work; and shall not be construed to authorize the use of any apparatus for radio communications in any other station than that specified.

Acting under these provisions of the statute, the Department of Commerce first licensed all broadcasting stations on two frequencies only, using one wave length for stations ". . . broadcasting news, concerts, lectures, and such matter;" and the other for stations ". . . broadcasting crop reports and weather forecasts." [1] [*Department of Commerce, Bureau of Navigation, Radio Service Bulletin No. 57, January 3, 1922, p. 10; No. 60, April 1, 1922, p. 23.*] On August 8, 1922, a new class of stations, "Class B" was created, to be licensed on yet a third wave length, with a minimum power of 500 watts and a maximum power of 1,000 watts (all other stations being limited to a maximum power of 500 watts). Class B stations were subject to the requirements that: "The programs must be carefully supervised and maintained to insure satisfactory service to the public." And that: "Mechanically operated musical instruments may be used only in an emergency and during intermission periods in regular program." [2] Furthermore, ". . . failure to maintain the standards prescribed for such stations may result in the cancellation of the license . . ." which would require the station to return to the wave length used by ordinary stations. [*Radio Service Bulletin No. 65, September 1, 1922, pp. 10–11.*]

The Secretary's assumption of authority over the matter broadcast, moreover, went further than the designation of classes of stations. *Radio Service Bulletin No. 69, January 2, 1923* contains at page 8 a warning to the operators of broadcast stations not to communicate with other stations. Nor was the "transmission of acknowledgments to individuals relating to the receipt of letters, telegrams and telephone calls" to be allowed, since it constituted "direct communication" and was not authorized in the licenses of broadcast stations. The Secretary's reasoning as to his authority was significant:

Section 2 of the Act of August 13, 1912 states that the license of a station "shall state the purpose of the station," and as broadcast stations are licensed for the specific purpose of broadcasting, any operator using a broadcast station for point-to-point communication may have his license suspended or revoked in the discretion of the Secretary of Commerce. Owners of broadcast stations should see that the above-cited Act is not violated, as the use of their stations for purposes other than specified in the station license is sufficient cause for the suspension or revocation of their station license.

---

[1] "License to broadcast weather forecasts and information and crop and market reports shall be revocable at any time that it may be in the public interest to do so." *Radio Service Bulletin No. 60, April 1, 1922, p. 23.*

[2] On September 22, 1922, the specifications applying to the new Class B stations were amended to prohibit absolutely "the use of mechanically operated instruments" for the production of music. *Radio Service Bulletin No. 66, October 2, 1922, p. 8.*

On February 5, 1923, the Court of Appeals for the District of Columbia, as noted above, affirmed the lower court holding that the Secretary of Commerce lacked discretion to refuse a license not specifically barred by the Radio Act of 1912. [*Hoover* v. *Intercity Radio Company*, 52 App. D.C. 339, 286 Fed. 1003.] In dictum, however, the Court of Appeals indicated that the selection by the Secretary of ". . . a wave-length, within the limitations prescribed in the statute, which, in his judgment, will result in the least possible interference" *was* a discretionary act. "It is a restriction entering into the license. The wave-length selected by the Secretary . . . measures the extent of the privilege granted to the licensee." [52 App. D.C. at 343.]

Its authority thus bolstered in one respect (though weakened in another), the Department of Commerce amended its regulations to provide for assigning specific frequencies to broadcast stations within a band prescribed for a specified class. The country was divided into five zones, with separate wave lengths designated for certain localities in each zone. Class B stations, with a minimum power of 500 watts and a maximum of 1,000 watts, were to be assigned wave lengths between 300 and 345 and 375 and 545 meters. They were to continue to be subject to programming and other qualifications, and would forfeit the Class B privilege upon failure to maintain any of the standards prescribed. Class A stations were not to use power exceeding 500 watts and were to be assigned frequencies between 222 meters and 300 meters. No new licenses were to be issued for the 360 meter frequency, but the old Class A stations on the frequency were to be allowed to remain there if so desired. As such, they were designated Class C stations. Finally, it was provided that "The reading of telegrams or letters by broadcasting stations will not be construed as point-to-point communications so long as the signer is not addressed in person and so long as the text matter is of general interest." [*Radio Service Bulletin No. 73, May 1, 1923*, pp. 11–13.]

Describing this move a few years later, the Solicitor of the Department of Commerce, Mr. Stephen B. Davis, Jr., remarked:

> There were at that time a great many stations that had no programs of their own. In other words, a man would put up a broadcasting station, and he did not want to go to the expense of putting up a program and he would put the phonograph up in front of the microphone and play into the microphone with that phonograph. I think of a large part of the stations that I have spoken of that was true.

* * *

There were certain stations, at any rate, willing, not only willing, but anxious to put on original programs: I mean, songs, speeches, and that sort of thing, but they were willing to subject themselves to an inspection as to the character of their studios, their equipment, and that sort of thing which went to the intelligibility and the character of their transmission. At that time, then, there were set up two classes of stations, what we called Class A stations, and what we called Class B stations. The Class B stations were the stations of 500 watts and over which were willing to put on original programs and were willing to subject themselves to certain qualifications as to character of their apparatus. The Class A stations covered the wide open radio field. Everybody then in existence had the choice as to whether he would go into Class A or Class B, and a large part of them elected to go into Class A, because, obviously, it was very much less expensive to operate in Class A than to operate in Class B; and also because the great mass of those stations were small powered, intended only to serve a very limited locality. [*Hearings Before the Committee on Interstate Commerce, United States Senate, 69th Cong., on S. 1 and S. 1754,* January 8 and 9, 1926, p. 267.]

In 1929, Mr. William D. Terrell, the Chief of the Radio Division of the Department of Commerce, who had been with the Department since the commencement of the regulation of broadcasting described the old Class B license in the course of the following colloquy:

SENATOR WHEELER: What, if anything, did your department have to do with censoring the kind of speeches or music, or anything that went over the radio?

MR. TERRELL: We had not any legal authority to do that, and we, of course, could not do it. About the only thing I can say that would approach that was the creation of a special class of license known as Class B license under our administration. Under that class of license we would not permit the station owner—and he agreed to it—to use mechanical music, phonographs, and things of that kind. The reason we did that was because at the beginning all the stations were turning to phonographs. It was a cheap way of putting on entertainments, and at the beginning the people were appreciating it. But later they were tiring of it, and if we had not checked it, it would have had a bad effect on broadcasting. So we created this special license, and they had to have talent. [*Hearings Before the Committee on Interstate Commerce, United States*

Senate, 71st Cong., 1st Sess. on S. 6, May 24, 27, 28, 29, June 5 and 7, 1929, p. 1071.]

2. Narrative History of Radio Act of 1927

Notwithstanding the relatively strong assumption of authority by the Department of Commerce, it was definitely felt on all sides that the Radio Act of 1912 was inadequate in its grant of authority to the government, and that further legislation was needed, particularly in view of the limited nature of the radio spectrum and the judicial holdings that the Department had no discretion in the issuance of a license. From February 27 to March 2, 1922 and from April 17 through April 19, 1922, a conference of representatives of the government, the broadcasting industry, amateur, educational and other interests, met at the invitation of Secretary of Commerce Hoover ". . . to consider general questions concerning the regulation of radio communication." [*Hearings on H.R. 11964,* p. 32 *et seq.*] The First National Radio Conference resolved "That it is the sense of the conference that radio communication is a public utility and as such should be regulated and controlled by the Federal Government in the public interest." It recommended

". . . that the radio laws be amended so as to give the Secretary of Commerce adequate legal authority for the effective control of: 1) The establishment of all radio transmitting stations except amateur, experimental, and Government stations. 2) The operation of non-governmental radio transmitting stations." That is, that ". . . the present authority of the Secretary of Commerce over the operation of radio transmitting stations be extended and that the Secretary of Commerce be granted authority to control the erection or establishment of certain classes of radio stations." [3]

In his annual report for the fiscal year 1922, Secretary Hoover noted that the Conference had drafted a bill for submission to Congress and urged its passage. [See *10 Secretary of Commerce Ann. Rep.* 13, 35, 217.] The bill was H.R. 11964, 67th Cong., and was introduced on June 9, 1922 by Representative (later Senator) Wallace H. White, Jr., of Maine, who had been a member of the Conference. [See *Hearings on H.R. 11964,* p. 32 and passim; 62 Cong. Rec. 8508.] The Committee on the Merchant Marine and Fisheries, however, to which the bill was referred, was busy with other matters, and hearings on

---

[3] Other recommendations of significance which were made by the First National Radio Conference will be referred to below.

the bill were not held until January 2 and 3, 1923. [*Hearings on H.R. 11964*, p. 50.] After redrafting by the Committee it was reintroduced by Mr. White as H.R. 13773, 67th Cong., (64 Cong. Rec. 1617) and reported out on January 16, 1923. [H.R. Rep. No. 1416, 67th Cong., 4th Sess.]

The House Committee Report noted the contribution of the First National Radio Conference and emphasized a theme which had run through the proceedings of the Conference and the Committee hearings: [4]

The radio art changes overnight. It is neither standardized nor stabilized. * * * Improvements in old methods and instruments and radical departures from accepted standards come with every passing day. The members of the conference and of this committee recognized fully that the recommendations so laboriously worked out by the technical committee of the conference [as to allocations of wave-lengths, time of operation, etc. which the Secretary of Commerce should make under the Act of 1912] might be out of date, demanding drastic revision, in a month's time. In these facts is found the compelling reasons (*sic*) for drafting the proposed legislation in most general terms. Statute law cannot be speedily changed. It is vital that the provisions of the law and of the regulations thereunder be so framed that the regulations may be changed as the art itself changes. Of necessity there is no way of meeting this unprecedented situation except by conferring in general terms, broad powers of supervisions, of regulation and of control, upon the designated regulatory body. We have conferred upon the Secretary of Commerce, designated by the basic law of 1912 as the agency of the Government for the control of this means of communication, the powers required in the premises. [H.R. Rep. No. 1416, *supra*, pp. 2–3.]

Without going into detail at this point, it is sufficient to note that most of the basic provisions of the Radio Act of 1927 take

[4] See the statements of Mr. White and Mr. L. C. F. Horle of the Federal Telephone and Telegraph Company in the *Minutes of the Open Meetings of the Department of Commerce Conference on Radio Telephony*, February 27 and 28, 1922, pp. 53, 81, 84, 93 (hereinafter cited as *Minutes*). See also the colloquy between Mr. White and Mr. Alfred P. Thom, general counsel for the American Railway Association, as well as the letter from Mr. William Brown, vice-president and general attorney of the Radio Corporation of America in *Hearings on H.R. 11964*, pp. 58–60. Similar statements were made in explanation of the bill during the course of the floor debate by members of the House Committee. 64 Cong. Rec. 2346, 2350.

their origin in this bill, and that it placed the issuance of licenses in the absolute discretion of the Secretary of Commerce.[5] With only slight amendment, it passed the House, but failed to emerge from the Senate Committee to which it was referred. [64 Cong. Rec. 2328–2355, 2781–2798, 3238.]

Mr. White introduced his bill again (with changes which will be noted later) early in 1924. [H.R. 7357, 68th Cong., 1st Sess.] Senator Howell introduced a bill into the Senate in the same session, which related to radio communications. [S. 2930, 68th Cong., 1st Sess.] The Senate bill was not, as was the House bill, an attempt at comprehensive regulation of radio. It merely reaffirmed the use of the ether for radio communication or otherwise to be the inalienable possession of the people of the United States and their government, limited grants of the privilege of this use to two years, and provided for temporary suspension by the President of privileges granted licensees in case of war or other national emergency.

The idea that "the ether" was a public possession, and that its use should be considered a mere privilege granted to individuals for some public purpose was not new. It had been voiced by Secretary Hoover at the First National Radio Conference. *Minutes*, pp. 4–5, and the bill passed by the House in 1923 had provided that every license contain the condition that "There shall be no vested property right in the license issued for such station or in the bands of wave length authorized to be used therein, . . ." [*Hearings on H.R. 11964;* 64 Cong. Rec. 2329.] But the belief ". . . that certain companies and interests have been endeavoring to establish a monopoly in wireless communication . . ." [H.R. Rep. No. 1416, 67th Cong., 4th Sess., p. 4] lent urgency to the demand that Congress act before rights which the courts might construe as vested and immune to governmental action could be established. The 1923 bill had been strongly criticized on the floor of the House as being inadequate in its provisions for the control and prevention of monopoly. [64 Cong. Rec. 2334–2336, 2341–2342, 2781–2783.] Shortly after passage of the bill, the House had requested the Federal Trade Commission to inquire whether the radio field was being restricted by the acquisition of basic patents by closely affiliated interests. [H. Res. No. 548, 67th Cong., 4th Sess. Agreed to, 64 Cong. Rec. 5544.] [6] The Hearings on H.R. 7357, Mr. White's

---

[5] See *Hearings on H.R. 11964*, p. 2; 64 Cong. Rec. 2329, 2331.
[6] The report was transmitted to Congress on December 5, 1923. 68 Cong. Rec. 24. It was published as the Report of the Federal Trade Commission on the Radio Industry (Government Printing Office, 1924).

bill, are replete with charges, defenses and countercharges. [See, *e.g.,* Hearings before the Committee on the Merchant Marine and Fisheries, House of Representatives, 68th Cong. 1st Sess. on H.R. 7357 (hereinafter cited as *Hearings on H.R. 7357*), pp. 40–51, 52–63, 70–98, 157–207.] The Senate Committee stated:

> . . . it would be unthinkable for Congress, through any laches on its part, to encourage any person or interest to assume the possibility of securing a right to any use of the ether whatever, other than a mere privilege for a limited period of time. [Sen. Rep. No. 311, 68th Cong., 1st Sess., p. 1.]

The Senate passed S. 2930 quickly and sent it to the House where it was referred to the Committee on the Merchant Marine and Fisheries. [65 Cong. Rec. 5733, 5737, 5907.] The House Committee incorporated the provisions of the White bill into the Senate bill and reported it out on May 13, 1924. [65 Cong. Rec. 8496; H.R. Rep. No. 719, 68th Cong., 1st Sess.] At this point, however, the Department of Commerce withdrew its support from the bill.[7] On December 5, 1924, Secretary Hoover sent a letter to Mr. White, portions of which were inserted in the Congressional Record by Mr. Davis of Tennessee (a member of the Committee on the Merchant Marine and Fisheries) a few years later. Mr. Hoover wrote:

> I feel, however, that the new developments in the art during the last 12 months have taken such a departure as to require somewhat further time for ascertaining its ultimate result to the public before we can adequately determine the proper course of legislation. There is a probability that by the end of that time we may require wholly new legislative provisions * * *
> During the past year there have been discoveries in the use of higher power and therefore larger areas of broadcasting, which may result in a single station being able to cover a large portion if not all of the country. This raises questions of the rights of local stations and rights of local listeners. Still another development has been the fact that it has been found possible by indirect advertising to turn broadcasting to highly profitable use. If this were misused, we would be confronted

---

[7] According to Representative Davis of the House Committee on the Merchant Marine and Fisheries, there was also much opposition by "certain representatives of the radio monopoly," and a majority of the Committee on rules refused to report a rule providing for consideration of the bill. H.R. Rep. No. 404, 69th Cong., 1st Sess., p. 16.

with the fact that service more advantageous to the listeners would be crowded out for advertising purposes.

Because of this situation *there is growing up a demand for the limitation of the number of stations in a given area,* and *that such a limitation would be based on the service needs of the community,* just as public utilities are generally limited by the rule of public convenience and necessity. Again, this enters a dangerous field of recognizing monopoly and implied censorship.

The public interest of radio broadcasting is rapidly widening. Entertainment and amusement have ceased to be its principal purposes. The public, especially our people on farms and in isolated communities, are coming to rely on it for the information necessary to the conduct of their daily affairs. It is rapidly becoming a necessity, and they rightly feel that since the public medium of the ether is used to reach them they have a direct and justifiable interest in the manner in which it is conducted.

From all of this, it seems to me, that there is a tendency which may require an entirely different basis in character, theory, and extent of legislation than any we have contemplated in the past. The basis of regulation and the fundamental policies to be followed must be finally declared by Congress, not left to an administrative officer. *Hitherto we have conceived the problem to be one of interference, but there is now opening before us a whole vista of difficult problems.* The development of the art is such that the whole situation is changing rapidly, and the opinion of to-day on the solution for a given difficulty is worthless to-morrow. I hope that another year's experience will show what direction of legislative course must be pursued * * * (emphasis added). [68 Cong. Rec. 2572–2573.]

The Secretary recommended enactment of S. 2930 in the form in which it had passed the Senate "to enable the department to retain firm control of the situation." [68 Cong. Rec. 2572.] On January 23, 1925, the bill was re-referred back to the Committee. [66 Cong. Rec. 2361.] Its failure to emerge again was undoubtedly due, at least in part, to advice from the Department of Commerce to the effect that applications for new licenses and the total number of stations operating appeared to be decreasing and that, if technological developments would reveal a method of eliminating interference between stations operating on the same or nearly the same wave-length, ". . . there might be a natural working out of the situation without the ne-

cessity for direct Government regulation." [Hearings before the
Committee on the Merchant Marine and Fisheries, House of
Representatives, 69th Cong., 1st Sess. on H.R. 5589 (hereinafter
cited as *Hearings on H.R. 5589*), p. 37.]

By November of 1925 these hopes had withered, as the number of new stations rose sharply and no scientific solution to the
problem of the limited scope of the radio spectrum appeared.
Without any express statutory authority, the Department of
Commerce stopped issuing new licenses, thus causing bitter
complaints of discrimination, etc. [See, *e.g.*, *Hearings Before the
Committee on Interstate Commerce, United States Senate, 69th
Cong., 1st Sess. on S. 1 and S. 1754*, pp. 37, 216–220, 250–252,
268–270, 275–283; *Hearings on H.R. 5589*, pp. 34–35. See also
the remarks of Senator Dill, 67 Cong. Rec. 12352, 12353.] Addressing the Fourth National Radio Conference on November 9, 1925, Secretary Hoover said:

> It is a simple physical fact that we have no more channels.
> It is not possible to furnish them under the present state of
> technical development. It takes no argument to demonstrate
> that 89 wave lengths (and no more are available) cannot be
> made to serve innumerable stations, no matter how ingenious
> we may be in arranging time divisions and geographical
> separations. It is not a question of what we would like to do
> but what we must do. [*Proceedings of the Fourth National
> Radio Conference* (Government Printing Office, 1926), p. 6
> (hereinafter cited as *Fourth National Radio Conference*).
> See also *Hearings on S. 1 and S. 1754*, p. 48 *et seq.*, where
> the proceedings of the conference are set out in full.]

After rejecting attempts to solve the problem by further division of time between stations on the same frequency (largely
on the grounds of the deterioration in program quality which
would result) or by widening the broadcasting band at the expense of non-broadcasting radio services, Mr. Hoover went on
to say:

> All of these things bring us face to face with the problem
> which we have all along dreaded and for which we have
> hoped the development of the art might give us a solution;
> but that appears to be far off, and we must now decide the issue
> of whether we shall have more stations in conflicting localities
> until new discoveries in the art solve the problem.
> We hear a great deal about the freedom of the air; but
> there are two parties to freedom of the air, and to freedom of
> speech, for that matter. There is the speechmaker and the lis-

tener. Certainly in radio I believe in freedom for the listener. He has much less option upon what he can reject, for the other fellow is occupying his receiving set. The listener's only option is to abandon his right to use his receiver. Freedom cannot mean a license to every person or corporation who wishes to broadcast his name or his wares, and thus monopolize the listener's set.

We do not get much freedom of speech if 50 people speak at the same place at the same time, nor is there any freedom in a right to come into my sitting room to make a speech whether I like it or not. So far as opportunity goes to explain one's views upon questions of controversy, political, religious, or social, it would seem that 578 independent stations, many competing in each locality, might give ample opportunity for great latitude in remarks; *and in any event, without trying out all this question, we can surely agree that no one can raise a cry of deprivation of free speech if he is compelled to prove that there is something more than naked commercial selfishness in his purpose.*

The ether is a public medium, and its use must be for public benefit. The use of radio channel is justified only if there is public benefit. The dominant elements for consideration in the radio field is, and always will be, the great body of the listening public . . .

*   *   *

We simply must say that conditions absolutely preclude increasing the total number of stations in congested areas. It is a condition, not an emotion; but *this implies a determination of who shall occupy these channels, in what manner, and under what test.*

I can see no alternative to abandonment of the present system, which gives the broadcasting privilege to everyone who can raise the funds necessary to erect a station, *irrespective of his motive, the service he proposes to render,* or the number of others already serving his community. Moreover, we should not freeze the present users of wave lengths permanently in their favored positions *irrespective of their service.* This would confer a monopoly of a channel in the air and deprive us of public control over it. It would destroy the public assurance that it will be used for public benefit. [(emphasis added.) *Fourth National Radio Conference,* pp. 6–8.]

The Conference, which was attended by Representative White and "other members of the House and Senate committees"

[*Fourth National Radio Conference*, p. 9],[8] adopted both the proposal that no new stations be licensed "until through discontinuance the number of stations is reduced and until it shall be in the interest of public service to add new stations" and the proposition tht "public interest as represented by service to the listener shall be the basis for the broadcasting privilege." [*Fourth National Radio Conference*, pp. 22–23.] Its Committee on Legislation drafted a set of principles which Congressman White later inserted in the Congressional Record as the basis for the bill which he introduced in the House. [*Fourth National Radio Conference*, pp. 34–35; 67 Cong. Rec. 5479.]

That bill, H.R. 5589, 69th Cong., 1st Sess., was redrafted by the Committee on the Merchant Marine and Fisheries and reintroduced by Mr. White as H.R. 9108, 69th Cong., 1st Sess. As such it was reported out [H.R. Rep. No. 404, 69th Cong., 1st Sess.] and then withdrawn in order to eliminate an antimonopoly provision with regard to radio tubes and apparatus over which it was felt the Committee had no jurisdiction. Introduced again as H.R. 9971, 69th Cong., 1st Sess., it was again reported out of committee. [H.R. Rep. No. 464, 69th Cong., 1st Sess.] With relatively slight amendment, it passed the House on March 15, 1926. [68 Cong. Rec. 5647.]

A companion bill had been introduced in the Senate by Senator Dill. [S. 1754, 69th Cong., 1st Sess.] After redrafting by the Senate Committee on Interstate Commerce, that bill was reintroduced as S. 4057, 69th Cong., 1st Sess. [See 67 Cong. Rec. 8574.] Before it could be reported out, however, H.R. 9971 passed the House and was referred to the Senate Committee on Interstate Commerce. The Committee inserted S. 4057 as an amendment to the House bill and reported it out. [Sen. Rep. No. 772, 69th Cong., 1st Sess.] After further amendment, the bill was passed on July 2, 1926. [67 Cong. Rec. 12618.]

There were a number of differences between the House and Senate bills, perhaps the most important one being that the House bill vested the licensing function in the Secretary of Commerce, with an appeal to a commission representing the various sections of the country, while the Senate bill placed such functions in the commission *ab initio*. On July 3, 1926, the conferees reported that they would be unable to come to agreement before the impending end of the session, and urged the passage of a Senate Joint Resolution [S.J. Res. 125, 69th Cong.,

[8] The Congressmen and Senators evidently attended but did not formally participate as members of the Conference. See the statement of Mr. White in *Hearings on H.R. 5589*, pp. 15–16.

1st Sess.] along the lines of S. 2930, which had passed the Senate in the 68th Congress, to preserve the status quo between sessions and until the conferees could draft a compromise. [See 67 Cong. Rec. 12959, 13046.] The resolution, which limited broadcasting licenses to 90 days and other licenses to two years and required a waiver of any claim of right, as against the United States, ". . . to any wave length or to the use of the ether in radio transmission because of previous license to use the same or because of the use thereof" as a prerequisite to the grant of a license or a renewal thereof, was swiftly passed by both houses. [67 Cong. Rec. 12959, 13047.] [9]

But the legislative machinery had not kept pace with the speed of events. Even while the Senate bill was pending before the committee, a United States District Court for the Northern District of Illinois had held that a licensee using another wave length than that authorized and operating at times other than authorized could not be prosecuted under the Act of 1912, since if the Act were construed to authorize the Secretary of Commerce to fix wave lengths, time of operation, etc. it would be unconstitutional as a delegation of the legislative power to make acts criminally punishable to an administrative official, without providing any standard for the guidance of his discretion. [*United States* v. *Zenith Radio Corp.*, 12 F.2d 614 (April 16, 1926).] [10] On June 4, 1926, the Secretary requested an opinion on this point from the Attorney General, and on July 8, 1926, the Attorney General issued an opinion to the effect that, under the law of 1912, the Secretary had no authority to assign wave lengths, specify hours of operation, limit the power to be used, or limit the duration of a license. [35 Ops. Atty. Gen. 126 (1926).] The Secretary of Commerce thereupon abandoned any attempt at regulation, and the ensuing chaos on the airways is the phenomenon which has been called "the breakdown of the act."

By the time Congress reconvened in December of 1926, matters had gone far enough to stir President Coolidge to speech:

---

[9] It was too late in the session to present this resolution to the President, so that it was not approved until December 8, 1926. 68 Cong. Rec. 93. See 44 Stat. 917.

[10] The statement above is slightly inaccurate. The Act of 1912 itself required that private stations operate within a certain band of frequencies and the holding of the court was that the Secretary had no authority to fix a wave length within the authorized band or to specify periods of operation so as to make operation on any other frequency or at any other time a crime.

Due to the decisions of the courts, the authority of the department under the law of 1912 has broken down; many more stations have been operating than can be accommodated within the limited number of wave-lengths available; further stations are in course of construction; many stations have departed from the scheme of allocation set down by the department, and the whole service of this most important public function has drifted into such chaos as seems likely, if not remedied, to destroy its great value. I most urgently recommend that this legislation should be speedily enacted. [H. Doc. No. 483, 69th Cong., 2nd Sess., p. 10.]

The conferees brought out their bill on January 27, 1927. [See 68 Cong. Rec. 2404. H.R. Rep. No. 1886, 69th Cong., 2nd Sess.; Sen. Doc. No. 200, 69th Cong., 2nd Sess.] Upon the basic issue of the authority of commission, as opposed to the Secretary of Commerce, the compromise reached was the vesting of the primary licensing functions in the commission for a period of one year, after which all of these functions save the revocation of licenses would revert to the Secretary of Commerce, and the commission, outside of the field of revocations, would assume the appellate role which had been planned for it in the House bill. [H.R. Rep. No. 1886, *supra* at pp. 5–6; Sen. Doc. No. 200, *supra* at pp. 3–4, 16–17.] The House concurred in the Conference Report on January 29, 1927. [68 Cong. Rec. 2580.] The Senate agreed on February 18, 1927. [68 Cong. Rec. 4155.]

3. Analysis

Several conclusions of importance to this memorandum flow from the mere narrative recital of the history which is given above. It is clear, at the outset, that Congress did not imagine the commission it created ". . . as a kind of traffic officer, policing the wave lengths to prevent stations from interfering with each other." [*National Broadcasting Co.* v. *United States,* 319 U.S. 190, 215.] The Department of Commerce had exercised such "traffic control" powers under the Radio Act of 1912 to the limit, without being able to avoid the crisis brought on by the fact that "the radio spectrum simply is not large enough to accommodate everybody." [*National Broadcasting Co.* v. *United States,* 319 U.S. 190, 213.] The bills reviewed above, starting with Mr. White's bill of 1922, were aimed at curing the feature of the 1912 law which limited the Secretary to "traffic control," namely, his lack of discretion in the issuance of licenses.[11]

It is just as clear that the distribution of licenses on the basis of priority in the time of application—the practice under the Act of 1912—was repudiated. The new principle of distribution was to be "service to the listeners" [*Fourth National Radio Conference*, p. 23] and "assurance of public interest to be served." (Mr. White, introducing the House bill, 67 Cong. Rec. 5479). And it is impossible to avoid the conclusion that this principle was intended to comprehend consideration by the commission of the programs to be broadcast.

Certainly this was the case in regard to the reservation of specific frequencies and periods of operation for different classes of stations. As noted above, the Department of Commerce had included specific restrictions on program content when it created Class B stations in 1922 and 1923. The classification system thus administered, in part at least, upon considerations of program content was continued with the advice and assistance of the industry. [See *Recommendations for Regulation of Radio*, adopted by the Third National Radio Conference (hereinafter cited as *Third National Radio Conference*), October 6–10, 1924, pp. 16–18.] And Congress was informed of this practice. [See the testimony of Solicitor Davis of the Department of Commerce in Hearings on S. 1 and S. 1754, pp. 266–267.] It was discontinued upon the recommendation of the Fourth National Radio Conference, not because it was felt to be improper regulation, but because ". . . the present distinction between Classes A and B is purely artificial, based originally on the proposition that Class B stations could not broadcast phonograph music. This result has been accomplished . . ." [*Fourth National Radio Conference*, p. 19; see also *Hearings on S. 1 and S. 1754*, p. 42.]

The provisions of Section 4(a) and (b) of the Radio Act [Section 303(a) and (b) of the Communications Act] were specifically intended to confirm and broaden this authority. The bill which Mr. White introduced in 1922 authorized the Secretary of Commerce to "(a) classify licensed radio stations and the operators required therein; (b) prescribe the nature of the

---

[11] See the remarks of Secretary Hoover concerning the "very large discretionary or . . . semi-judicial function" of determining "who shall use the traffic channels and under what conditions" (*Fourth National Radio Conference*, p. 8), and his similar remarks before the House Committee (*Hearings on H.R. 5589*, pp. 11–12). See also Sen. Rep. No. 772, 69th Cong., 1st Sess., p. 3, and the remarks of Senator Dill, introducing the Senate Committee bill on the floor of the Senate. 67 Cong. Rec. 12353–4.

service to be rendered by each class of licensed station and assign bands of wave lengths thereto; (c) make, alter, and revoke
regulations applicable to all licensed stations . . . concerning
the service to be rendered by each class of stations so established." [*Hearings on H.R. 11964*, p. 1.] Mr. White explained
during the course of the hearings on this bill that these provisions were ". . . broad enough to authorize the Secretary of
Commerce to allocate from 6 to 10 o'clock on Sunday evenings
available broadcasting wave lengths to the churches, but I am
not so sure that it is broad enough to enable the Secretary to
say to the church that, 'You shall broadcast a sermon instead of
an organ recital.' * * * But I do think the Secretary, in this
bill, undoubtedly has the power to put everybody out of the air
from 5 to 10 o'clock on Sunday evenings, except the churches of
the country, if he sees fit to do so." [*Hearings on H.R. 11964*,
pp. 63–64.] And on the floor, when apprehension was expressed
concerning the possibility that, under the bill, the Secretary of
Commerce might license commercial or amateur stations whose
broadcasts would interfere with the broadcast of crop or market
reports or sermons [64 Cong. Rec. 2337, 2787], both Mr. White
and members of the House Committee stated that the bill gave
the Secretary power to give priority to stations broadcasting
the crop reports or sermons. [64 Cong. Rec. 2787, 2340–2341,
2343–2344.]

Mr. White, moreover, had thought from the beginning that
government would have to go further and ". . . work out
priorities or preferences in this air as to subject matter." [*Hearings on H.R. 11964*, p. 63; see also Mr. White's statements at
the First National Radio Conference, *Minutes*, pp. 95–96.] The
bill which he introduced early in 1924, in the first Session of
the 68th Congress, contained a provision giving the Secretary of
Commerce authority to: ". . . prescribe the nature of the service to be rendered and the priorities as to subject matter to be
observed by each class of licensed stations and of each station
within any class. . . ;" and to: ". . . make, alter and revoke
regulations . . . concerning the service to be rendered and the
priorities as to subject matter to be observed by each class of
stations . . . and of each station within an established class."
[*Hearings on H.R. 7357*, p. 1.]

The bills which were introduced in both House and Senate in
1926 contained this provision in the final form in which it was
enacted as Section 4(a),(b). The reference to priorities as to
subject matter was dropped, according to Mr. White, ". . . because of the fear which had been expressed by so many to me
that that did confer something akin to censorship." [*Hearings*

on H.R. 5589, p. 39.] But the language allowing the licensing authority to prescribe the nature of the service not only of each class of licensed stations but of each station within any class was retained. [See *Hearings on H.R. 5589*, p. 2; *Hearings on S. 1 and S. 1754*, p. 2.] Commenting on this provision a year after the enactment of the Radio Act of 1927, Mr. White said:

> Now, I take it, under that authority, the commission has the right to say that a particular station may broadcast jazz music or that it may be used for the broadcasting of weather reports, stock reports, or market reports; *that it may generally prescribe the nature and the character of the service which a class of stations or which a particular station is to render.* Now, I am inclined to believe, myself, that the language of present law is broad enough to permit the commission to say that on a particular station you may or may not put out advertising, direct or indirect; but, . . . I recognize there is some doubt about that construction . . . (emphasis added).

Again, at the commencement of the hearings on the final White bill in 1926, various members of the House Committee asked that a general statement of the scope, meaning and content of the bill be made, and Solicitor Davis of the Department of Commerce took the stand (with the consent of Mr. White) to provide such a statement. [*Hearings on H.R. 5589*, pp. 16–18, *et seq.*] Mr. Davis of Tennessee inquired of the Solicitor whether some provision might not be made for university stations, so as "to afford a better and more wholesome set of programs than sometimes exist." The Solicitor replied:

> I think that could be done, Judge Davis, under this draft. Of course the difficulty at present is that we have absolutely no authority whatever over that class of station. We have no right to make any preferences whatever as between different types of stations. This bill provides that we may classify stations and may prescribe the nature of service and may assign wave lengths in accordance with the necessities of those different classes. Now, I take it that under that the department could set up a class of church stations, it could set up a class of educational stations, and make due provisions for them; which, under the present law, we cannot do. [*Hearings on H.R. 5589*, pp. 38–39.] [12]

[12] Moreover, a provision inserted by the House Committee, which would have required the commission, in determining the location of classes of stations or individual stations to give "due consideration" to "the right of each

The evidence is also convincing that program content was expected to be a prime consideration in the licensing of individual applicants. This is unquestionably what Secretary of Commerce Hoover had in mind when he urged that each applicant be required to prove "that there is something more than naked commercial selfishness in his purpose," and when he argued that "we should not freeze the present users of wave lengths permanently in their favored positions, irrespective of their service." [*Fourth National Radio Conference*, pp. 7–8.] And it is difficult to believe that Congressman White could have meant anything else when he said [*Hearings on H.R. 5589*, p. 208]:

> When a license expires, the holder of it must make out, de novo, his right to a license, and his right to a license depends under the terms of the bill upon whether the station in actual operation or proposed, will serve a public interest or a public convenience.

Certainly the burden of explanation is upon those who would argue to the contrary.

This conclusion is buttressed by the history of Section 4(i) of the Radio Act [Section 303(j) of the Communications Act], which granted the commission authority to ". . . make general rules and regulations requiring stations to keep such records of programs . . . as it may deem desirable." This provision originated in an amendment of the Senate Committee, which would have provided: "The license shall require the keeping of a log of all programs, messages, or transmissions of radio energy, communications, or signals for each twenty-four-hour pe-

---

State to have allocated to it, or to some person, firm, company, or corporation within it, the use of a wave length for at least one broadcasting station located or to be located in such State," was dropped by the Conference Committee. The provision had been inserted largely at the behest of ". . . agricultural and educational institutions, which want the right to broadcast during certain hours of the week." 67 Cong. Rec. 12618 (See *Hearings on H.R. 5589*, pp. 128–130; *Hearings on S. 1 and S. 1754*, pp. 95–100; 68 Cong. Rec. 2568–2569.) Defending the action of the conferees against the claim that the bill would deny to each State the opportunity to have educational programs broadcast from its own university (68 Cong. Rec. 2568–2569), Mr. Scott (who was Chairman of the House Committee, a manager on the part of the House in conference, and had charge of the Conference Report on the floor) stated: "I am sure the gentleman does not mean to convey the impression to the House that the thing he seeks to accomplish is not capable of accomplishment under the provisions of the bill."

riod for the hours the station is operated." [*Calendar No. 774,
H.R. 9971. In the Senate of the United States,* 69th Cong., 1st
Sess., May 6 (Calendar Day May 8), 1926, p. 44.]

Senator Howell, a member of the Committee, stated that this
provision was inserted in order ". . . to render more certain
the responsibility of a station operator and anyone speaking
into the microphone" for criminal libels. [68 Cong. Rec. 4152.]
And indeed, the bill as reported and passed by the Senate contained a provision which would have made the knowing utterance of "any false or fraudulent radio communication" or "any
libelous or slanderous communication by radio" a crime punishable by $1,000 fine or one year in jail, or both. [H.R. 9971,
In the House of Representatives, 69th Cong., 1st Sess., July 2,
1926, ordered to be printed with the amendment of the Senate,
p. 55.] This criminal libel provision was dropped in conference,
and the program log provision, which Mr. Scott (introducing
the conference report on the floor of the House) characterized
as one of ". . . the important matters which were the subject of
controversy in conference," [68 Cong. Rec. 2564], was changed
to its final form and shifted to Section 4. Senator Howell complained bitterly [68 Cong. Rec. 4152], as might be expected,
for nothing less than a complete *verbatim* log of all programs
would have served his purpose. The provision which was reported out by the Conference Committee and enacted could only
have been meant to serve the *commission*'s purposes, and it is
difficult if not impossible to conceive of any purpose which such
records could serve other than the provision of a record on
which judgments could be made in renewing or revoking a license.[13]

[13] In the Senate hearings, Mr. M. L. Ernst, representing the American Civil
Liberties Union, raised the question of "private censorship" by the licensee
station—of a refusal to allow various interests in the community to express
themselves over the radio. He urged:

". . . that there should be an opportunity for the public to argue on the
question of the revocation of a license so that people could come in and
complain to the commissioner that this station is not taking this kind of
material, as these public questions, these interests, to these people. Now
I do not say that the commissioner should be given the blanket power to
decide whether each station in each case must accept what any person
offers that station, but *if you please on the question of the renewal of the
license on application, there should be a record* . . . * * * I submit that
that ought to be a matter of very vital public record so that the commissioner in determining, when there is a free wave length or opportunity for
assignment may have that information so that that part of public opinion
can also have some expression.

"And it seems to me that for that purpose the bill should provide a

One must note further, that the problem of "private censorship" by the broadcast licensee was of primary concern to the Congress of 1927. The House bill, as passed, contained a provision directed, *inter alia,* at this problem. It authorized revocation of a license

> . . . whenever the Interstate Commerce Commission, or any other Federal body in the exercise of authority conferred upon it by law, shall find and shall certify to the Secretary of Commerce that any licensee bound so to do, has failed to provide reasonable facilities for the transmission of radio communications, or has made any unjust and unreasonable charge, *or has been guilty of any discrimination, either as to charge or as to service* or has made or prescribed any unjust and unreasonable classification, regulation, or practice with respect to the transmission of radio communications or service. [*H.R. 9971, In the Senate of the United States,* March 15 (Calendar Day March 16), 1926, pp. 10–11.] [14]

The language which is emphasized, concerning discriminations "as to charge or as to service," was added on the floor of the House, through an amendment offered by Mr. Johnson of Texas. [67 Cong. Rec. 5560] Congressman Johnson explained his concern as follows [67 Cong. Rec. 5558]:

> There is no agency so fraught with possibilities for service of good or evil to the American people as the radio. As a means of entertainment, education, information, and communication, it has limitless possibilities. The power of the press will not be comparable to that of broadcasting stations when the industry is fully developed. If the development continues as rapidly in the future as in the past, it will only be a few years before these broadcasting stations, if operated by chain stations, will simultaneously reach an audience of over half of our entire citizenship, and bring messages to the fireside of nearly every home in America. They can mold and crystallize sentiment as no agency in the past has been able to do. If the strong arm of the law does not prevent monopoly ownership and make discrimination by such stations illegal,

---

completest (sic) kind of record, accessible to the department and to the public, as to the operation of these stations." (Emphasis added) *Hearings on S. 1 and S. 1754,* p. 128.

[14] This provision originated in Mr. White's bill of 1922–23, in the 67th Congress, as an anti-monopoly measure. See H.R. Rep. No. 1416, 67th Cong., 4th Sess. p. 4; 64 Cong. Rec. 2329.

American thought and American politics will be largely at the mercy of those who operate these stations. For publicity is the most powerful weapon that can be wielded in a Republic, and when such a weapon is placed in the hands of one, or a single selfish group is permitted to either tacitly or otherwise acquire ownership and dominate these broadcasting stations throughout the country, then woe be to those who dare to differ with them. It will be impossible to compete with them in reaching the ears of the American people.

Because he feared, moreover, that ". . . the Interstate Commerce Commission is so busily engaged with affairs concerning the railroads that it would not have the time to hear complaints with reference to discrimination or other acts of omission or commission by these licensees," Congressman Johnson offered another amendment, which would have provided: "That equal facilities and rates, without discrimination, shall be accorded to all political parties and all candidates for office, and to both proponents and opponents of all political questions or issues." [67 Cong. Rec. 5559.] This amendment was ruled out of order, as not germane to the section then under consideration, and was not offered again in the House. [67 Cong. Rec. 5560–61.] But the Senate committee was more impressed with the gravity of the problem, which had been raised at length in its hearings. [*Hearings on S. 1 and S. 1754*, pp. 125–134, 257–258.] It reported out a provision as follows [Calendar No. 774, *supra*, p. 50; Sen. Rep. No. 772, 69th Cong., 1st Sess., p. 4; 67 Cong. Rec. 12503]:

> If any licensee shall permit a broadcasting station to be used . . . [to broadcast any matter for a valuable consideration], or by a candidate or candidates for any public office, or for the discussion of any question affecting the public, he shall make no discrimination as to the use of such broadcasting station, and with respect to said matters the licensee shall be deemed a common carrier in interstate commerce: Provided, that such licensee shall have no power to censor the material broadcast.

The "common carrier" language and the requirement of nondiscrimination with respect to "the discussion of any question affecting the public" were deleted on the floor of the Senate, through an amendment offered by Senator Dill. [67 Cong. Rec. 12501–12502.] His reasons for deleting the common carrier requirement for all matter broadcast for hire were expressed as follows [67 Cong. Rec. 12502]:

When we recall that broadcasting today is purely voluntary, and the listener-in pays nothing for it, that the broadcaster gives it for the purpose of building up his reputation, it seemed unwise to put the broadcaster under the hampering control of being a common carrier and compelled to accept anything and everything that was offered him so long as the price was paid.

His reason for striking the requirement concerning "the discussion of any question affecting the public" was that ". . . a radio station would be placed in the position . . . that they would have to give all their time to that kind of discussion, or no public question could be discussed." [67 Cong. Rec. 12504.] Equal opportunities were thus required only in the use of broadcasting *facilities by candidates* for public office.[15]

But this did not end the matter. The Senate committee reported and the Senate adopted a provision on revocation of licenses which placed responsibility for making the judgment as to when a "discrimination, either as to charge or as to service" had occurred upon the Radio Commission, rather than the Interstate Commerce Commission. The Conference Committee adopted the House provision which is quoted above, in place of the Senate provision. [Sen. Doc. No. 200, 69th Cong., 2nd Sess., p. 8; Sen. Rep. No. 772, 69th Cong., 1st Sess., p. 4; *Hearings on S. 1 and S. 1754*, p. 4.] This action was attacked, both in the House and in the Senate, on the ground that ". . . the Interstate Commerce Commission, the only body authorized to exercise any jurisdiction over that subject, has never endeavored to exercise any jurisdiction over radio, and plainly so stated." [68 Cong. Rec. 2567; see also 67 Cong. Rec. 5559, 68 Cong. Rec. 3028, 3032, 3036, 3258.]

Senator Dill in the Senate, and Congressman White in the House, defended the handiwork of the conferees, claiming that the Interstate Commerce Commission had full power to control discriminations. [68 Cong. Rec. 2580, 3032.] Senator Dill argued that discriminations were not as such major problems in the radio field at that point. [68 Cong. Rec. 3028, 3258.] But he also went further. He pointed out that the provision requiring the Radio Commission to await action by another Federal body was applicable only to ". . . a licensee who already has a

---

[15] The Conference Committee struck certain other phrases not relevant to this memorandum and added a final sentence: "No obligation is hereby imposed upon any licensee to allow the use of its station by any such candidate." Sen. Doc. No. 200, 69th Cong., 2nd Sess., pp. 10, 18.

license." [68 Cong. Rec. 3258.] He denied that the conference bill gave no authority over the "service" of licensees to the commission:

MR. DILL: I know the Senator does not want to make a misstatement. He says there is nothing in this bill that would empower the radio commission to compel radio broadcasters to give service. I think he did not mean to say that.

MR. PITTMAN: I did mean to say that.

MR. DILL: Then the Senator is mistaken.

MR. PITTMAN: The Senator can answer me in his own time.

MR. DILL: I just wanted to call attention to the fact that the whole basis of the bill is public service to the listeners in. [68 Cong. Rec. 4111.]

And he made yet more significant reply to Senator Pittman:

MR. DILL: The Senator from Nevada evidently overlooks two lines in section 14 [dealing with authority to revoke a license]; namely, that the commission may revoke a license when it finds certain conditions which would warrant it in refusing to grant a license. It has the authority to refuse to grant a license, if it finds, from the statement of facts when presented to it, that the granting of a license would not be in conformity with the public interest, convenience, or necessity, and *if it finds that a licensee has been guilty of acts which make it no longer desirable for it to operate a station it can revoke the license* under the basic principle laid down in section 14, and also in section 9, which lays down the basic grounds for the granting of licenses.

MR. PITTMAN: If that was the admitted intention of the section, it never would have had to be framed in that way and no one would have framed it in that way. It would simply have provided that upon certification of the Interstate Commerce Commission—

MR. DILL: I am perfectly willing to accept criticism of the arrangement of the language to which the Senator calls attention, because while admitting that the act may not be framed as it should have been framed, nevertheless I think its meaning is clear when the two sections are taken together. (Emphasis added.) [16] [68 Cong. Rec. 3036.]

---

[16] Senator Dill here referred to the provision in Section 14 of the Radio Act of 1927 authorizing revocation of a license "because of conditions revealed by such statements of fact as may be required from time to time which would warrant the licensing authority in refusing to grant a license on an original application." See Communications Act, Section 312(a)(2).

The primary answer which might be made to these observations is that there *was* one important countervailing consideration which had the assent of everyone involved, both within and without the Congress. This was that the right of free speech should not be abridged and that the Commission should not be empowered to censor material broadcast. As noted above, Mr. White had dropped the provision giving authority to prescribe "priorities as to subject matter" because it conferred "a power akin to censorship." The Fourth National Radio Conference had resolved that governmental authority should not ". . . under any circumstances enter the forbidden field of censorship" and had incorporated into its legislative recommendations the principle that "the doctrine of free speech be held inviolate." [*Fourth National Radio Conference*, pp. 34–35.] On the floor of the House Mr. LaGuardia referred to this recommendation of the conference and asked, "What provision does the bill make to carry that out?" The following exchange then ensued:

> MR. WHITE of Maine: It does not touch that matter specifically. Personally, I felt that we could go no further than the Federal Constitution goes in that respect. The pending bill gives the Secretary no power of interfering with freedom of speech in any degree.
> MR. LaGUARDIA: It is the belief of the gentleman and the intent of Congress in passing this bill not to give the Secretary any power whatever in that respect in considering a license or the revocation of a license.
> MR. WHITE of Maine: No power at all. [67 Cong. Rec. 5480.]

Moreover, of course, the Senate bill contained the provision which was enacted finally as Section 29 of the Radio Act of 1927, forbidding either censorship or infringement of "the right of free speech by means of radio communication." [See Section 326 of the Communications Act.] On the floor of the Senate Senator Dill was quick to react to the suggestion that the bill gave the commission the authority to censor broadcasts:

> MR. DILL: Mr. President, I want to correct a statement which the Senator has made. * * * The bill does not give to the commission the power to censor programs, but instead there is a provision in the bill which specifically prohibits the commission from censoring programs in any way. I wish that statement to go in the RECORD, to clear up any misapprehension that might arise. [67 Cong. Rec. 12615.]

The relevant question, however, is *not* whether Congress favored free speech over the radio and opposed censorship *in the abstract,* but whether and to what extent it was thought that such considerations precluded any judgment on program content by the commission in the course of its licensing or other functions.

The evidence which can be marshalled on this point is not absolutely conclusive, for the issue was not taken up, discussed and decided by the Congress in so many words. The weight of the evidence, however, supports the conclusion that Congress—like Secretary Hoover, who did face the issue squarely in his speech to the Fourth National Radio Conference—saw neither "censorship" nor infringement of free speech in a distribution of broadcasting licenses based upon reasonable judgments as to the overall program service which serves the public interest.

It is clear, at the outset, that both House and Senate were aware that action by the Commission in performing the licensing function might impinge upon First Amendment freedoms. Thus, Mr. Reid of the House Committee asked Solicitor Davis of the Commerce Department, with regard to the license renewal provisions [*Hearings on H.R. 5589,* p. 26]:

> . . . suppose some broadcasting station, during the Republican administration of the Government, is broadcasting a lot of Democratic documents which we thought were not for the good of the country. Would it be possible for him [the licensing authority] to refuse the license if, in his discretion, he thought that? Would it not be a limitation in the freedom of speech?

And Senator Dill, introducing the Senate bill on the floor of the Senate, spoke at some length of "a gentleman in New York," who was refused permission to broadcast "an attack upon the present administration" by the managers of a radio station because "they were compelled to go to Washington to get their license renewed and they could not afford to take the chance of displeasing the administration in Washington." [67 Cong. Rec. 12356.]

But this awareness did not lead to any proposal to prohibit or limit consideration of program content. Solicitor Davis' answer to Mr. Reid was: "If you can imagine a Secretary doing that, he would have the power, but his action would be reviewable by a court on a direct appeal, under the terms of this bill." And another member of the Committee added: "Under this act it would be arbitrary action and might be reviewed by the court without any doubt." [*Hearings on H.R. 5589,* p. 26.] Similarly, Senator

Dill's illustration was not used to support any restriction on the commission's authority or—for that matter—as a basis for the Senate bill's anti-censorship section, but rather as a reason for placing the licensing function in a bi-partisan, independent commission, so that stations need not be "under the fear which they must necessarily feel, regardless of which party may be in power, when the control is placed in the hands of an administrative branch of the Government." [67 Cong. Rec. 12356.]

The history of Section 29 itself indicates that it was not intended to impose a limit on the commission's authority additional to that of the Constitution, and that neither the section nor the Constitution was thought to conflict with the programming judgments which the licensing authority was expected to make. Mr. White, as noted, thought that the House bill, *without such a section*, went "no further than the Federal Constitution" and conferred "no power of interfering with freedom of speech in any degree." This attitude was closely paralleled by that of Solicitor Davis of the Department of Commerce, who remarked during the Senate hearings [*Hearings on S. 1 and S. 1754*, p. 121]:

> Frankly, I do not think there is anything in the act which would give the power of censorship. I fully agree that there should be nothing to give the Secretary the power of censorship, and it is perhaps wise to give this formal declaration of that policy. Anyway, that is the purpose of this section.[17]

The bill in which Section 29 originated, moreover, was attacked during the Senate hearings on the ground that it gave *too much* authority over program content. [Statement of Norman Baker, President, American Broadcasters, *Hearings on S. 1 and S. 1754*, p. 166]:

> Who is going to decide what public interest is? * * * Is it what the larger Class B stations, that kind of program, those stations which give sort of a home-like program, or is it again the schools or colleges that have intellectual talks at various times? * * * Some think that the only program is an operatic singer who sings in a foreign language that you can't

---

[17] This was one of the two lone remarks in the Senate hearings directed specifically at Section 29. The other was made by Mr. M. L. Ernst of the American Civil Liberties Union, who said: "I have read over the House record, and over the Senate record, and I have never heard a word said, except the constitutional fiat that there shall be no impairment of the right of free speech." (*Hearings on S. 1 and S. 1754*, p. 132.)

understand. * * * But who is to decide what the public interest is? It seems to me that is a big burden. In other words, I would not want to sit here and tell you gentlemen that all of your wives and your children could not go to the theater except what theater I told you to go to, whether to a vaudeville or to an operatic kind.

No senator pointed in response to Section 29; and when the bill was reported to the Senate, the committee deleted without comment protection for the right of "free entertainment," which the original section had placed on a par with the right of "free speech." [Compare *Hearings on S. 1 and S. 1754*, p. 5 with *Calendar No. 774*, H.R. 9971, In the Senate of the United States, 69th Cong., 1st Sess., May 6 (calendar day May 8), 1926, p. 51.]

The Senate Committee report stated merely that "The commission shall not be permitted to exercise the power of censorship over radio programs. . . ." [Sen. Rep. No. 772, 69th Cong., 1st Sess., p. 4.] The Conference Report said only that "That part of section 29 which refers to the power of censorship and to the freedom of speech is taken from the Senate amendment, there being no similar provisions in the House bill." [Sen. Doc. No. 200, 69th Cong., 2nd Sess., p. 19; 68 Cong. Rec. 2564.] There is nothing to indicate that the House considered the addition of this section as more than the "formal declaration" which Solicitor Davis had described. It accepted the conference report without a single inquiry or comment as to the effect of Section 29. [68 Cong. Rec. 2556–2580.]

Events occurring on the Senate floor do afford some insight into the meaning which the Congress of 1927 ascribed to the term "censorship." Senator Blease offered an amendment which provided that "The Commission is further empowered to make and enforce regulations to censor and prohibit all discourses broadcast from stations under its control regarding the subject of evolution." He argued that the committee bill gave the commission power to censor everything "except religion," and it was at this point that Senator Dill entered the categorical denial quoted above, to the effect that the bill gave no power of censorship "in any degree." After several jokes about evolution and an impassioned statement from Senator Copeland, testifying to his belief in both religion and evolution, the Blease amendment was defeated. [67 Cong. Rec. 12615.]

In addition, we have Congressman White's statement that his proposal to authorize the prescription of "priorities as to subject matter" was thought by many to confer a power "akin to censorship." [*Hearings on H.R. 5589*, p. 39.] His proposal, as his remarks at the First National Radio Conference make clear, was intended to extend the process of allocating space in the spectrum, beyond the distribution of frequencies among classes of stations and individual stations, down to the distribution of specific time periods between various kinds of programs. This was to be accomplished either by particular orders or general rules, which would determine the relative preferences to be given to sermons, sacred concerts, prize fights, baseball, horse-racing, etc. [*Minutes*, pp. 11, 95–96.]

Thus, neither censorship in the classical sense—suppression of individual publications on the ground that their content is objectionable—nor establishment by the commission of a scale of values which would govern the selection of individual programs was thought to be within the power conferred by the Act. Neither type of action, however, is involved in the overall programming judgment which Secretary Hoover had proposed and which—it has been argued above—the Congress adopted.

There are, to be sure, indications which might be construed as pointing in the opposite direction. As introduced, reported and passed by the Senate, Section 29 forbade censorship and infringement of the right of free speech "except as herein specifically stated and declared" and "except as specifically stated and declared in this act." [*Hearings on S. 1 and S. 1754*, p. 5; *Calendar No. 774, supra*, p. 51; H.R. 9971, In the House of Representatives, July 2, 1956. [(Ordered to be printed with the amendment of the Senate), p. 55.] The conference committee deleted the quoted phrases without comment, and there was no other comment on the floor of either house during the final stages of enactment. It might be argued that the removal of this restriction made the section's prohibition all-encompassing.

Secondly, two members of the House committee indicated during the course of the hearings that they considered any attempt on the part of the licensing authority to provide "a more wholesome set of programs through the use of its authority in the issuance and renewal of licenses almost the entering wedge to censorship." [*Hearings on H.R. 5589*, p. 39.] Finally, when the conference bill was attacked in the House, on the ground that its protection against "private censorship" and discrimination rested *only* on the provision allowing revocation upon certification of discrimination to the Radio Commission by the Interstate Commerce Commission or some "other Federal body" and that this provision was ineffective because the Interstate

Commerce Commission had never exercised any jurisdiction over radio stations, Mr. Scott, who was one of the House conferees and floor manager for the conference report, said:

> Yes; and you are trespassing very closely on sacred ground when you attempt to control the right of free speech. It has become axiomatic to allow the freedom of the press, and when Congress attempts by indirection to coerce and place a supervision over the right of a man to say from a radio station what he believes to be just and proper, I think Congress is trespassing upon a very sacred principle. [67 Cong. Rec. 2567.]

The colloquy continued:

> Mr. Davis: I am opposed to any such authority, but I am in favor of provisions that will prevent an abuse of that kind.
> Mr. Scott: I think the gentleman's statement is correct. I think his views on the subject are the same as mine. But my fear is that through a desire to protect, he will unintentionally strike a blow which would produce the very opposite effect to that intended. [67 Cong. Rec. 2567.] [18]

[18] One should also list here the history of provisions dealing with advertising. The White bill which was reported out in the 68th Congress in 1924 contained the original of what was to be Section 19 of the Radio Act of 1927 (see Communications Act, Section 317), requiring that all matter broadcast for a valuable consideration be announced as paid for by the sponsor. The House committee report stated: "One of the subjects of public discussion at the present time is the extent to which broadcasting stations should be utilized for advertising purposes. *Your committee has not felt justified in forbidding or in undertaking to limit advertising through this medium*, but we are unanimous in the opinion that much the same rule should apply to this form of advertising as applies in the case of newspaper advertising. It should not be hidden from the knowledge of the hearer. Section 6 accordingly requires that all matter broadcasted for which any money . . . is paid shall be announced as advertising at the time the same is broadcasted. The section contains a provision that when the advertising or publicity consists solely of the announcement of the name and business of the person paying for the feature broadcasted, it shall be sufficient to announce that the feature is 'paid for' or is 'furnished by' such person." (emphasis added). H.R. Rep. No. 719, 68th Cong., 1st Sess., pp. 5–6. The same provision was carried by Mr. White's bill in the 69th Congress (*Hearings on H.R. 5589*, p. 5), but the requirement that material broadcast for a valuable consideration be announced as "advertising" was dropped by the committee. See H.R. Rep. No. 404, 69th Cong., 1st Sess., p. 3; Sen. Rep. No. 772, 69th Cong., 1st Sess., p. 4.

On the floor of the Senate, Senator Pittman attacked the conference bill at length, setting out its alleged inadequacies. Among them were the claim

On balance, however, such evidence is more than outweighed by the indications to the contrary. If the Congress saw no conflict between commission consideration of program content in its issuance of broadcast licenses and the anti-censorship provision, then the "except as specifically declared" phrase was surplusage, and was stricken for that reason. This interpretation is supported by the extraordinary lack of comment on the provision both before and after the phrase was stricken. Mr. Scott's defense of free speech is similarly equivocal, for an invasion of such freedom by the Interstate Commerce Commission can hardly be distinguished from an invasion of free speech by the Radio Commission.

In the final analysis, evidence of this nature simply will not bear the burden of explaining away the explicit position of Secretary Hoover, the statements of Congressman White, the provisions authorizing prescription of the nature of the service to be rendered by each class of stations and each station within any class, the requirement of program logs, and the statement by Senator Dill that the commission could take into account acts of discrimination "which make it no longer desirable" for a licensee to operate a station. By far the most probable conclusion is that Solicitor Davis of the Department of Commerce was expressing the understanding of Congress when he wrote, less than six months after the enactment of the Radio Act:

The character of the programs furnished is an essential factor in the determination of public interest but a most difficult test to apply, for to classify on this basis is to verge on censorship. Consideration of programs involves questions of taste, for which standards are impossible. It necessitates the determination of the relative importance of the broadcast-

that "No authority is given to the commission or the Secretary of Commerce to limit the extent to which broadcasting stations may be utilized for purely advertising purposes. The owners of the 15,000,000 purchased radio receiving sets in the United States are interested in the character of matter that is broadcast. This subject becomes particularly material when it is understood that there are only 89 effective broadcasting channels." 68 Cong. Rec. 4109. *Query*, however, whether this statement is consistent with the statements by Mr. White to the effect that the bill was drafted on the principle that ". . . the right of the public to service is superior to the right of any individual to use the ether." (67 Cong. Rec. 5479.) And that the conference bill ". . . starts out by asserting in the first place that the right to broadcast is to be based not upon the right of the individual, not upon the selfish desire of the individual, but upon a public interest to be served by the granting of these licenses." (68 Cong. Rec. 2579.)

ing of religion, instruction, news market reports, entertainment, and a dozen other subjects. It may require the determination of preferences as between stations devoted to service of the public generally and those servicing only special groups, however important. But in spite of the troublesomeness, these very features may be the controlling considerations in commission decision. [Davis, The Law of Radio Communications, p. 62 (1927).]

B. Administrative, Judicial and Legislative History of Communications Regulation under the Radio Act of (1927–1934)

1. Administration by the Radio Commission

The interpretation which the Federal Radio Commission gave between 1927 and 1934 to its authority under the Radio Act of 1927 is the same as that which has been advanced above as a result of consulting the legislative history of the Act, namely, that it was authorized to take the content of radio programs into account in making judgments under the standard of the public interest, convenience or necessity in assigning power, time, allocating wave lengths, etc., *and* in its licensing functions. It construed the prohibition of censorship as preventing its suppression of particular programs through the exercise of "prior restraints," and it construed the First Amendment so as to leave a substantial field for the exercise of its judgment upon radio programs.

For present purposes it is neither necessary nor appropriate to provide more than an outline of the essential steps taken.[19] In the very first general allocation of wave lengths, time of operation, etc., ". . . stations were recognized in terms of position and time on the basis of their demonstrated capacity to serve the public." [1 F.R.C. Ann. Rep. 11 (1927).] Similarly, in passing on applications for greater power, better frequencies, hours of operation, etc., the Commission ". . . required the contending stations to make complete showings of their past rec-

---

[19] It should be borne in mind throughout the following discussion that the Commission had, under the technological conditions then obtaining, no unused frequencies to allocate. "Every broadcasting channel is filled to its apparent capacity and in some cases possibly overcrowded. Accordingly, any listener who wants a different allocation of frequency or power for his favorite station, or any broadcaster who seeks increased facilities for service, must be prepared to show specifically what other station should be required to give up its frequency or have its own power reduced in order to make possible the desired reallocation." 1 F.R.C. Ann. Rep. 9 (1927)

ord of service, their program resources, etc." [2 F.R.C. Ann. Rep. 9 (1928).] [20]

Control of programs through the issuance of general orders (regulations), outside of the requirement of the announcement of call letters, was exercised only to the extent of the requirement that broadcasting by means of mechanical reproductions was to be announced as such. [See General Orders Nos. 16, 49, 45, and 78 in 2 F.R.C. Ann. Rep. 41, 55 (1928); 3 F.R.C. Ann. Rep. 56 (1929); 4 F.R.C. Ann. Rep. 13 (1930). See also 3 F.R.C. Ann. Rep. 16–18 (1929).]

The Commission was concerned with ". . . the extent and character of advertising which will be permitted by broadcasting stations," and it took the firm stand that ". . . the advertising must not be of a nature such as to destroy or harm the benefit to which the public is entitled from the proper use of broadcasting channels," but, in view of the fact that it had no power to censor programs, it felt that it ". . . must proceed cautiously in its regulations on this subject." [2 F.R.C. Ann. Rep. 19–20 (1928).]

It was in renewing licenses, however, that program content was of greatest moment.[21] The Commission's fundamental policies in this regard developed originally in the course of proceedings under General Order No. 32, which required 164 specified stations, with regard to which "The Commission had in its files reports . . . and other records of information indicating that it was very doubtful whether any of these broadcasting stations was performing any service entitling it to a renewed license," to ". . . make a showing that their continued operation would serve public interest, convenience, or necessity." [2 F.R.C. Ann. Rep. 15 (1928).] [22]

[20] See also General Order No. 10, May 18, 1927, reprinted in 1 F.R.C. Ann. Rep. 14 (1927): "For the purpose of facilitating wider and better reception of daytime service programs, such as those of educational and religious institutions, civic organizations, and distributors of market and other news, the Federal Radio Commission will consider applications . . . for a larger power output than is authorized by such licenses."

[21] The Commission's forms for applications for renewal of license early required such information as the average amount of time per week devoted to "Entertainment," "Religious," "Educational," "Agricultural," etc. programs, and whether or not direct advertising, including the quotation of merchandise prices was conducted. Hearings before the Committee on the Merchant Marine and Fisheries, House of Representatives, 70th Cong., 1st Sess. on H.R. 8825, pp. 21–23 (January, 1928).

[22] The background of this order is as follows: Section 9 of the Radio Act of 1927 had required the Commission to ". . . make such a distribution of

In making decisions under General Order No. 32, the Commission took the position that too much duplication of programs and types of programs in a particular area should be avoided; [23] that "A station which devotes the main portion of its hours of operation to broadcasting such phonograph records is not giving the public anything which it cannot readily have without such a station." [24] That ". . . broadcasting stations are not given these great privileges by the United States Government for the primary benefit of advertisers. Such benefit as derived by advertisers must be incidental and entirely secondary to the interest of the public."; [25] and that broadcasters ". . . who con-

---

licenses, bands of frequency or wave lengths, periods of time for operation, and of power among the different States and communities as to give fair, efficient, and equitable radio service to each of the same." 44 Stat. 1162, 1166. Congress amended this section in 1928, requiring the Commission to make, as nearly as possible, an *equal* allocation of licenses, etc., to each of the zones set up in Section 2 of the Act and "fair and equitable" allocation to each of the States and communities within any zone. 45 Stat. 373. (The original provision was substantially restored in 1936. 49 Stat. 1475.) "The Commission had before it requests of approximately 700 broadcasting stations for renewals of their licenses prior to January 15, 1928. Obviously, before it could intelligently fix upon the quota of each zone the Commission had to ascertain approximately how many stations were to remain in operation." 2 F.R.C. Ann. Rep. 15 (1928).

Out of the 164 stations cited, ". . . 81 escaped action by the Commission, 12 were substantially reduced in power, 4 were placed on probation, and 5 were left on as the result of consolidations with other stations . . ." "All told, 62 stations were deleted—4 as the result of surrender of license, 26 as the result of action by the Commission, and 32 as the result of default." 2 F.R.C. Ann. Rep. 16 (1928).

[23] Statement made by the Commission on August 23, 1928, relative to public interest, convenience, or necessity. 2 F.R.C. Ann. Rep. 166, 168: "Where one community is underserved and another community is receiving duplication of the same order of programs, the second community should be restricted in order to benefit the first. Where one type of service is being rendered by several stations in the same region, consideration should be given to a station which renders a type of service which is not such a duplication."

[24] 2 F.R.C. Ann. Rep. 168 (1928). The use of phonograph records was not completely proscribed, in view of the lack of resources for original programs in small towns and the development of transcriptions for broadcasting use only, but "The Commission cannot close its eyes to the fact that the real purpose of the use of phonograph records in most communities is to provide a cheaper method of advertising for advertisers who are thereby saved the expense of providing an original program." *Ibid.*

[25] 2 F.R.C. Ann. Rep. 168 (1928). See also 3 F.R.C. Ann. Rep. 32, 35 (1929). Also in 1929, in response to a complaint from Mr. Adrian M. Kelly, Chair-

sume much of the valuable time allotted to them under their licenses in matters of a distinctly private nature, which are not only uninteresting but also distasteful to the listening public," *e.g.* "where two rival broadcasters in the same community spend their time in abusing each other over the air" or where a station was used by its owner "(1) As a means of direct advertising, (2) for the promotion of its candidacy for mayor of Providence, (3) for expressing his views on all private matters, (4) as a medium for his attacks on his personal enemies," were not serving the public interest.[26]

It also took the position that ". . . the constitutional guaranty of freedom of speech applies to the expression of political and religious opinions, to discussions, fair comments, and criticisms on matters of general public interest, of candidates, of men holding public office, and of political, social and economic issues," but that it did not apply to ". . . the airing of personal disputes and private matters" or to ". . . entertainment programs as such." [2 F.R.C. Ann. Rep. 160–161 (1928).]

In 1929, the Commission committed to writing ". . . the broad underlying principles which, in its opinion, must control its decision on controversies arising between broadcasting stations in their competition for favorable assignments on the limited number of channels available." [Statement of Facts and Grounds for Decisions, *Great Lakes Broadcasting Co. et al.* v. *Federal Radio Commission*, Cases Nos. 4900, 4901, 4902. In the Court of Appeals for the District of Columbia, p. 17. (This state-

---

man of the National Food Products Protective Committee that certain advertisements by the American Tobacco Company for Lucky Strike Cigarettes amounted to a "clear and conscienceless attack upon public health, public morals and public welfare," the General Counsel of the Federal Radio Commission issued an opinion holding that, while the transmission of advertisements which were shown to be not in the public interest could not, under the circumstances there involved, be a ground for revocation of the licenses of radio stations carrying such advertisements, still such facts, if proven, would be material upon consideration of an application for renewal of license. In the course of his opinion, the General Counsel took the position that advertising was not as such protected by the Constitutional and statutory guarantees of free speech. Opinions of the General Counsel, Federal Radio Commission, August 1, 1928—August 1, 1929, pp. 77–82 (Opinion No. 32). The offending advertisements were apparently discontinued without any further action by the Commission. See Hearings before the Committee on Interstate Commerce, United States Senate, 71st Cong., 1st Sess. on S. 6, p. 88.

[26] 2 F.R.C. Ann. Rep. 152–153, 169 (1928). See also Opinion of the General Counsel No. 3, Federal Radio Commission, Opinions of the General Counsel, August 1, 1928—August 1, 1929, p. 20.

ment is reprinted in part in 3 F.R.C. Ann. Rep. 32 *et seq.* [1929] and citations will be to that source where possible.)] Stations which operated in the sole interest of individuals or specific groups were, as a general policy, no longer to be licensed. "There is not room in the broadcast band for every school of thought, religious, political, social, and economic, each to have its separate broadcasting, its mouthpiece in the ether. If franchises are extended to some it gives them an unfair advantage over others, and results in a corresponding cutting down of general public-service stations. It favors the interests and desires of a portion of the listening public at the expense of the rest. * * * As a general rule, . . . , particular doctrines, creeds and beliefs must find their way into the market of ideas by the existing public-service stations, . . ." [3 F.R.C. Ann. Rep. 34 (1929).] On the other hand, in passing on the applications of "general public-service stations," ". . . the tastes, needs, and desires of all substantial groups among the listening public should be met, in some fair proportion, by a well-rounded program, in which entertainment, consisting of music of both classical and lighter grades, religion, education and instruction, important public events, discussions of public questions, weather, market reports, and news, and matters of interest to all members of the family find a place." [*Ibid.*] [27] Again,

---

[27] This standard was by no means unqualified or rigid: "With so few channels in the spectrum and so few hours in the day, there are obvious limitations on the emphasis which can appropriately be placed on any portion of the program. There are parts of the day and of the evening when one type of service is more appropriate than another. There are differences between communities as to the need for one type as against another. The Commission does not propose to erect a rigid schedule specifying the hours or minutes that may be devoted to one kind of program or another. What it wishes to emphasize is the *general* character which it believes must be conformed to by a station in order best to serve the public.

"A somewhat different situation will obtain in regions which, like the thickly populated Chicago area and surrounding agricultural country, are served by several cleared channel stations and a less thickly populated region served by only one cleared channel station. A greater diversity of program is possible in the former case than the latter; by apportioning the types of service among several stations, each may perform any one type in more detail and completeness. This is only the natural result of disparities in population and in other aspects. The principle is the same." 3 F.R.C. Ann. Rep. 34. Statement of Facts and Grounds for Decisions, *supra*, pp. 35–36.

Moreover, the discussion was confined to clear channel stations: "The same basic principles will, of course, apply to regional and local stations, but cannot be as rigorously enforced against them because of the smaller

"Insofar as a program consists of discussion of public questions, public interest requires ample play for the free and fair competition of opposing views, and the Commission believes that the principle applies not only to addresses by political candidates but to all discussions of issues of importance to the public." [3 F.R.C. Ann. Rep. 33.]

Guides to the evaluation of broadcasting stations were found in "the injunctions of the statute itself, such, for example, as the requirement for non-discrimination between political candidates, and the prohibition against the utterance of 'any obscene, indecent or profane language' (Section 29)," in the rules and regulations of the Commission, such as "the requirements as to the announcing of call-letters and as to the accurate description of mechanical reproductions," and in "decisions of the Commission bearing on particular practices, such as the broadcasting of private disputes and offensive direct advertising, the excessive use of phonograph records of the ordinary commercial type, and the fraudulent solicitation of contributions by radio. . . ." [Statement of Facts and Grounds for Decisions, *supra* at p. 33.]

With regard to the restrictions of Section 29 on the Commission's authority, it was stated:

The Commission is convinced that in setting up the standards it does, it is not transgressing the provisions of Section 29 of the Radio Act of 1927 prohibiting it from assuming the power of censorship or infringing the right of free speech. It does not, either by rule, regulation or order, forbid or curtail the full scope of the free exchange of ideas on all matters of interest or importance to the *public;* it simply is applying the standard of *public* interest, convenience or necessity which, under the statute, must control its every action. It desires to eliminate matters of private interest only to make room for the already excessive demand of matters of public interest. It is not imposing any prior restriction on utterances (the usual conception of censorship) but it is reserving the right to take into account a station's past conduct, measured by the legal standard, in its future actions. If any restriction

---

areas served, the smaller capital available for programs, and the extensive time-divisions which have been imposed on nearly all of them in order to make possible the forty cleared channels, and the satisfactory use of the regional channels. Furthermore, program service of general or national interest appropriate to stations serving large areas will be replaced in part by program service of regional or local interest appropriate to stations serving lesser areas." Statement of Facts and Grounds for Decisions, *supra*, p. 23.

is imposed on free speech it is by the laws of radio physics which make it impossible to crowd the same amount of utterance into the few channels of the ether that can be accommodated in the press or on the public platform. Even in the press or in public places speech is not unrestricted; matters of private interest become public nuisances, grounds for actions for damages, and even crimes.[28] [Statement of Facts and Grounds for Decisions, *supra*, p. 43.]

Two aspects of this statement of policy by the Commission are of particular significance. The first is that the context of the policy was, as indicated, one of competition by two or more stations for the same facilities, or what would now be called a "comparative" hearing context. The Commission referred to its decisions under General Order No. 32 discussed above, as ". . . statements of its application of the standard of public interest, convenience or necessity to particular stations in cases where the question was as to whether renewal licenses should be granted and no controversy *between* stations was involved . . ." (emphasis in original). [Statement of Facts and Grounds for Decisions, *supra*, p. 18.] There is a clear difference between a minimum standard which all licensees must meet at the peril of losing their license and a comparative standard which will determine the outcome of a contest with more than one horse in the race. The significance of this difference, however, can be overemphasized. The ". . . concept of service, capable of practical application," which could be ". . . maintained as the ideal by which all contestants shall be measured . . ." [Statement of Facts and Grounds for Decisions, *supra*, p. 28] was to be the same in either context. ["It may be urged that if what has heretofore been said is law, the listening public is left at the mercy of the broadcaster. * * * . . . the licensing authority will

---

[28] This construction of Section 29 of the Radio Act of 1927 is in general based upon two opinions of the Commission's General Counsel, which were issued on January 26, 1929. One was signed by the Commission's first General Counsel, Mr. Louis G. Caldwell, and the other "approved" by Bethuel M. Webster, Jr., the Commission's second General Counsel. Both opinions agreed that consideration of program content in the context of renewal applications was not "censorship," since it was not a prior restraint. Both took the position that the second clause of Section 29, prohibiting the infringement of the right of free speech was an additional and independent limitation upon the Commission's authority and that only certain kinds of judgment upon program content made in deciding upon applications for renewals would interfere with that right. Opinions of the General Counsel of the Federal Radio Commission, Nos. 29 and 42.

have occasion, both in connection with renewals of his license
and in connection with applications of others for his privileges
to review his past performances and to determine whether he
has met with the standard." 3 F.R.C. Ann. Rep. 35 (1929).]
The difference between a judgment that a station's performance
does not entitle it to renewal of its license where there are other
better qualified applicants and a similar judgment where the apparent alternative is to leave a frequency unused in a particular
area is in the end one of degree only. The standard of program
service is one set by the Commission in either case. It should be
noted, however, that the difference between the two situations
was of little significance in the early life of the Radio Commission because, as indicated above, under the technological conditions then obtaining, there was so little space in the radio spectrum assigned to broadcasting that there was little chance that a
position which was lost by one station would remain unused for
long.

The second point of importance to be noted is that the Commission here turned away from the idea that its responsibility to
the various elements of the listening public could in general be
met by the licensing of special purpose stations, such as "educational," "religious," etc.[29] Its imposition of the obligation of a
"balanced" program upon "general public-service" stations was
a strict corollary of this decision and of the proposition, accepted by everyone, that it was responsible for the over-all use
to be made of the limited radio spectrum.

2. Judicial Interpretation of the Radio Act.

Turning to the judicial history of the Radio Act of 1927, one
finds a construction of the Act which also sustains the position
taken above on the basis of the legislative history. The Court of
Appeals for the District of Columbia uniformly assumed that
the content and quality of program service was a prime consideration in the allocation of power, time of operation and frequency. [City of New York v. Federal Radio Commission (November 4, 1929) 59 App. D.C. 129, 36 F.2d 115 cert. denied,
281 U.S. 729; Great Lakes Broadcasting Co. v. Federal Radio
Commission (January 6, 1930) 59 App. D.C. 197, 37 F.2d 993,
995 cert. dismissed 281 U.S. 706; Chicago Federation of Labor
v. Federal Radio Commission (May 5, 1930) 59 App. D.C. 333,
41 F.2d 422; Woodmen of the World Life Insurance Assn. v.

[29] As noted above, the policy against special purpose stations was carefully
qualified so as not to apply ". . . in regions which, like the thickly populated Chicago area and surrounding agricultural country, are served by
several cleared channel stations. . . ." See note 31, supra.

Federal Radio Commission (February 29, 1932) 61 App. D.C.
54, 57 F.2d 420; *Radio Investment Co.* v. *Federal Radio Commission* (November 21, 1932) 61 App. D.C. 296, 62 F.2d 381,
cert. denied 288 U.S. 612; *Unity School of Christianity* v. *Federal Radio Commission* (February 19, 1934) 63 App. D.C. 84,
69 F.2d 570, *cert. denied* 292 U.S. 646. It made a similar assumption with regard to the renewal of licenses. *Technical Radio Laboratory* v. *Federal Radio Commission* (November 4,
1929) 59 App. D.C. 125, 129, 36 F.2d 111; *Riker* v. *Federal
Radio Commission* (December 21, 1931) 60 App. D.C. 373, 55
F.2d 535; *Brahy* v. *Federal Radio Commission* (June 6, 1932)
61 App. D.C. 204, 59 F.2d 879.] [30]

The Supreme Court of the United States made the same assumption in *Federal Radio Commission* v. *Nelson Brothers
Bond & Mortgage Co.* 289 U.S. 266. The standard of public interest, convenience or necessity, held the Court, ". . . is to be
interpreted by its context, by the nature of radio transmission
and reception, *by the scope, character and quality of services,*
and . . . by the relative advantages in service which will be
enjoyed by the public through the distribution of facilities."
(Emphasis added.) [289 U.S. at p. 285.] The Court went on to
hold that the Commission was entitled to consider ". . . the
special requirements of radio service at Gary." [*Ibid.*], *i.e.*,
the need of a steel producing center, over 60 per cent of whose
population were foreign born, for a program service tailored to
the needs of that population by the inclusion of foreign language broadcasts, talks on ". . . the application of new safeguards of various types of machinery used in the steel mills."
(289 U.S. at p. 271), etc., in granting an application by one
station for authority to operate on a particular frequency for
unlimited time and deleting two other stations operating on the
same frequency.

The question of authority to consider program content was
faced squarely in two cases during the period under consideration. The first, *KFKB Broadcasting Assn.* v. *Federal Radio Com-*

[30] Prior to July 1, 1930, when the Radio Act was amended (46 Stat. 844), the
Court of Appeals for the District of Columbia acted as ". . . a superior
and revising agency . . ." over the Commission. *Federal Radio Commission* v. *General Electric Co.* 281 U.S. 464, 467. Its proceedings on appeal
from the Commission were "administrative" proceedings, and it was authorized to take additional evidence, revise or alter the Commission's decision, and enter such judgment as to it seemed just. In the light of this *de
novo* function of the Court, its assumption, in cases prior to the 1930 amendment, that program content was relevant to the Commission's functions has
added significance.

mission (February 2, 1931) 60 App. D.C. 79, 47 F.2d 670, involved a denial of an application for renewal by a license held by a Dr. J. R. Brinkley of Milford, Kansas. Dr. Brinkley operated Station KFKB, the Brinkley Hospital and the Brinkley Pharmaceutical Association, as the Court put it, ". . . in a common interest." Dr. Brinkley, through the medium of a program known as the "medical question box," prescribed over the air in response to letters from the public, referring to prescriptions by number only; the prescriptions, in turn, could only be obtained from druggists who were members of the pharmaceutical association and who paid a fee to the station upon each sale of certain of the Brinkley preparations. The Commission found that the practice thus outlined was inimical to the public health and safety and that the station was being operated only in the personal interest of the licensee and not in the interest of the public. The Court squarely upheld this consideration of program content:

> It is apparent, we think, that the business is impressed with a public interest and that, because the number of available broadcasting frequencies is limited, the Commission is necessarily called upon to consider the character and quality of the service to be rendered. In considering an application for a renewal of the license, an important consideration is the past conduct of the applicant, for "by their fruits ye shall know them" [Matt. VII:20].

It also specifically agreed with the Commission's interpretation of the statute as excluding the broadcasting of ". . . matters of a private nature." [2 F.R.C. Ann. Rep. 169 (1928). (See p. 43, *supra*)]:

> When Congress provided that the question whether a license should be issued or renewed should be dependent upon a finding of public interest, convenience, or necessity, it very evidently had in mind that broadcasting should not be a mere adjunct of a particular business but should be of a public character. Obviously, there is no room in the broadcast band for every business or school of thought. [47 F.2d at p. 672.]

Finally, it rejected the contention of the appellant that such consideration of program content conflicted with the prohibition of censorship in Section 29 of the Radio Act of 1927:

> This contention is without merit. There has been no attempt on the part of the Commission to subject any part of appellant's broadcasting matter to scrutiny prior to its re-

lease. In considering the question whether the public interest, convenience, or necessity will be served by a renewal of appellant's license, the Commission has merely exercised its undoubted right to take note of appellant's past conduct, which is not censorship. [47 F.2d at p. 672.]

The second case turning on the question of the Commission's authority over programming was *Trinity Methodist Church, South* v. *Federal Radio Commission* (November 28, 1932) 61 App. D.C. 311, 62 F.2d 850, *cert. denied* 284 U.S. 685, 288 U.S. 599. The station whose license was not renewed was operated by a Reverend Doctor Shuler. Dr. Shuler's station had been used to attack a religious organization, namely, the Roman Catholic Church, to allude slightingly to Jews as a race, to attack judges in cases pending before them,[31] to defame the board of health, and to attack the local bar association for its activities in recommending judges. "In none of these matters, when called on to explain or justify his statements, was he able to do more than declare that the statements expressed his own sentiments." [61 App. D.C. at p. 313.] Further, "on one occasion he announced over the radio that he had certain damaging information against a prominent unnamed man which, unless a contribution (presumably to the church) of a hundred dollars was forthcoming, he would disclose. As a result, he received contributions from several persons. He freely spoke of 'pimps' and prostitutes." [*Ibid.*] The Court held that it was the Commission's *duty* to consider these actions of the appellant in deciding whether to renew its license. It held further that a refusal to renew on the basis of this record was ". . . neither censorship nor previous restraint, nor is it a whittling away of the rights guaranteed by the First Amendment, or an impairment of their free exercise." [61 App. D.C. at pp. 313, 314.]

It should be noted that this first judicial construction of the First Amendment as it related to radio took the position that the guarantee of free speech prevented "previous restraints," but that the application of "subsequent punishment" in the exercise of proper regulatory power in the interests of the general welfare was not proscribed. [61 App. D.C. at pp. 312–313.] The Court also implied that the denial of ". . . the continued

---

[31] As the Court noted, the Supreme Court of California had stated that these utterances by Dr. Shuler ". . . disclosed throughout the determination on his part to impose on the trial courts his own will and views with respect to certain causes then pending or on trial, and amounted to contempt of court." 61 App. D.C. at p. 313.

use of an instrumentality of commerce . . . except in subordi-
nation to all reasonable rules and regulations Congress, acting
through the Commission, may prescribe" *could not* interfere
with the appellant's right of free speech: "Appellant may continue to indulge his strictures upon the characters of men in
public office. He may just as freely as ever criticize religious
practices of which he does not approve. He may even indulge
private malice or personal slander—subject, of course, to be required to answer for the abuse thereof . . ." [61 App. D.C. at
p. 314.]

3. Legislative History 1927–1934

The evidence that Congress was aware of these administrative and judicial constructions of the statute is little short of
overwhelming.[32] Between 1927 and 1934, Congress extended
the provisions of the Radio Act of 1927 which vested original
authority in the Radio Commission, rather than the Secretary of
Commerce, three times—twice for limited periods and finally
"until otherwise provided by law." [45 Stat. 373. 1559; 46 Stat.
50.] In 1929 and 1930, extensive hearings were held on a bill
which would have created a unified communications commission
exercising jurisdiction over both "wire and wireless" communication. [Hearings Before the Committee on Interstate Commerce, United States Senate, 71st Cong. 1st and 2nd Sess. on
S. 6.] Moreover, bills providing extensive revisions of proce-
dural sections of the Act passed both Houses of Congress between 1930 and 1933. [H.R. 11635, 71st Congress; H.R. 7716,
72nd Congress.] [33]

During the course of the hearings on these legislative actions
and in confirming the appointments of radio Commissioners,
Congress was informed not once but many times of the Commission's interpretation of its authority. [See, *e.g.*, Hearings Be-

---

[32] The evidence presented in the text, *infra*, is of course in addition to the
Commission's annual reports to Congress, which have already been discussed.

[33] The first was passed by the Senate too late in the session to allow time for
a conference committee to reconcile differences between the House and
Senate bills. See H.R. Rep. No. 1179, 71st Cong., 2nd Sess.; Sen. Rep. No.
1578, 71st Cong., 3rd Sess.; 72 Cong. Rec. 8055, 74 Cong. Rec. 5206, 5256.
Action on the second bill, which largely incorporated the provisions of the
first, was completed, but the bill was pocket-vetoed by President Hoover.
See H.R. Rep. No. 221, 72nd Cong., 1st Sess.; Sen. Rep. No. 564, 72nd
Cong., 1st Sess.; Sen. Rep. No. 1004, 72nd Cong., 2nd Sess., Sen. Rep. No.
1045, 72nd Cong., 2nd Sess., H.R. Rep. No. 2106, 72nd Cong., 2nd Sess.;
75 Cong. Rec. 3705; 76 Cong. Rec. 3770, 5039, 5212, 5397.

fore the Committee on the Merchant Marine and Fisheries, House of Representatives, 70th Cong., 1st Sess. on H.R. 8825, pp. 21–25, 63, 78–79, 135–136, 188–189, 203–204; Hearings Before the Committee on Interstate Commerce, United States Senate, 70th Cong., 1st Sess. on the Confirmation of Federal Radio Commissioners, pp. 17–19, 83–84, 136; Hearings Before the Committee on Interstate Commerce, United States Senate, 70th Cong., 2nd Sess. on S. 4937, pp. 20, 40; Hearings Before the Committee on the Merchant Marine and Fisheries, House of Representatives, 70th Cong., 2nd Sess. on H.R. 15430, pp. 8, 55; Hearings Before the Committee on Interstate Commerce, United States Senate, 71st Cong., 1st and 2nd Sess., on S. 6, pp. 68–69, 77–78, 88–90, 91–92, 95, 126–144, 157, 1607–1608, 1616, 1636, 1642–1643.]

The Commission's Statement of Facts and Grounds for Decisions in the *Great Lakes Broadcasting Company* case, discussed *supra* on p. 133 which explained the Commission's standards for the evaluation of program content in detail, was inserted in the record of the hearings on S. 6, in the 71st Congress. [Hearings Before the Committee on Interstate Commerce, United States Senate, 71st Cong., 1st Sess. on S. 6, pp. 126–144.] And the effect of the *KFKB* case, discussed *supra* p. 138 was the subject of specific comment on the floor of the House during the passage of H.R. 7716 in the 72nd Congress. [75 Cong. Rec. 3682, 3684.] [34]

[34] "MR. DAVIS: The present radio law specifically provides that the Radio Commission and broadcasting stations shall not have the right of censorship. However, I want to state that some confusion has arisen in the public mind on this ground. They have refused to grant renewal of licenses perhaps because that station was broadcasting speeches or material which the Commission conceived to be distasteful to a large portion of the public. The Supreme Court (*sic*) has held that that is not censorship; that they do not censor; they do not pass upon anything as broadcast; but when a station over a period of time has been permitting the broadcasting of programs of any kind, that the Commission has a right to take that into consideration in determining whether or not a renewal of that license is in the public interest or necessity." 75 Cong. Rec. 3682.

"MR. WILLIAMSON: The gentleman is familiar with the radio law and the powers of the Commission. Does not the Commission have authority to regulate the character of advertising that goes over the air?

"MR. LEHLBACH: The Commission has the right of granting or withholding or canceling licenses for broadcasting of all radio programs; the canceling of all broadcasts if they are not in the public interest. It has no specific authority to censor, but in the application of these broad general powers it is within its discretion how far it shall go.

"MR. WILLIAMSON: So that if a radio station persists in sending out

Moreover, in 1932 the Senate passed a resolution instructing the Radio Commission to make a survey and to report to the Senate on such questions as the feasibility of Government ownership and operation of broadcasting facilities, the plans which might be adopted to reduce, limit, control or eliminate the use of radio facilities for commercial advertising purposes, and means which had been and might be used to provide greater access to radio facilities by educational institutions. [S. Res. No. 129, 72nd Cong., 1st Sess.] In an extensive report the Commission stated, *inter alia,* that, while specific power to prescribe the character and limits of advertising *by regulation* was not within its authority and would require further legislation, it could take the character of commercial advertising into account in renewing or revoking a license.[35] [Sen. Doc. No. 137, 72nd Cong., 1st Sess., p. 33.] It also took the position (in response to a specific question) that "The present attitude of broadcasters, as indicated herein, justifies the Commission in believing that educational programs can be safely left to the voluntary gift of the use of facilities by commercial stations." [Sen. Doc. No. 137, *supra,* p. 101.]

Finally, it should be noted that H.R. 7716, which was pocket vetoed by President Hoover, contained a provision which would have broadened the requirement of Section 18 of the Radio Act of 1927 so as to require "equal opportunities" not only for candidates for public office, but also for persons using a station in support of or in opposition to a candidate ". . . or in the presentation of views on a public question to be voted upon at an election . . ." and which would have added to the same section: "Furthermore, it shall be considered in the public interest for a licensee, so far as possible, to permit equal opportunity for the presentation of both sides of public questions." [H.R. Rep. No. 2106, 72nd Cong., 2nd Sess., p. 4.] There was some question whether the latter provision was necessary to *authorize*

what the Commission considers as objectionable advertising, the Commission could refuse to renew the license?

"MR. LEHLBACH: Absolutely." 75 Cong. Rec. 3684.

[35] The history of attitudes toward advertising prior and up to the enactment of the Radio Act of 1927 and of the Commission's doubts as to its authority to proceed in this field by way of regulation has been given above. See footnote *18,* and p. 131, *supra.* A bare majority of three of the five commissioners concurred in the statement that additional legislation would be needed if control of advertising by means of direct regulation was to be assumed, the other two commissioners holding that Section 4 of the Radio Act (Section 303 of the Communications Act) provided ample authority. Sen. Doc. No. 137, *supra,* p. iii.

action by the Commission. Senator Dill, for instance, was on
record to the effect that the Commission could promulgate regulations requiring such "equal opportunities" with regard to
"public questions" *under the original Act of 1927.* [See Hearings Before the Committee on Interstate Commerce, United
States Senate, 71st Cong., 2nd Sess. on S. 6, p. 1616.]

It is hardly too much to say that such ambiguities as the legislative history of the Radio Act of 1927 reveals with regard to
the Commission's statutory authority over programming in considering renewals of licenses had, by 1934, been dispelled by
the administrative, judicial and legislative developments which
have been described. There was, as noted, some doubt as to
whether authority for any direct control over programming by
means of rules or regulations might not conflict with the "censorship" prohibition of Section 29. But the Commission's authority to take program content into account in renewing licenses, in assigning frequencies, power, time of operation and
location of station, was clearly understood to be limited only by
the First Amendment's ban on infringements of the right of free
speech. It remained for the future to provide a clear understanding of those Constitutional limits, but it was generally
presumed that they left a large field for the play of the Commission's judgment.[36]

---

[36] MR. CALDWELL: In section 27 on page 33, I want to mention a matter for
a possible later recommendation simply, as a possibility of a future need
for an amendment.

This section provides that nothing in this act shall be understood or
construed to give this Commission the power of censorship.

I believe that was intended to mean, and does mean, the power of censorship over the dissemination of questions of public interest, and does not
refer to program service or matters of advertising, and all that sort of
thing. That construction is being regularly followed by the Commission
and, so far, has not been seriously challenged by anyone. If the time should
come when a different construction were given the provision by the courts,
that it takes away from the Commission the power of considering program
service and advertising, then I think some change should be made.

I have just been through a very complete study of the historical evolution of the meaning of censorship and freedom of speech in a case concerning the validity of a law in Minnesota. I am convinced that the construction giving this Commission the power I mention is the correct one,
restricting it only from exercising any power to discipline stations in any
manner, for views on questions of public interest or importance.

SENATOR GLENN: In other words, you think this does not need amendment?

MR. CALDWELL: I think now it is all right if properly construed by the

C. Immediate Legislative History of the Communications Act of 1934

As the Supreme Court indicated in *Federal Communications Commission* v. *Pottsville Broadcasting Co.* 309 U.S. 134, 137, the fundamental provisions of the Radio Act of 1927 were not altered in the course of its re-enactment as Title III of the Communications Act of 1934. With one exception, such changes as were made stemmed from the Senate bill and had, for the most part, been portions of H.R. 7716, which had passed both houses in the previous Congress only to be pocket-vetoed by the President. [See H.R. Rep. No. 1850, 73rd Cong., 2nd Sess., pp. 2, 7; Sen. Rep. No. 781, 73rd Cong., 2nd Sess., pp. 6–8; H.R. Rep. No. 1918, 73rd Cong., 2nd Sess., pp. 47–49.]

Three provisions which *were* added throw light upon the Congressional understanding of the authority which the Commission had exercised in the programming field under the Act of 1927 and of the authority which the new Communications Commission was intended to exercise. The requirement of Section 325(b) and (c) that a permit be obtained from the Commission as a prerequisite to the location, maintenance or use of studios or apparatus in the United States from which programs are transmitted to a station in a foreign country for the purpose of broadcasting such programs back into the United States originated in S. 2660, a bill which had passed the Senate and had been reported out favorably by a House committee earlier in the same session of the 73rd Congress. [Sen. Rep. No. 781, 73rd Cong., 2nd Sess., p. 8; H.R. Rep. No. 1918, 73rd Cong., 2nd Sess., p. 49.] The clear intent of this legislation was to prevent the use of American studios and apparatus for the broad-

---

courts, but I think that there is a possibility that there might be trouble later if, contrary to my expectation, a different construction is placed upon it.

SENATOR GLENN: In other words, it might be cleared up?

MR. CALDWELL: I am not sure that it is important enough as a potential danger.

SENATOR GLENN: I think it is an important situation.

MR. CALDWELL: I mean, until a later time, if and when the necessity arises. Perhaps it would be better to have the question thoroughly decided as it stands.

SENATOR GLENN: It is sure to come, I think. Hearings before the Committee on Interstate Commerce, United States Senate, 71st Cong., 1st Sess. on S. 6, p. 157 (1929).

(Mr. Caldwell was Mr. Louis G. Caldwell, the first General Counsel of the Federal Radio Commission.)

casting into the United States of programs which did not meet the standards imposed by the Federal Radio Commission.[37] Indeed, one of the prime malefactors at whom this provision was aimed was the same Dr. Brinkley whose application for renewal of license had been denied in the *KFKB* case, *supra,* and who had moved his studio to Texas and his transmitter to Mexico. [Hearings before the Committee on the Merchant Marine, Radio and Fisheries, House of Representatives, 73rd Cong., 2nd Sess. on H.R. 7800, pp. 2–10, 40–43, 57–79.]

Section 307(c), which originated in the Senate committee, also has relevance to the programming authority of the Commission. Senators Wagner and Hatfield offered on the floor of the Senate an amendment, which was also urged in both House and Senate committee hearings, requiring that one fourth of all radio broadcasting facilities within the Commission's jurisdiction be allocated to educational, religious, agricultural, labor, cooperative and "similar non-profit-making associations." [78 Cong. Rec. 8828. See also Hearings before the Committee on Interstate Commerce, United States Senate, 73rd Cong., 2nd Sess. on S. 2910, pp. 184–193 (hereafter cited as *Hearings on S. 2910*); Hearings before the Committee on Interstate and Foreign Commerce, House of Representatives, 73rd Cong., 2nd Sess. on H.R. 8301, pp. 147–163 (hereafter cited as *Hearings on H.R. 8301*).] This proposal must be viewed against the background of the Commission's policy statement in the *Great Lakes Broadcasting Co.* case, discussed *supra,* taking the position that "special purpose" stations, operated in the interests of particular groups, would no longer be licensed unless it appeared that a particular area was already adequately served by "general public-service" commercial stations, upon whom the Commission imposed its "balanced programming" standard.

Opposing the Wagner-Hatfield proposal in the House committee hearings, the National Association of Broadcasters took exactly the position which the Commission had taken in the *Great Lakes* case and in its report to Congress:

---

[37] "Certain persons who have been forbidden to operate broadcasting stations in the United States have set up stations in Mexico and are operating studios on the American side of the line. This bill will give the Commission power to stop such outlaw broadcasting." Sen. Rep. No. 319, 73rd Cong., 2nd Sess., accompanying S. 2660. "Two of the stations are operated by persons who have been denied licenses by the Federal Radio Commission, and are sending out programs which the Federal Radio Commission has found not to be in the public interest." H.R. Rep. No. 1037, 73rd Cong., 2nd Sess., accompanying S. 2660, p. 2. See also Senator Dill's statement, introducing S. 2660 on the floor of the Senate, 78 Cong. Rec. 2865.

It is the manifest duty of the licensing authority, in passing upon applications for licenses or the renewal thereof, to determine whether or not the applicant is rendering or can render an adequate public service. Such service necessarily includes the broadcasting of a considerable proportion of programs devoted to education, religion, labor, agriculture, and similar activities concerned with human betterment.

In actual practice, over a period of 7 years, as the records of the Federal Radio Commission amply prove, this has been the principal test which the Commission has applied in dealing with broadcasting applications. Most of the evidence presented by applicants with regard to program service has been concerned with programs of a public-service character from which no revenue has been received.

The National Association of Broadcasters fully agree that the facilities of broadcasting should be made available in the fullest possible measure, as it maintains they now are, and either free of all charge or at the lowest possible cost, in the service of education, religion, and other activities for human betterment, but it insists that these facilities should be those of stations serving the public as a whole. [Hearings on H.R. 8301, p. 117.] [38]

Opposing the Wagner-Hatfield amendment in both committee hearings and on the Senate floor, both Senators Dill and White, the co-authors of the Radio Act of 1927, pointed to the difficulties of allocation upon the basis of special purpose to specific educational, religious or other organizations without unfair discrimination, to the fact that educational and religious institutions could not support full-time radio stations without going into commercial broadcasting themselves, to the fact that then existing commercial stations devoted substantial time to religious and educational programs—in short to the considerations which had led the Commission to adopt and maintain its "balanced program" standard for "general public-service" commercial stations rather than to attempt such an allocation. [*Hearings on S. 2910*, pp. 190–191; 78 Cong. Rec. 8830, 8837, 8843–8845.] As Senator White formulated the question before the Senate: "Manifestly, we should either go ahead as a Congress

[38] In the Senate hearings, the representative of the broadcasting industry association indicated general satisfaction with the Radio Act and opposed any changes: "Almost every one recognizes that, despite minor defects, the Radio Act of 1927, as amended, *and the court decisions under it,* have established a solid, workable and sound basis for Government regulation of radio." (Emphasis added.) *Hearings on S. 2910*, p. 54.

and divide up the entire spectrum among persons and organizations for uses here in the United States or we should leave it alone in its entirety and place the responsibility of allocation where it already is—upon the Federal Radio Commission." [78 Cong. Rec. 8845.]

Neither Senator White nor Senator Dill endorsed the Commission's solution of the problem, as had the National Association of Broadcasters. Senator Dill did suggest that a condition be inserted in the licenses of ordinary commercial broadcasting stations, requiring them to devote a specified portion of their time to educational, religious, and similar non-profit users. [78 Cong. Rec. 8837, 8843, 8844.] But he indicated that his suggestion was tentative, and strongly supported the committee substitute for the Wagner-Hatfield amendment, which required the Commission to study the proposal embodied in that amendment and report to Congress. This was the course which Congress followed, rejecting the Wagner-Hatfield amendment and enacting the provision carried in Section 307(c) of the Communications Act.[39]

Section 3(h) of the Communications Act, which declares that radio broadcasters are not to be deemed common carriers, is unlike either of the two sections just discussed in that its relevant portion appeared in its final form in both the Senate and House bills as they were introduced. [S. 2910, In the Senate of the United States, February 20 (Calendar Day, February 27), 1934, p. 4; H.R. 8301, In the House of Representatives, February 27, 1934, p. 4.] The provision received no comment in any

---

[39] The report which the Commission made in 1935 pursuant to this section of the statute reaffirmed its position that educational and religious interests could and should find expression through the use of the facilities of general "public-service" stations. It recommended that ". . . at this time no fixed percentages of radio broadcast facilities be allocated by statute to particular types or kinds of non-profit radio programs or to persons identified with particular types or kinds of non-profit activities," and stated:

"It would appear that the interests of the non-profit organizations may be better served by the use of the existing facilities, thus giving them access to costly and efficient equipment and to established audiences, than by the establishment of new stations for their peculiar needs. In order for non-profit organizations to obtain the maximum service possible, cooperation in good faith by the broadcasters is required. *Such cooperation should, therefore, be under the direction and supervision of the Commission.*" (Emphasis added.)

Again, the Commission stated: "It is our firm intention to assist the non-profit organizations to obtain the fullest opportunities for expression."

Report of the Federal Communications Commission to Congress to Section 307(c) of the Communications Act of 1934, pp. 5, 6, 9–10.

of the committee reports or on the floor of either House. Its intent, however, can be established by recourse to prior history.

In adopting the Radio Act of 1927, it will be remembered,
the Senate eliminated a provision which would have made all
radio broadcasters common carriers with regard to controversial public questions, on the ground that it would be impractical, in view of the limited time available, to impose upon
broadcasters the obligation to allow the use of their facilities to
everyone who might wish to speak. See p. 121, *supra*. Senator
Couzens' premature proposal in 1929 to unify the regulation of
all communications industries under one commission would have
made the common carrier provisions applicable to telegraph
and telephone companies also applicable to all uses of radio, including radio broadcasting. [See Hearings Before the Committee on Interstate Commerce, United States Senate, 71st
Cong., 1st and 2nd Sess. on S. 6, pp. 1–2.] This provision was
stoutly supported by Chairman Robinson of the Radio Commission [Hearings on S. 6, pp. 189–195, 1614–1617], but it was
just as stoutly opposed by the Commission's former General
Counsel, Mr. Louis G. Caldwell, by the National Association of
Broadcasters, the National Broadcasting Company, and by the
majority of the Radio Commission, whose General Counsel (Mr.
Bethuel M. Webster, Jr.) submitted comments to the Senate
committee recommending that broadcasters be specifically ex-
empted from common carrier status. [See Hearings on S. 6, pp.
75, 87–88, 104, 241, 1715, 1757; Letter, General Counsel of
Federal Radio Commission to Senator Couzens and Suggested
Amendments to S. 6, August 26, 1929, F.R.C. Mimeo No. 1271,
pp. 1, 2, 7.] The ground of this opposition was again the im-
practicality rather than the impropriety of the suggestion that
anyone who wished to speak must be allowed to do so. As Senator Dill phrased it, ". . . in theory I have agreed for a long
time with the idea that all broadcasting stations should be common carriers, but in practice I have never been able to convince
myself that it could be worked out without seriously breaking
down the radio service, and that is why I have never insisted
upon it." [*Hearings on S. 6, p. 193.*]

There is not the slightest evidence that anyone who proposed
the removal of broadcasters from the common carrier category
thought that by so doing they were urging that the Commission
abandon its concern with program content. On the contrary,
the four majority members of the Commission (other than Commissioner Robinson) had taken the position in the *Great Lakes*
case that, while broadcasting should not be analogized to such
common carrier services as "wire telegraphy or telephony or

point-to-point wireless telephony or telegraphy" whose duty to serve all without discrimination ran to the sender of the message transmitted, it *should* be considered comparable to those public utilities ". . . engaged in purveying commodities to the general public, such, for example, as heat, water, light, and power companies, whose duties are to consumers, just as the duties of broadcasting stations are to listeners." [3 F.R.C. Ann. Rep. 32, 33 (1929).] [40] On the basis of this comparison, they proceeded to announce the "balanced program" standard and the requirement of ". . . free and fair competition of opposing views . . ." with regard to ". . . all discussions of issues of importance to the public." [*Ibid.*]

Mr. Caldwell, having expressed his opposition to the classification of broadcasters as common carriers on the ground that "If the broadcasting station which ordinarily has to rely on advertisers for its income has to receive every advertiser on an equal basis, it, and its listening public may be the prey to all sorts of quack advertising, and it is felt that it is safer to allow the station owner the same discretion which a newspaper or magazine has—that of rejecting or accepting advertising, and relying on his self-interest to see to it that no unfairness is done," was then asked his opinion with regard to the advertising of cigarettes and ". . . the broad subject of going into homes with the creation of a habit which, if not deleterious, is at least not beneficial?" He replied, *inter alia*, ". . . if the Commission has discretion, as I am firmly convinced it has, and as its present general counsel has given an opinion that it has, that in considering renewals of licenses it may take into consideration the past performances of stations on their programs, including that sort of advertising, it seems to me you have a sufficient safeguard." [*Hearings on S. 6, pp. 87–89.*] Without laboring the point further, the hearings on Senator Couzens' bill, S. 6, are replete with statements by members of the Commission and by Senator Dill which recognize and affirm the Commission's authority to consider program content in the performance of its licensing functions. [See in particular Senator Dill's statements, *Hearings on S. 6*, pp. 1607–1610, 1636, 1637, 1751.]

Turning back to the legislation of 1934, the provision of Section 3(h) declaring that broadcasters are not common carriers, on its face and by its position as part of the definition of the phrase "common carrier" for the purposes of the Act, evidences

[40] Commissioner Robinson had not participated in the *Great Lakes* decision and statement.

an intent only to exempt broadcasters from obligations imposed upon telephone and telegraph common carriers by Title II. There is again no indication of any kind that Congress intended by this definition to undo the interpretation which the Commission and the courts had placed upon the Act as regards authority over programming. On the contrary, the legislative history of Section 325(b) and (c) evidences clear intent to reaffirm that interpretation.

Other indications support this conclusion. Both during the hearings and on the floor of the House it was charged that the Commission was using its authority to consider program content on applications for renewal of a license in such a manner as to discriminate unfairly against a particular religious group, namely Jehovah's Witnesses. [*Hearings on H.R. 8301*, p. 300 *et seq.*; 78 Cong. Rec. 10325–10326.] A bill was introduced by Mr. McFadden of Pennsylvania which would have amended the Radio Act by adding sections forbidding discrimination by any broadcasting station against programs sponsored by any religious, charitable, or educational association and making such discrimination a crime. [See Hearings before the Committee on the Merchant Marine, Radio, and Fisheries, House of Representatives, 73rd Cong., 2nd Sess. on H.R. 7986, p. 1 and *passim.*] In reply to the charges of unfair "censorship" by the Commission and as the Commission's comment on the proposal to incorporate the McFadden bill into the House version of the Communications Act, Chairman Sykes of the Commission asked that his testimony in the hearings on the McFadden bill be inserted in the hearings on the bill for a Communications Act. [*Hearings on H.R. 8301*, p. 349 *et seq.*] The very opening of that statement reads:

> Mr. Chairman, I would like to say first, that the provisions of this bill would make broadcasting stations in the United States to that extent public-service companies of programs of that character. That is directly contrary to broadcasting as it has grown up in the United States prior to the Act of 1927 and is directly contrary to the theory of broadcasting under the act under which we operate . . .

* * *

> That act puts upon the individual licensee of a broadcast station the private initiative to see that those programs that he broadcasts are in the public interest, bearing in mind that many broadcasting stations are located in different parts of the United States and what might be in the public interest in one part of the United States might not be of interest to other

listeners in an entirely different community . . . Now this particular bill, as I say, would do away with that.

Then that act makes those individual licensees responsible to the licensing authority to see that their operations are in the public interest. If you pass a bill of that kind, then, if the Commission should think that their programs are not in the public interest, the reply would be, "We are now made public-service companies; we have to take programs that are offered to us, if we have the time to take those programs." [*Hearings on H.R. 8301*, pp. 349–350.]

In reply to a specific question as to the Commission's authority to pass on the subject matter of programs, Chairman Sykes said flatly:

We have no power of censorship under section 29 of the Radio Act, which is a very wise provision, indeed. Our licenses to broadcasting stations last for 6 months. The law says that they must operate in the public interest, convenience, and necessity. When the time for a renewal of those station licenses comes up, it is the duty of the Commission, in passing on whether or not that station should be relicensed for another licensing period, to say whether or not their past performance during the last license period has been in the public interest. [*Hearings on H.R. 8301*, p. 352.]

The fact that the McFadden bill was never reported out of committee, the fact that neither the House nor the Senate saw fit to incorporate it into the Communications Act and the fact that the renewal provisions of the Radio Act were re-enacted in the face of the charges of "censorship" serve to confirm the view that the Congressional decision not to impose common carrier obligations upon radio broadcasters or to grant the Commission regulatory authority with regard to broadcasters akin to that granted with regard to common carrier communication services in no way affected the Commission's authority to consider the content of radio programs.[41]

[41] For similar reasons, the fact that the broadened version of the "equal opportunities" provision, intended to prevent discrimination by licensees between proponents and opponents of positions on "public questions," as well as between candidates, was taken over by the Senate Committee from H.R. 7716 of the 72nd Congress, passed by the Senate and then eliminated by the conference committee, has no effect upon the authority of the Commission to impose an obligation of "fairness" with regard to public questions in the context of its licensing functions, as it had done in the *Great Lakes* case. See Sen. Rep. No. 781, 73rd Cong., 2nd Sess., p. 8; S. 3285,

D. Post-1934 Developments

As has already been indicated, the basic provisions of the Communications Act took their present form in 1934. Legislative developments and administrative constructions thereafter are not crucial for purposes of this memorandum. In any event, it is well known that the Federal Communications Commission has maintained substantially the same position on the question of its authority over programming as that taken by its predecessor, the Federal Radio Commission. [See *In re McGlasham et al.*, 2 FCC 145, 149 (1935); *Report on Public Service Responsibility of Broadcast Licensees* (1946); *Report and Statement of Policy Re: Commission En Banc Programming Inquiry* (July 29, 1960).]

Two developments are worthy of note, as an indication of the attitude which Congress has adopted toward its handiwork. Section 307(d) of the Act deals with renewal of licenses; as enacted in 1934, it contained a provision requiring that the same considerations govern the Commission's action on renewal applications as those which govern its action on applications for initial licenses.[42] The purpose of this provision, according to Senator White (its author), was as follows [*Hearings Before the Senate Committee on Interstate Commerce, 72nd Cong., 1st Sess. on H.R. 7716*]:

It is an effort to negative the suggestion that because you are in possession of a license you have any rights which carry over from the granting of that license. * * * It is an effort to negative the thought that because you are once possessed of a license you acquire any—

73rd Cong., 2nd Sess., In the House of Representatives, May 21, 1934, p. 62; H.R. Rep. No. 1918, 73rd Cong., 2nd Sess., p. 49.

It is of some interest to note, in this regard, that that part of Section 14 of the Radio Act of 1927 which authorized revocation of a license upon certification of a discrimination in service by the Interstate Commerce Commission or some "other Federal body" had proved, as its opponents had predicted in 1927, to be ineffective. In *Sta-Shine Products Co.* v. *Station WGBB*, 188 I.C.C. 271 (1932), the Interstate Commerce Commission declined to take jurisdiction over radio broadcasting companies. See the discussion of this case in Herring and Gross, Telecommunications, pp. 226–227. This provision of the Radio Act was one of the ". . . matters no longer effective . . ." which were eliminated in 1934. H.R. Rep. No. 1918, 73rd Cong., 2nd Sess., p. 47.

[42] This provision originated in H.R. 7716, 72nd Cong. See Sen. Rep. No. 781, 73rd Cong., 2nd Sess., p. 6; H.R. Rep. No. 1918, 73rd Cong., 2nd Sess., p. 48).

SENATOR BROOKHART (*interposing*): Vested right.

SENATOR WHITE: Yes, or anything kindred with that idea.

In 1952, this language was eliminated, and the present language, to the effect that renewals shall be granted "if the Commission finds that public interest, convenience, and necessity would be served thereby," was inserted. [66 Stat. 711.] The Senate Committee reporting on the 1952 amendments went out of the way to stress that it was not in any way limiting the Commission's traditional review of program operations [Sen. Rep. No. 44, 82nd Cong., 1st Sess., p. 7]:

> It should be emphasized that while the recommended amendment does eliminate the necessity for the type of involved and searching examination which the Commission must make in granting an original license, it does not in any way impair the Commission's right and duty to consider, in the case of a station which has been in operation and is applying for renewal, the overall performance of that station against the broad standard of public interest, convenience, and necessity. This authority of the Commission is made explicit by specifying that such renewal grants are subject to findings by the Commission that the "public interest, convenience, or necessity would be served thereby."

Again, in 1949 the Commission issued a *Report on Editorializing* by Broadcast Licensees, 13 FCC 1246, 1 Pike & Fischer, R.R. (Pt. Three), p. 91:201, which took the position, *inter alia*, that licensees are required "to devote a reasonable percentage of their broadcasting time to the discussion of public issues of interest in the community served by their stations" and further to design such programs so that "the public has a reasonable opportunity to hear opposing positions on the public issues of interest and importance in the community." [13 FCC 1257–8, 1 Pike & Fischer, R.R. (Pt. Three), p. 91:211.] In 1959, the Congress amended Section 315 of the Act, to exempt appearances by candidates on various types of news programs from the "equal opportunities" requirement. [73 Stat. 557.] The amended statute adds, however, that nothing in the exemption is to be construed as relieving broadcasters, in connection with their presentation of such news programs, of "the obligations imposed upon them under this Act to operate in the public interest and to afford reasonable opportunity for the discussion of conflicting views on issue of public importance." The legislative history makes it more than clear that this sentence was intended as an adoption and affirmation of the basic policies expressed in the Commission's *Report on Editorializing, supra.* [See H.R. Rep. No. 1069, 86th Cong., 1st Sess., p. 5; Sen. Rep. No. 562, 86th Cong., 1st Sess., pp. 13, 19 (at fn. 3); 105 Cong. Rec. 14457–14463.]

IV. JUDICIAL CONSTRUCTION

One of the reasons why it is sometimes thought that the critical issues concerning the Commission's authority in the programming field are still unanswered is the absence of any specific decision of the Supreme Court in which those questions were squarely presented and squarely ruled upon. The Court has had ample occasion, however, to make its attitude on the subject known, and its actions confirm the propositions which have been gleaned from the history of the Act. The Court of Appeals for the District of Columbia Circuit, moreover, has faced the issue squarely, not once but several times; its decisions likewise confirm the position which has been advanced in this memorandum. Finally, other Federal courts, to the extent the question has been raised, have uniformly followed the lead of the Supreme Court and the Court of Appeals for the District of Columbia. It is this picture of uniform judicial acceptance of the degree of authority which the Commission has attempted to exercise, together with the legislative history already described, which justifies the statement that the basic issues are settled.

The relevant decisions under the Radio Act of 1927 have already been described. The discussion which follows is therefore limited to decisions under the Communications Act of 1934, as amended.

A. *The Supreme Court*

In *FCC* v. *Pottsville Broadcasting Co.* 309 U.S. 134, the Supreme Court reversed a mandate of the Court of Appeals for the District of Columbia which directed the Commission *not* to hold a comparative hearing on an application for construction permit for a standard broadcast station. The Court of Appeals had previously reversed the Commission's denial of a construction permit to the Pottsville Broadcasting Company and, on remand, the Commission had set the Pottsville application for hearing together with two rival applications for the same facilities which had been filed subsequent to the Pottsville application. [See *Federal Communications Commission* v. *Pottsville Broadcasting Co.* 309 U.S. 134, 139–140.] The Supreme Court held that the Court of Appeals' mandate exceeded the reviewing power which Congress had conferred upon the courts under Article II of the Constitution and that the attempt to give the applicant prior in point of time a priority in the race for the permit was ". . . at war with the basic policy underlying the statute." [309 U.S. at p. 145.]

Characterizing the function assigned to the Commission by the Communications Act, the Court remarked:

Underlying the whole law is recognition of the rapidly fluctuating factors characteristic of the evolution of broadcasting and of the corresponding requirement that the administrative process possess sufficient flexibility to adjust itself to these factors. Thus, it is highly significant that although investment in broadcasting stations may be large, a license may not be issued for more than three years; and in deciding whether to renew the license, just as in deciding whether to issue it in the first place, the Commission must judge by the standard of "public convenience, interest, or necessity." The Communications Act is not designed primarily as a new code for the adjustment of conflicting private rights through adjudication. Rather it expresses a desire on the part of Congress to maintain, through appropriate administrative control, a grip on the dynamic aspects of radio transmission." [*Federal Communications Commission* v. *Pottsville Broadcasting Co.* 309 U.S. 134, 138.]

In a footnote to the last sentence quoted, the Court said:

Since the beginning of regulation under the Act of 1927 comparative considerations have governed the application of standards of "public convenience, interest, or necessity" laid down by the law. ". . . the Commission desires to point out that the test—'public interest, convenience, or necessity'— becomes a matter of a comparative and not an absolute standard when applied to broadcasting stations. Since the number of channels is limited and the number of persons desiring to broadcast is far greater than can be accommodated, the Commission must determine from among the applicants before it which of them will, if licensed, best serve the public. In a measure, perhaps, all of them give more or less service. Those who give the least, however, must be sacrificed for those who give the most. The emphasis must be first and foremost on the interest, the convenience, and the necessity of the listening public, and not on the interest, convenience, or necessity of the individual broadcaster or the advertiser." [Second Annual Report, Federal Radio Commission, 1928, pp. 169–70.]

It is to be noted that the Court here quoted with approval the concluding portion of the statement which the Federal Radio Commission issued in 1928 in explanation of its decisions *on the renewal of licenses* under General Order No. 32, the decisions in which it first developed standards for the judgment of program content. The significance of this fact should not be overemphasized, of course. In the early history of the Radio Commission, as has been noted, the difference between a comparative standard by which to judge competing applicants and a minimum standard to be enforced on all licensees was blurred by the fact that, under the conditions of that period, ". . . the number of channels is limited and the number of persons desiring to broadcast is far greater than can be accommodated . . ." In *Pottsville*, moreover, the Supreme Court, in repudiating the principle of priority, clearly referred to a comparative proceeding rather than one where the Commission was faced with only one applicant. Nonetheless, the Court here plainly pointed to the Commission's authority and duty to consider the nature of the service which an applicant was likely to give as the basis for its distribution of licenses, rather than priority in the time of application.

In *FCC* v. *Sanders Brothers Radio Station* 309 U.S. 470, the Supreme Court reversed a decision of the Court of Appeals for the District of Columbia which had in turn reversed a decision by the Commission granting a construction permit for a new standard broadcast station over the protest of the existing station in the same general radio market. The Court of Appeals had taken the position that the Commission was required to consider and to make findings as to the potential economic injury which the entry of the new station might cause to the existing station. In repudiating this position the Supreme Court stated that ". . . the Act recognizes that the field of broadcasting is one of free competition," and, contrasting the broadcasting industry with such common carrier industries as the railroads, said:

> But the Act does not essay to regulate the business of the licensee. The Commission is given no supervisory control of the programs, of business management or of policy. In short, the broadcasting field is open to anyone, provided there be an available frequency over which he can broadcast without interference to others, if he shows his competency, the adequacy of his equipment, and financial ability to make good use of the assigned channel. [309 U.S. at pp. 474, 475.]

It is highly improbable, to say the least, that by this general dictum in a case not raising the question of programming the

Supreme Court intended to sweep away some thirteen years of administrative, judicial and legislative history under the Communications Act. The addition of the qualifying adjective "supervisory" to the control over programs which, the Court said, the Act did not give suggests that the reference was to the ban on censorship contained in Section 326. Such an interpretation finds support in the paragraph which immediately follows the dictum which has been quoted:

> The policy of the Act is clear that no person is to have anything in the nature of a property right as a result of the granting of a license. Licenses are limited to a maximum of three years' duration, may be revoked, and need not be renewed. *Thus the channels presently occupied remain free for a new assignment to another licensee in the interest of the listening public.* [309 U.S. at p. 475 (emphasis added).]

In addition, the Court specifically indicated that financial qualifications were only one aspect of ". . . the ability of the licensee to render the best practicable service to the community reached by his broadcasts," and stated that an applicant must show his "competency," in addition to the adequacy of his equipment and his financial ability. It would, to be sure, be difficult to draw a specific recognition of the Commission's authority to consider programming in issuing and renewing licenses out of such language, but the attempt to make the *Sanders* dictum stand for the proposition that *no* control whatsoever is to be exercised faces, as indicated above, even greater difficulties. In the last analysis, the ambiguities which the opinion displays when one attempts to draw definitive rulings on the question of the Commission's authority in the programming field out of it are due to the fact that the programming question was simply not the one with which the Court was faced.[43] It *was* faced with the assertion that the broadcasting field was one of "natural monopoly," in which existing licensees were to be protected against the incursions of potential competitors, an assertion which it rejected. But the Commission's concern with program content stemmed historically *not* from any belief in the economic soundness of monopoly in the broadcasting field but from the fact that the radio spectrum was so limited physically that only a few could use it in relation to those who might

---

[43] "Questions which merely lurk in the record, neither brought to the attention of the court nor ruled upon, are not to be considered as having been so decided as to constitute precedents." *Webster* v. *Fall*, 266 U.S. 507, 511. See also *KVOS, Inc.* v. *Associated Press* 299 U.S. 269, 279.

desire to so express themselves. Nor could its obligations with regard to program content be fulfilled simply by fostering as much competition as possible. The policy which it sought to effectuate by means of the "balanced program" standard, for instance, could not be effectuated by the mere addition of a second station serving Dubuque, Iowa (the result of the *Sanders* case), since the practically innumerable elements and interests of the listening public would not thus be assured of a reasonable chance for expression.

The correctness of this interpretation of the *Sanders* case dictum is confirmed by the opinion of the Supreme Court in *National Broadcasting Co.* v. *United States* 319 U.S. 190. The Supreme Court there affirmed a district court's dismissal of suits to enjoin enforcement of the Commission's Chain Broadcasting Regulations. In so doing it upheld the Commission's authority to insist that its licensees maintain full and free control of the programs which they presented, unhampered by contractual relations with network organizations. [319 U.S. at pp. 196–209–218.] It rejected any interpretation of the Act which would limit the Commission to ". . . technical and engineering impediments to the 'larger and more effective use of radio in the public interest.' " [319 U.S. at p. 217.] It confirmed the view of the history of the Radio Act of 1927 taken above, to the effect that the Act stemmed basically from the limitations of the radio spectrum, rather than technical problems of "interference" and that the Commission had clearly been intended to have more than "traffic control" functions. As the Court's famous phrase runs, the Commission has ". . . the burden of determining the composition of that traffic." [319 U.S. at pp. 213, 215–216.]

The Court moreover specifically stated:

> The Commission's licensing function cannot be discharged, therefore, merely by finding that there are no technological objections to the granting of a license. If the criterion of "public interest" were limited to such matters, how could the Commission choose between two applicants for the same facilities, each of whom is financially and technically qualified to operate a station? Since the very inception of federal regulation by radio, comparative considerations *as to the services to be rendered* have governed the application of the standard of "public interest, convenience, or necessity." [See *Federal Communications Commission* v. *Pottsville Broadcasting Co.*, 309 U.S. 134, 138 n. 2. (emphasis added) 319 U.S. at pp. 216–217.]

It should be noted that in referring with approval to the foot-note in the *Pottsville* case which is discussed above, the Supreme Court, speaking through the same Justice, added the words which are emphasized, making it quite clear that it referred to the Commission's long-established practice of considering program content. Moreover, though it pointed to comparative hearings as a limiting case in which the Commission was obviously authorized to go beyond "technical and engineering matters," the standards which the Court approved in the *National Broadcasting Co.* case were minimal standards, applicable to all licensees. The position taken throughout this memorandum, *i.e.*, that the standard of the public interest, convenience or necessity comprehends considerations of program content in any situation not governed by specific countervailing factors such as Section 326 and the Constitutional right of free speech thus finds strong support in this ruling precedent.

The *National Broadcasting Co.* case also throws some light on the limitations which the Constitution imposes. As against the contention that the Chain Broadcasting Regulations abridged the licensee's right of free speech, the Court said:

If that be so, it would follow that every person whose application for a license is denied by the Commission is thereby denied his constitutional right of free speech. Freedom of utterance is abridged to many who wish to use the limited facilities of radio. Unlike other modes of expression, radio inherently is not available to all. That is its unique characteristic, and that is why, unlike other modes of expression, it is subject to governmental regulation. Because it cannot be used by all, some who wish to use it must be denied. But Congress did not authorize the Commission to choose among applicants upon the basis of their political, economic or social views, or upon any other capricious basis. If it did, or if the Commission by these Regulations proposed a choice among applicants upon some such basis, the issue before us would be wholly different. The question here is simply whether the Commission, by announcing that it will refuse licenses to persons who engage in specified network practices (a basis for choice which we hold is comprehended within the statutory criterion of "public interest"), is thereby denying such persons the constitutional right of free speech. The right of free speech does not include, however, the right to use the facilities of radio without a license. The licensing system established by Congress in the Communications Act of 1934 was a proper exercise of its power over commerce. The standard it provided for the licensing of stations was the "public interest, convenience, or necessity." Denial of a station license on that ground, is valid under the Act, is not a denial of free speech. [319 U.S. at pp. 226–227.]

As this passage is the sole pronouncement by the Supreme Court on the limits which the First Amendment places upon the Commission in the exercise of its licensing functions, it warrants careful scrutiny. The limits of the radio spectrum, the Court has said, themselves restrict freedom of speech by means of radio communication and impose upon the Commission the burden of choosing those who may speak; hence, the denial of a license is not, *per se*, a governmental abridgment of free speech. The Court stressed the proposition that this is a unique characteristic of radio, differentiating it from other modes of expression and requiring that it, unlike other modes, be subject to special governmental controls, *i.e.*, a licensing system. (The elimination of a system of regulation by licensing it should be remembered, stands historically at the very beginning of the development of the freedom of the press which is guaranteed by the First Amendment, and the absence of such a licensing system is a minimal element of that freedom.) [See *Grosjean* v. *American Press Co.* 297 U.S. 233, 245–246.]

Moreover, the principles upon which the Commission may choose those who are to speak are not restricted by the First Amendment to technical or financial matters. The holding of this case means nothing if it does not mean that the Commission may concern itself with the nature of the programs which a financially and technically qualified applicant is likely to give, for if the Constitution forbids *any* evaluation by the Commission of the licensee's selection of programs then it must equally forbid interference with the *means* by which those programs are selected—particularly when the interference is based on the Commission's belief that the effect of such means ". . . has been that broadcasting service has been maintained at a level below that possible under a system of free competition." [*National Broadcasting Co.* v. *United States*, 319 U.S. 190, 218.] Such interference, however, was here firmly held to be within both the statute and the Constitution.

This is not to say that the Constitution imposes no limits upon the Commission's judgment. The Court specifically stated that if Congress or the Commission had proposed a choice of licensees ". . . upon the basis of their political, economic or social views, or upon any other capricious basis . . . the issue before us would be wholly different." This enumeration of

bases of choice by the Commission which are proscribed by the
First Amendment should not, of course, be taken to exhaust all
conceivable limitations, nor can the question of the constitutional limits of the Commission's authority in the programming field be solved on the basis of this language by the simple
statement that any non-capricious choice by the Commission
would be constitutionally sanctioned, but the position that *any*
consideration of program content by the Commission violates
the First Amendment cannot be maintained in the face of the
National Broadcasting Company case.

There is, further, no need to speculate whether the interpretation of the *Sanders* and *National Broadcasting Co.* cases which
has been advanced is that which the Supreme Court intended,
for the Court has endorsed precisely this interpretation. In *Regents of the University System of Georgia* v. *Carroll,* 338 U.S.
586, 598, the Supreme Court stated flatly, "Although the licensee's business as such is not regulated, the qualifications of
the licensee and the character of its broadcasts may be weighed
in determining whether or not to grant a license." [*Federal
Communications Commission* v. *Sanders Radio Station,* 309 U.S.
470, 475; *National Broadcasting Co.* v. *United States,* 319 U.S.
190, 218, 227. (Emphasis added.)] [44]

Other decisions serve to confirm the same view. In *FCC* v.
WOKO, Inc., 329 U.S. 223, the Supreme Court reversed the
Court of Appeals for the District of Columbia Circuit and affirmed the Commission's refusal to renew the license of Station
WOKO. The Commission had based its action on a long-con-
tinued pattern of misrepresentations in the licensee's statements
to the Commission. Although there was evidence in the record
as to the nature of the station's program service, the Commis-

---

[44] It should also be noted that in *FCC* v. *American Broadcasting Company,*
347 U.S. 284, the Supreme Court recognized the Commission's authority to
consider in the context of its licensing functions programs violating statutes
other than the Communications Act, in that case the other statute being the
prohibition of radio lotteries contained in 18 U.S.C. § 1304. This provision had formerly been Section 316 of the Communications Act, but the
Supreme Court did not limit such authority to provisions which originated
in the Communications Act. "The 'public interest, convenience, or necessity' standard for the issuance of licenses would seem to imply a requirement that the applicant be law-abiding. In any event, the standard is sufficiently broad to permit the Commission to consider the applicant's past
or prospective violation of a federal criminal statute especially designed to
bar certain conduct by operators of radio and television stations." 347 U.S.
at pp. 289–290, n. 7.

sion had refused to make findings or consider the subject. The Court of Appeals thought it "obvious that, in dealing with an application for the renewal of a license, the quality of the applicant's programs and the adequacy of the applicant's mechanical and scientific broadcasting facilities are principal among the elements to be considered." [*WOKO, Inc.* v. *FCC*, 80 U.S. App. D.C. 333, 339, 153 F.2d 623.] It reversed for this and other reasons. While the Supreme Court disagreed and held that the Commission was not bound to consider WOKO's programming, it did not do so on the ground that the Commission was without authority. On the contrary, it stated, "It may very well be that this Station has established such a standard of public service that the Commission would be justified in considering that its deception was not a matter that affected its qualifications to serve the public." [*FCC* v. *WOKO, Inc.*, 329 U.S. 223, 229.]

Finally, in *Farmers Educational and Cooperative Union of America* v. *WDAY, Inc.*, 360 U.S. 525, the Supreme Court held that Section 315 of the Act forbade censorship of candidates' broadcasts by the licensee, and that in light of this prohibition, the Act immunized the licensee from liability for defamatory remarks which the candidate might make. One of the arguments made by the petitioner union was that a licensee could protect himself against liability by exercising his right, under Section 315, not to allow the use of his facilities by any candidate. To this the Court replied [360 U.S. 525, 534-5]:

Petitioner's reliance on the station's freedom from obligation "to allow the use of its station by any such candidate" seems equally misplaced. While denying all candidates use of stations would protect broadcasters from liability, it would also effectively withdraw political discussion from the air. Instead the thrust of § 315 is to facilitate political debate over radio and television. Recognizing this, the Communications Commission considers the carrying of political broadcasts a public service criterion to be considered both in license renewal proceedings, and in comparative contests for a radio or television construction permit. [Citing *City of Jacksonville*, 12 Pike & Fischer, R.R. 113, 125-6, 180i-j; *Loyola University*, 12 Pike & Fischer, R.R. 1017, 1099; *Homer P. Rainey*, 11 FCC 898; *Report on Editorializing by Broadcast Licensees*, 1 Pike & Fischer R.R. (Pt. Three), p. 91:201, 13 FCC 1246.] Certainly Congress knew the obvious—that if a licensee could protect himself from liability in no other way but refusing to broadcast candidates' speeches, the necessary effect would be to hamper the congressional plan to develop broadcasting as a political outlet, rather than to foster it.

If the Court had believed that the Commission's authority to require the carrying of political broadcasts was doubtful, it could hardly have reached the conclusion which it did. And the four dissenting justices would surely have seized upon this argument if they had any doubts concerning the Commission's authority. Instead, their treatment of this issue ran as follows [360 U.S. 525, 544]:

> Conflict between the North Dakota libel law and § 315 might be attributed to the fact that broadcasters, to avoid being held liable without fault, will refrain from permitting any political candidate to buy time. This result, the argument would conclude, is contrary to the congressional command that stations operate in the 'public convenience, interest, or necessity." [48 Stat. 1083, as amended, 47 U.S.C. § 307, 47 U.S.C. § 307.] The Federal Communications Commission has determined that to fulfill this congressional command stations must carry some political broadcasts. But the state libel laws do not prohibit them from airing speeches by political candidates. They merely make such broadcasts potentially less profitable (or unprofitable) since the station may have to compensate someone libeled during the candidate's broadcast. The Federal Act was intended not to establish a mode of supervising the income of broadcasters—not of protecting or limiting their profits—but of insuring "a rapid, efficient, Nation-wide, and world-wide wire and radio communication service" for the benefit of "all the people of the United States." [48 Stat. 1064, as amended, 47 U.S.C. § 151, 47 U.S.C. § 151.]

B. The Court of Appeals for the District of Columbia Circuit

The Court of Appeals for the District of Columbia Circuit is the most significant single source of judicial control over the Commission's actions, for appeals from standard Commission licensing actions must be brought before it, and petitions for review of all other Commission actions may—and often are—brought to it rather than to other Federal courts. [Communications Act, Section 402(a), (b), 47 U.S.C. § 402(a), (b).] As noted above, it has faced the question of the Commission's authority with respect to programming in a number of cases.

In *Simmons* v. *FCC*, 83 U.S. App. D.C. 262, 169 F.2d 670, *cert. denied* 335 U.S. 846, the Court upheld the Commission's denial of an application for increased power and change of frequency by an applicant who proposed, *without so binding himself contractually*, to broadcast all programs, commercial and sustaining, offered by the CBS network, exercising his discretion in the selection of programs only as to the remaining time not used by CBS. The majority of the court, like the Commission, could see no distinction between the voluntary adoption by a licensee of a policy in selecting programs which the Commission found contrary to the public interest and the embodiment of that policy in binding contracts. The court based its decision squarely on the *National Broadcasting Company* case and brushed aside the claim that the Commission's action amounted to censorship with the statement that "Even if the *National Broadcasting Company* case had not foreclosed any such contention, censorship would be a curious term to apply to the requirement that licensees select their own programs by applying their own judgment to the conditions that arise from time to time." [169 F.2d at p. 672.]

It should be noted that although there was a mutually exclusive application for the same facilities before the Commission and the Court in the *Simmons* case, the decision made by the Commission and upheld by the Court was based not upon comparative merit but upon a minimum standard applicable to all licensees, the Simmons application being denied without regard to comparative considerations. [See 169 F.2d at p. 672.] Together with the *National Broadcasting Company, Trinity Methodist Church* and *KFKB* cases, this holding makes it clear that the Commission's *authority* to consider program content does not rest upon the question of whether a proceeding is comparative or not.[45] To turn away an applicant because he pro-

---

[45] To these decisions should be added *Noe* v. *FCC*, U.S. App. D.C., 260 F.2d 739, *cert. den.*, 359 U.S. 924, and *Independent Broadcasting Co.* v. *FCC*, 89 U.S. App. D.C. 396, 193 F.2d 900. In the *Noe* case, the Court rejected a claim that a successful applicant, because of its religious orientation, might not treat other religious faiths fairly or properly meet its community's religious needs, stating (260 F.2d at 743) : "Of course, should Loyola in the future fall short of the rules and regulations of the Commission in regard to proper programming, the Commission may always review the matter in a renewal proceeding or otherwise." See *Trinity Methodist Church, South* v. *Federal Radio Commission*, 1932, 61 App. D.C. 311, 62 F.2d 850, certiorari denied, 1933, 288 U.S. 599, 53 S.Ct. 317, 77 L.Ed. 975. In the *Independent Broadcasting Co.* case, the Court upheld the Commission's refusal of a license to an applicant on grounds that a consistent pattern of action, displayed in broadcast programs, indicated a lack of the requisite character qualifications. The applicant's dominant stockholder had "used

poses to broadcast political, economic or social views of which the Commission disapproves would be an invasion of free speech regardless of the presence or absence of mutually exclusive applications, and the validity of a denial of a license because of a failure to meet the "balanced program" standard would depend upon the presence or absence of other applicants only in the sense that what is reasonable to require in the presence of other better-qualified applicants might be arbitrary in their absence.[46]

For this reason, the holdings in *Bay State Beacon, Inc.* v. *FCC*, 84 U.S. App. D.C. 216, 171 F.2d 826, *Johnston Broadcasting Co.* v. *FCC*, 85 U.S. App. D.C. 40, 175 F.2d 351, and *W. S. Butterfield Theatres, Inc.* v. *FCC*, 99 U.S. App. D.C. 71, 237 F.2d 552, to the effect that the Commission is authorized, in comparative proceedings, to consider and evaluate as an element of the public interest the amount of sustaining time a prospective licensee proposes to reserve, the effort which he proposes to make to encourage broadcasts on controversial issues or topics of current interest to the community such as education,

---

intemperate language in his writings, sermons and broadcasts . . . had a constant habit of attacking the honesty and sincerity of those individuals and groups who did not agree with him . . . had attempted to institute economic boycotts of persons and groups who did not cooperate with him as he demanded . . . and . . . had constantly solicited funds on the basis of statements which were contrary to fact." 89 U.S. App. D.C. at 398.

[46] To phrase the issue in a slightly different manner, it has been pointed out that during and immediately after the enactment of the Radio Act of 1927, broadcasting frequencies were so limited relative to the demand for them that every proceeding was, in effect, a comparative proceeding—whether or not the Commission was faced with more than one applicant for the same facilities at the same time. But the development of techniques much less wasteful of spectrum than those used in the late twenties and the general increase in the amount of usable space assigned to broadcasting, relative to the demand, raises issues of policy rather than jurisdiction. For broadcasting is not the only service which needs and uses the radio spectrum and—from many points of view—it is far from the most important. Radio services which protect the safety of life and property, which are essential to the national defense, or which are critical to the development of important industries—to name but a few—are constantly expanding. Many portions of the spectrum are now congested, and requests for the use of frequencies now allocated to broadcasting are far from uncommon. Every grant of a broadcasting license withdraws spectrum space not only from use by other potential broadcasters but also—in the long run—from nonbroadcasting uses which the country truly needs. In this sense, there is no such thing as a Commission licensing proceeding which is wholly noncomparative.

labor and civic enterprises, or the relative amount and character
of network, filmed and local live programming which he pro-
poses to present, have significance beyond their specific facts.
[See also *Kentucky Broadcasting Corp.* v. *FCC,* 84 U.S. App.
D.C. 383, 174 F.2d 38; *Easton Publishing Co.* v. *FCC,* 85 U.S.
App. D.C. 33, 37–38, 175 F.2d 344; *Plains* v. *FCC,* 85 U.S. App.
D.C. 48, 51–52, 175 F.2d 359.]

It is particularly significant that in the *Bay State* and *Johnston* cases the Court rejected the proposition that such consideration by the Commission constituted "censorship" or violated the
First Amendment. In *Bay State Beacon* the Court said [84 U.S.
App. D.C. at 217, 171 F.2d at 827]:

> To argue that the Commission may not in the performance
> of its plain duty inquire into the amount of sustaining time a
> prospective licensee purports to reserve if granted a license,
> and to further argue that if it does, such inquiry is in excess
> of its authority, contravenes the First Amendment and con-
> stitutes censorship prohibited by Sec. 326 of the Act, is to
> suggest that Congress intended to create the Commission and
> then by the very act of its creation, stultify and immobilize it
> in the performance of the specific functions that called it into
> being. Congress obviously intended no such thing. * * *
> While with reference to the alleged constitutional violation,
> certainly if a denial of a license would be violative of the
> First Amendment, then every unsuccessful applicant would
> have the right of free speech throttled and abridged—a palpa-
> bly absurd conclusion. [*National Broadcasting Company* v.
> *United States,* 319 U.S. 190, 226 (1943).]

Again, in *Johnston* the Court said [85 U.S. App. D.C. at 48,
175 F.2d at 359]:

> As to appellant's contention that the Commission's consid-
> eration of the proposed programs was a form of censorship,
> it is true that the Commission cannot choose on the basis of
> political, economic or social views of an applicant. But in a
> comparative consideration, it is well recognized that com-
> parative service to the listening public is the vital element,
> and programs are the essence of that service. So, while the
> Commission cannot proscribe any type of program (except
> for prohibitions against obscenity, profanity, etc.), it can
> make a comparison on the basis of public interest and, there-
> fore, of public service. Such a comparison of proposals is not
> a form of censorship within the meaning of the statute. As we
> read the Commission's findings, the nature of the views of the

applicants was not part of the consideration. The nature of the programs was.

Indeed, the Court has made it clear that, in its view, the Commission has not only the right but the duty to consider programming. Aside from remarks like those in the *Bay State Beacon* decision, *supra*, the Court has reversed Commission decisions on the ground that they failed to consider programming. Thus, in the *Butterfield* decision, *supra*, one of the grounds for reversal was stated as follows [99 U.S. App. D.C. at 76–77, 237 F.2d at 557–58]:

> The Commission erroneously disregarded the sharp curtailment of film programming upon the ground that the film programs proposed by an applicant are not "the Commission's concern." Film programs make up a very substantial part of the program fare of television audiences. WJR's original proposal, for example, was to devote about 40 per cent of its broadcast time to films. Moreover, unlike network programs, over which perhaps the licensee has relatively little control, films are the free and independent selection of the licensee and are, therefore, as much a part of and a measure of his responsibility to the public and the Commission as are the live programs he produces. We pointed out in *Johnston Broadcasting Co.* v. *Federal Communications Commission* that "in a comparative consideration, it is well recognized that comparative service to the listening public is the vital element, and programs are the essence of that service." Some television stations devote only an insignificant portion of their time to live programming. If the network and film programs which occupy the bulk of their broadcast time are not "the Commission's concern," then the Commission has little left to consider in determining the relative merit of such stations.

And in *Wrather-Alvarez Broadcasting, Inc.* v. *FCC.* 101 U.S. App. D.C. 324, 248 F.2d 646, the Court reversed a Commission decision under Section 325(b) of the Act, which would have permitted an American network to transmit programs to Mexican Station XETV, which would in turn broadcast those programs to an audience composed largely of Americans. The Court said [101 U.S. App. D.C. at 329, 248 F.2d at 651]:

> Obviously American network programs would make XETV a more attractive station to its San Diego viewers and the larger audience it would attract would also be available to it for its locally originated programs. While the Commission

has no power to prevent XETV from broadcasting to San Diego locally originated programs which are objectionable by American standards, it has power to refrain from issuing a permit which would give those programs a larger American audience. We do not suggest that such programming imperfections as would militate against an American station applicant in a comparative proceeding are necessarily relevant in deciding whether a foreign station is to be permitted to affiliate with an American network. We hold only that, in making the latter decision, the Commission may not altogether exclude from consideration such serious defects of the foreign station's programming as would affect the public interest.

C. Other Federal Courts

It remains only to note that the interpretation of the Commission's authority which has been put forward in this memorandum has been accepted and acted upon by courts in a number of cases not involving appeals from actions of the Commission. Thus, in *Allen B. Dumont Laboratories* v. *Carroll*, 184 F.2d 153 (C.A. 3), the Court of Appeals for the Third Circuit held that the control over the content of television programs which the Communications Act vests in the Commission is extensive enough to exclude an attempt by the state of Pennsylvania to censor films used in projecting television programs in that state. "Congress thus set up a species of 'program control' far broader and more effective than the antique method of censorship which Pennsylvania endeavors to effectuate in the instant case." [184 F.2d at p. 156.] And in a series of cases, persons claiming that station licensees have violated obligations imposed by contract or the Communications Act to present or allow the presentation of specific programs over their facilities have been told that the Commission, under the Communications Act, imposes upon its licensees a non-delegable duty to retain discretion in the selection of all programs presented, and that that discretion is reviewable by the Commission upon application for renewal of a license. Thus it has been stated: "The authority of the Commission as defined in Section 303, 47 U.S.C.A. § 303 includes the power to pass upon such allegations of unfair treatment as the plaintiffs make here respecting the defendant. The Commission may refuse to renew the defendant's license if he has failed to act in the public interest." [*McIntire* v. *William Penn Broadcasting Co.* (C.A. 3) 151 F.2d 597, 599.] Similarly, another Court has said, "This freedom of the licensee to determine what programs his station shall broadcast is not, of course, an absolute and unfettered one. The exercise of the right is subject to review by the administrative agency, the Federal Communications Commission. At least once every three years the Commission must determine whether a renewal of the license is in the public interest, 47 U.S.C.A. § 307, and it may review the action of the licensee in selecting programs at any time in proceedings under 47 U.S.C.A. § 312." [*Massachusetts Universalist Convention* v. *Hildreth & Rogers Co.* (D. Ct., D. Mass.) 87 F. Supp. 822, 824–825, *aff'd and adopted* (C.A. 1) 183 F.2d 497.] "Plaintiff's performance of this legal duty to choose, select, and schedule programs in the interest of the listening public is subject to review by the Federal Communications Commission in a proper proceeding under Sections 309 or 312 of Federal Communications Commission Act and defendant can always invoke the administrative discretion of that agency if it is of the opinion that the plaintiff is not broadcasting the defendant's programs that are in the interest of the listening public." [*Albuquerque Broadcasting Co.* v. *Regents of New Mexico College of Agriculture and Mechanic Arts* (D. Ct., D. N.M.) 70 F. Supp. 198, 202, *aff'd sub nom. Regents of New Mexico* v. *Albuquerque Broadcasting Co.* (C.A. 10) 158 F.2d 900; see also *Voliva* v. *WCBD, Inc.* 313 Ill. App. 177, 39 N.E. 2d 685.]

Appendix II

DISCUSSION
[*Following is the transcript of the questioning which came after the address of Chairman Minow at the public session on Thursday, August 3, 1961, which appears earlier in this book.*]

NATHANSON: Mr. Chairman, I thought Governor Collins asked a pretty good question. I'll just repeat it. I think he raised the question of whether balanced programming may be achieved by allowing stations to specialize so that the total picture would be a balanced program.

MINOW: I think that the point Governor Collins made has a great deal in it. Historically, when the Federal Radio Commission first faced up to this identical question in the late twenties, it decided that each station should have to present a balanced program rather than classifying a lot of different categories of stations. Instead of saying this will be a religious station, it said every station will have to do some kind of religious program, some kind of educational program. Now at that time there were very few stations. Today with so much radio, I think you must distinguish between radio and television. I, myself, am sympathetic to the idea that they specialize. For example, you cannot have a good music station, which you so often now find in FM, unless you permit specialization. It raises some very difficult problems for us because this means that some stations may be less obligated to perform certain kinds of public service programming than others, but I still think that when you have many stations, as in radio, that the idea of the specialization should be encouraged by the Commission.

In television, I don't think you can do that at this stage, because there are so few stations we must still insist that each television station provide a more balanced format. Maybe there will be some differences of view on that.

McGILL: Does the Commission have any flexibility when it is faced with an application for a station, even though there may already be a lot of stations, or when the economics of adding another would raise some doubt?

MINOW: The answer, I believe, was decided by the courts in the *Sander's* case some years ago. Where the Court said no, the

171

act specifically says this is not a utility, it is a free enterprise system and if there is an available frequency for a broadcaster, the Commission cannot foreclose anybody from using it; and this has been the Commission's view to this time. Although I think there is some disagreement about it as expressed this morning. But this is what I understand the law to be just now.

NOVIK: Mr. Chairman, to get back to the specialization and the radio station. Given the basic facts that you now have—over five thousand radio stations—given the basic fact that somewhat between seventy and seventy-eight per cent of the stations are operating a specialized news and music format, then the twenty-two per cent of the stations are carrying the whole load. Why impose a condition on the twenty-two per cent that is not being carried on the others?

How long can you expect a presidential press conference to be carried by a radio station if all of his opponents in Chicago are carrying rock and roll, or classical music, or straight music?

MINOW: Well, this is the other side of it, and that is why I say it makes it such a difficult decision to make. I, myself, would welcome some suggestions from the broadcasters as to how there could be a sharing of the public service burdens on an equitable basis among the stations.

If this raises problems, as has been traditionally felt under the Anti-Trust Laws, I can promise I will certainly use my best efforts to go to the Department of Justice and enable them to at least meet and discuss this.

If there were ten radio stations in the community, and they wanted to talk over how they might jointly serve the need of public affairs and public service programs, and come up with a proposal, I certainly would want to see it.

JAFFE: Mr. Minow, I'd like to make a comment, something in the nature of a legal comment on your discussion of the censorship issue. I think I agree with you in everything you intend to do; that is, in your program of administration and the way I think you are going to carry it out, I think I agree with you. I certainly agree with the proposition that looking to the general character of the performance is not censorship. But I disagree quite strongly, and I think that there are very unsound and very, very dangerous implications in your distinction between prior restraint and subsequent examination.

The Supreme Court has abandoned this as a distinction for

the general application to the First Amendment, and I don't think
it should be understood, and there was a possible implication
from your statement, that the First Amendment is not applicable to TV and radio.

The First Amendment is clearly applicable, but, of course,
there always is the additional fact that given the peculiar character of TV and radio there are certain things that would not offend
the First Amendment that might offend if you tried to do it to
a newspaper. But I don't think the distinction is in terms of
whether it's prior restraint or later criticism. In other words, it
would equally offend the constitutional guarantee, I believe, to
punish people for having put on certain performances whether
they were on TV or anything else.

I think this is very clear Constitutional Law, and I think your
kind of broad distinction between prior restraint and what you
thereby imply, that is, namely, that there is an absolutely different situation constitutionally once the program has been put on, is
an extremely dangerous one, and if you make this argument, you
are going to play precisely into the hands of the people who are
complaining that the FCC is going to censor. I think it's an extremely dangerous statement.

MINOW: The implication that you drew from it, Professor
Jaffe, was certainly not intended. Certainly, the First Amendment applies to radio. It's only the question decided in the *NBC*
case that turning somebody down when he applies for a license is
not a denial of free speech contemplated by the First Amendment. That's all I think the *NBC* case says.

Now as to the difference between prior restraint and subsequent punishment—I tried very carefully in my talk to say that
what we are doing, and what I understand it our duty to do, is at
renewal time to review in the context of performance against
promise, whether a broadcaster has lived up to the public interest
standard. I don't think that involves subsequent punishment because, after all, a license is a privilege and not a right. This he
took on the basis of certain representations, and I don't think that
the implication you drew from what I said is what I meant.

JAFFE: Again it seems to me very mistaken to again draw implications of a Constitutional character from the fact that a license is a privilege. That isn't the point. You can't censor anything regardless of whether it's a privilege or whether it's before
or after. The point I agree with you on—I think it's all you mean

to say—is that you may, in examining the total performance, see whether this person has acted with the general sense of public responsibility, but if you make your emphasis on the distinction between prior restraint and subsequent, and if you make your emphasis on the fact that the radio thing is a privilege, I think you're getting on the wrong foot and I think you're getting on very dangerous ground.

MINOW: Well, I would accept everything that you've said, Professor Jaffe. If I didn't make my legal position clear, it's my fault, because I don't think I disagree at all.

CONE: Mr. Minow, I wouldn't like this audience to go home or to go out and repeat some of the things they've heard here today in the proportion that the number of words on the side of what is bad against what is good would seem to be. There's a very significant line in which you had to say, and I also want to say that I agree with you all the way along, but there was just one little line that said, and I think I have this right, that most broadcasters are trustworthy. You didn't say anything about the advertisers or the agencies. I'd like to say, I believe they, too, are mostly trustworthy. And some day there's going to be a meeting about television where what's bad doesn't get ninety-nine per cent of the time or space.

MINOW: I'd be very glad to say that I think most advertisers are trustworthy, too. I think particularly the agency that Mr. Cone is associated with has been conspicuous by its repeated and enduring contributions to the public interest. It is his agency that put on almost all the shows that the industry itself rewarded with its Emmys this year. But, I can only say to you, Mr. Cone, may your tribe increase! I, unfortunately, don't think there are enough of you!

GUIDER: Mr. Minow, I'm still worried about censorship in spite of not only the speech but the long brief that was filed in support of it. I believe we have a reason to feel worried about censorship, and I'd like to just ask this question very quietly and as carefully as I can. Let us suppose that we are in agreement that programs need improvement, it would be strange if they didn't in a business like ours, with passing tastes, and fancies, and events; and let us suppose that a broadcasting station has fully met its promises as to how much of its time it devoted to religion, and to agriculture, and to the discussion of public issues. Let us suppose that it is operated on the norm or the standard of the vast majority of the stations, which the chairman seems to feel intend to do the right thing, or are trying to do the right thing; let's suppose they come in for their renewal with no bad marks against them for violating any of the prohibitions against obscenity, or lottery, or unfairness in the handling of a political broadcast; let us suppose that everything about them is all right except they've had an awful lot of violence on their shows, and their children's shows, by a great many people, have not been considered good for children and perhaps of the sort that might induce juvenile delinquency.

Now I'm saying this is a station that is no worse than eighty or ninety per cent or is probably perfectly typical of the best. Now in view of all the chairman's remarks that have been reported in the press about there being too much violence and bloodshed and sadism on television, and the fact that children's shows are due for a big overhauling, and there is so much wrong with television, I want to ask the chairman, very frankly, if a broadcasting licensee fully lives up to his promise and is fully performing as the vast majority of licensees are performing, what is the Commission going to do at renewal time in order to reduce the murder, the bloodshed, the mayhem, and the trash, that so much has been said about in his public utterances?

MINOW: I think that's a very serious question that I want to give a serious answer. But first, I'd like to tell you about a letter I got from a mother the other day. She said, I know what to do about all this violence on television. She said, why don't you let those fellows use live bullets?

I wish there were a clear answer. I don't think that under the present regulatory system any individual licensee, who has done all these things and has lived up to the promises he made, can be held accountable for the violence and the mayhem that we see on television. This is why the Commission has taken the position that we must have authority to regulate the networks, because the source of most of these programs, or at least many of them, are the networks. They don't originate with the individual licensees. If you analyze it, very few individual licensees choose to put on these kind of programs. They receive them from New York or Hollywood on the cable or occasionally from some syndicators, but very few of the licensees produce them; so I would only say that I don't think the Commission, under the present state of the law or regulation, would hold a licensee accountable for that kind of programming. I think we must, the Commission must, do something in other directions. I think we must do it in terms of network regulations. I think that our network study involving the relationship that very often exists with the talent agencies and the syndicators is teaching us many things about how programs originate and how they are sold and how they get on the air; and this is the direction in which there will have to be improvement and not in the field of renewals of individual station licenses.

[*The conversations in this section of Appendix II followed the delivery of the paper by Professor Jaffe and the comment thereon by Commissioner King, both of which appear earlier in this book.*]

PIERSON: I was interested in the statement by Professor Jaffe, which was to the effect that we would have no warrant for doing anything about it—referring to present calibre of television programming—"unless we were similarly prepared to control the other media."

I rather gathered from that, that Professor Jaffe was of the view, at least as a matter of fairness and equity, that the other media should be subjected to the same restraints.

I'm not certain that he intended to say that a restraint upon broadcasting would be constitutional whereas a similar restraint upon the other media would be unconstitutional.

The difficulty that I've always had with this problem, in reading the output of the Supreme Court in about the last ten years, is trying to find what standard of restraint they would permit government to impose upon any medium.

I've been unable to find any standard that approaches the broadness of the "public interest" standard. And I also have been unable to find any distinction between prior restraints and subsequent punishment in determination of the broadness of the standard that government can apply.

I'd like to cite a few cases and the standards that were employed: There was the *Burstyn* case, which was a motion picture case, where a license was revoked. That was a "prior restraint." The standard that the Supreme Court refused to accept because it was too broad, was "sacrilegious." Certainly "sacrilegious" is much narrower than "public interest." The other case was the picture "M." This was a prior restraint, banning a motion picture, Ohio refusing to issue a license because it tended to promote crime. Again, this is a much narrower standard than public interest.

Then there's the famous "Lady Chatterly's Lover" case, where the State of New York refused to grant a license, because it presented adultery as a desirable and acceptable standard, or pattern of behavior. Again it seems to me this is much, much narrower than the public interest standard.

In the *Roth* case, the Postmaster General held a book nonmailable because of its effect upon the most susceptible persons. There was a subsequent punishment imposed by Michigan in the *Butler* case, because the book tended to corrupt youth. Again, a much narrower standard than public interest.

There was the *Winters* case, which was a magazine case, in which the state had banned the book and convicted the book seller for selling magazines containing crime stories that tended to incite crime and corrupt youth. And of course in the *Near* case, where there was both prior restraint, and subsequent punishment, they refused to uphold the standard which was that the newspaper was not operating in harmony with public welfare.

Now if it is true, or if Professor Jaffe intended to say, that constitutionally the standards could be no broader in broadcasting than they are in other media, then it seems to me that we have to say that the court has disapproved of standards that are vastly narrower than the public interest standard, which is the standard we would apply to broadcasting. At least no other has been suggested. And it seems to me that if broadcast communication and the other media have equal protection under the First Amendment, we would have to conclude that they would not approve such a broad standard as public interest.

JAFFE: Well I wanted to say first that, it doesn't seem to me you meet the argument at all, because the point I made was that the requirement of balance is distinct from positive control of programs. And I wonder how you answer the point I made which only as a matter of fact rather recently occurred to me, that the industry has uniformly and unqualifiedly accepted the proposition that political discussion can be conditioned on showing the opposite side. I can't imagine any greater restraint than for me to have to get up, for example, before I discuss an issue, and provide somebody else with a public hall to answer me. That seems about the most remarkable restraint. Now I guess you're saying this is unconstitutional—indeed it must be terrifically unconstitutional. Yet I think probably it's not, because it's based on the idea of requiring balance in a monopoly situation.

PIERSON: I'm not going to say that in my opinion Section 315 is constitutional—it's sufficient to say that it hasn't been tested. I do think there is a distinction however, between the Commission on the one hand invoking a broad standard of public interest which requires licensees to broadcast something that they would not otherwise broadcast, or to not broadcast something that we would otherwise broadcast; and on the other hand to say to the licensee that "If you propose to carry, in your own discretion, programs dealing with a controversial issue, your obligation is to provide the right of reply."

A very distinguished group commissioned on Freedom of Communications held that the right of reply, even as applied to newspapers, would probably not be unconstitutional; but, I don't think they ever got to the point, nor have I known anyone else since that has, that equates the right of reply to a requirement that your programs be balanced in the public interest, or that violence that would not be in the public interest be eliminated, or that programs tending to corrupt the youth would be eliminated. I think there's a great distinction between the two.

MINOW: I'm going to talk at length this afternoon about the law, as I understand it, as I believe the courts have understood it for many years. None of the cases which Mr. Pierson referred to involved broadcasting.

The whole point, it seems to me, of the course of the law, has been that broadcasting is unique. In the famous *NBC* case in the United States Supreme Court, the Supreme Court said that's the whole reason why we have Government regulation of broadcasting—because it is unique; it is the only medium of expression in which there aren't enough frequencies for everyone to go into the field. I'm going to go into this at some length later but I didn't want to leave the impression now that those cases remotely affect broadcasting. We're dealing with a very special kind of creature here, and that's why it seems to me that we're all in this room. There is no other medium of mass communication subject to government regulation. At the same time there is no other medium of communication, I think, that touches peoples' lives more closely and more intimately each day than the television. I'd like to go into this later this afternoon but for now, I'd like to try to put the discussion into more specific terms; Dean King mentioned the fact that in our new program forms we have asked the licensee who is a network affiliate to list the hours of network public affairs program which were offered to him.

I would go a lot further. As I said in the little concurring statement at the time, I would also ask, how many hours of public affairs programs were you offered by your network; how many hours did you run; if you didn't run them, what kind of a program did you put on instead? Never getting into a question of a specific program, but rather the hours involved in the offering, and the kind of program you ran instead.

Some people feel that this is an unwarranted government intrusion into licensee responsibility. Some people feel this involves the word "censorship" which I regard as a very curious use of that word since it doesn't involve any specific program in any sense. My point is, that when we give out these valuable licenses, particularly in television, often having to make a tortuous choice between five or six different competitors, it ought to go to the fellow who will give the most public service to his community in preference to the fellow who will give the least. And I feel that the whole role of the government here—I agree with Professor Jaffe—is to encourage as much of a public spotlight on these decisions as possible, as much publicity as possible. Then if people do care, if they are interested, they'll have a way of knowing.

GUIDER: I'd like to introduce into the discussion at this time, the proposition that simply calling for information about the number of network programs that were not accepted by the individual station might be more than just an unwarranted government intrusion; it might be an uninformed government intrusion.

Unless you're going to ask what time of day these programs were offered; and what the impact of the acceptance of that program would be; and what it would amount to in terms of the economic life of the station, I don't see how you can draw a proper conclusion as to whether the station should have taken it, or, shouldn't.

Now I think generally, a point that ought to be kept in the mind of everyone here if we're going to achieve any progress, is that it is the will of Congress and the law of the land that we're to operate within the framework of a free enterprise system. This is happily regarded by many people as a chance to make millions. But there are television stations in this country today that aren't making any money, and there are a great many more that didn't make money for many years until they turned the corner and started to make money.

It's very hard to do all these high and noble things when you have your payroll to meet. If a network contributes 25 per cent of your total income to you; and your bread and butter money is coming from the other 75 per cent of your time, and maybe 40 per cent of it or 50 per cent is coming from an early show that you're running from 5:30 to 7:15; and you're offered a one-half hour public service show at 6:00 o'clock—is it proper to expect that station to give up 105 minutes of its bread and butter money to accept a 30 minute show? They might take it at some different time, if the program were only going to replace a 30 minute show.

And I believe that if we will look into the situation of the individual station, and what its economic requirements are, and what the competitive situation is in its network, in its market, some stations could do almost anything they want to, because they're on easy street as far as income and outgo is concerned. Others find themselves in a situation where they have very, very heavy competition, and they have a hard time getting along.

Now unless the Commission is willing to go into the economic situation of the individual station and into the reasons for not taking a program, I don't think you can pass an informed judgment on whether or not they were "right" or "wrong" in accepting or rejecting a certain percentage of the public service shows offered to them by the network out of network time.

TAYLOR: The thing that was just pointed to by Mr. Guider interested me. I happen not only to be associated with the Chicago education television station, but for the past nine or ten months I have spent about two-fifths of my time in New York working at "Learning Resources Institute," which is an organization that over the past several years has developed "Continental Classroom" and produced it for NBC.

Six or seven months ago, we worked out another scheme. This "Continental Classroom" was offered as you know early in the morning, on the cables, and so we tried to find another scheme for two reasons: One to save some money, and another to find out if we couldn't get some different times. A biology course which is going to be offered at the college level this fall was first offered to the CBS stations, and as of yesterday 186 stations have agreed to telecast it. Incidentally, 144 was the greatest number that had accepted from the NBC group year before last and last year, too.

REINSCH: It might be interesting to indicate the time of the telecast.

TAYLOR: 6:30–7:00 A.M. was when it was offered by NBC last year and the two previous years. But the point I want to make now is, that when we offer the biology course this next fall, it will be over the cables. But any one, any station, can take a time of its own choosing—assuming that they are consistent. The course runs five days a week, and the spread of acceptance runs all the way from 6:00–6:30 A.M. to 11:00–11:30 at night; and there's a concentration, at a point that I think is going to be a good one, between 6:30–8:30 A.M.; and there's another concentration in the afternoon, just after lunch when it's being offered on the cables; and there's another one about 4:00 o'clock.

REINSCH: It's being fed at 1:00–1:30 P.M.—is that right?

TAYLOR: Yes, at 1:00 o'clock, as a matter of fact, that's the Eastern time, but it will be fed straight through and that becomes 12:00 o'clock on the Coast after they change it around.

But we are very interested in seeing this thing serve various levels as well as various types of schools. You'll catch some teachers before they go to school, you'll catch other teachers in off periods at school; you'll catch in-school college students. This can be, we think, a very fine way to get more education done by the networks.

MINOW: Just to clarify, in our proposal we have asked, whether, if you didn't run it when it was offered by the network, did you run it at another time.

MICKELSON: I was just going to suggest that almost any direction we take here gets around to the fact that at some point or other somebody has to make a subjective programming decision. With respect to this question of the acceptance of programs by stations, the assumption has to be made, either that all public service or public affairs programs that go out through networks are eminently worth while; are a high quality production, and should be taken by the stations; or, if that isn't true, somebody at some point or other has got to make a decision that maybe some one of these wasn't worth while for distributing, or a station had a right not to accept or to accept, in either case.

Now it so happens that for a long period of time at least as far as the history of television goes, I've had something to do with the production of a great number of these programs. And I can't say in good conscience here that 100 per cent of the programs which I was in a position to offer to the affiliates of that network were worth while accepting in any way, and I think in many cases the affiliates were fully justified in not accepting the program based on what turned out to be the quality and content of the program. However, at the same time I do think that these acceptances, the evidence will show, probably was much higher than the public is being led to believe by statements which have been made about acceptances of programs on the part of station managers affiliated with networks.

TAISHOFF: I should like to go back to the original premise of Professor Jaffe, "the element of scarcity in allocations which seems to justify all these things."

Now in radio broadcasting the argument of "scarcity" was used at the beginning—everyone wanted clear channels. Later on they accepted regional channels; and local channels; daytime assignments. There are now nearly 5,000 AM stations on the air. Is there scarcity in AM? Some broadcasters are now protesting that there are too many stations!

Now we get to television. Everyone wants from VHF the prime channels; greatest coverage. But there are 70 UHF channels available with a mutiplicity of assignments that can be handed out for the asking. Now I believe in excess of 150 UHF assignments have been turned back to the government, because the operators could not stand the economic gaff.

So is there actually a scarcity element? They can't all be clear channel stations in radio; you can't have all VHF stations in television with a limitation of 12 channels! You do have 70 UHF channels available, and probably several thousands of assignments that could be made.

REINSCH: I might add, that the Washington people will recall that in the 40's, those of us in the broadcasting business who went to Washington were urged by the Commission to apply for the VHF channels; there was a lack of interest in applications at that particular period. It's rather strange to think about it now that at one period in the television history the Commission was most anxious to have applicants for VHF channels.

JAFFE: I'm really rather surprised that you make the statement, Mr. Taishoff, because as I understand it, and as I think we all do, UHF cannot compete effectively commercially in an area that's predominantly VHF. I may be quite wrong about that.

TAISHOFF: Well all I was saying is, that now there's a monopoly in VHF, we're not saying it's going to be forever.

ANOTHER: I'm perfectly prepared to stand on my position, that if there no longer is a scarcity there's no basis whatever for regulation.

ANOTHER: But what constitutes "scarcity"? That is my question. If you have 70 UHF channels available for the asking, in most areas—now they can't all be in New York; they can't all be in Chicago.

JAFFE: Well for example, you can't run a radio station with gravel and rocks—there's lots of gravel and rocks all over the place! But that doesn't show that there's not a scarcity.

TAISHOFF: Doesn't the element of "pioneering" come into play in this picture? People invested their money; they took the risk; at one time there was not a single television station in the country that was returning a profit; and this was not too many years ago —I think ten.

JAFFE: Isn't it clear that if something sells for $15 million that there's a very strong scarcity element involved in it?

GUIDER: In that particular market, Professor.

JAFFE: Well, because it's limited! If you had 72 in that market it wouldn't sell for $15 million.

PIERSON: No more than if you have three in a smaller city it won't sell for a million. And you might have two million in it. I don't think these conditions are uniform throughout the area.

REINSCH: We're having considerable discussion about VHF and UHF, judging from the trade press. Chairman Minow, would you like to add to this?

MINOW: Well I'm a little startled too, I must say, by Mr. Taishoff's contribution. To put it in very simple terms, he knows as well as anyone in the room—you can't talk about UHF and VHF in the same breath!

VOICE: You can't except as to specific markets.

MINOW: You can in a market that's all UHF, period.

VOICE: That's right.

MINOW: But you can't talk about it in any place where it's in competition with a VHF channel, and many people, including Clair McCollough, know this by very hard experience and a lot of money down the drain. The only way you can use the UHF's is, if you have a market that's all UHF.

We just authorized a channel in Washington, D. C., to an educational group. Unfortunately the only channel we can give them is a UHF channel, Channel 26. I can't get it on my television set; you can't get it on your television set, Mr. Taishoff—no one who lives in Washington in this room can get it on their television set—unless we go out and either buy a new set, or get a converter for our present set, which is going to be at some cost and inconvenience.

Therefore, it seems to me totally beside the point to compare UHF and VHF in the same terms. Every time we have a VHF channel that is up for a license, we have a hot fight; we have many competitors.

VOICE: But we can't all drive Cadillacs!

MINOW: Well I know that, but the point is that the scarcity is exactly the argument that requires the government to be interested. If there were enough television stations for everybody, I would close up the FCC Broadcast Bureau this afternoon, I would be delighted. But the whole reason we're there is that there aren't enough microphones or television stations for everybody that wants to use them.

PIERSON: As I understood Mr. Taishoff's statement, it was that, what scarcity exists now exists as a result of limitations other than technical, or the scarcity of frequencies which the Commission can allocate to the television broadcaster. Scarcity arises from the practical problem of getting distribution of receivers that will receive the part of the band that's been allocated. And another very important problem is the current status of the economic support for television in general.

Now I think that the important thing to remember is that this same kind of situation existed in radio, and time cured it. And I would like to suggest that, if the scarcity that now exists in television is something that will be cured by time, through the efforts of Chairman Minow and his Commission to make UHF feasible, and the efforts of the New Frontier to tremendously increase our national growth or our gross national product, it's not unreasonable to say, that in a few years television also will reach the position that radio has reached, in terms of the number of stations, or at least a much lower scarcity than now.

And I suggest that if this can be cured by time, and if that hope exists, we certainly shouldn't barter away our liberties of speech and press, for a small temporary advantage.

McGILL: I would prefer not to speak to these points, but rather with regard to the newspaper at the moment, if I may. I would suggest that it's significant that we're meeting at a university, one of the distinguished universities of the country, and that the public opinion, about which we've been talking, is not going to come from Mr. Jaffe's "passive sponges." It's going to come from more articulate people. I don't like to use the word "from the intellectuals," because these words mean different things to many persons.

I think that we in the newspaper business, magazines, and the broadcasting media are certainly being subjected to new pressures, and some of which we don't well understand as yet. But this public opinion is going to come from a relatively small percentage, and these are the ones who will influence the Congress, who will influence editorial opinion; this I think is demonstrated by the fact of where we're meeting for our discussion.

Also it seems to me—well I think that all of the philosophers from Plato, perhaps ahead of Plato, have said it all along— "We are a part of what we have met." This is inescapably true. In New England its culture is a part of what it has met with along the way; in the South, God knows, its culture is a part of what it has met with along the way, and so on.

It seems to me that in this tremendous industrial revolution we're going through, that our culture is being wrenched and distorted and convulsed, and that out of it may come a "national culture" instead of regional cultures. This I think is important: more and more people are becoming concerned about children, whether it's from the viewpoint of delinquency, or education, or what not. I think it's important that we see that this public opinion which is going is concerned about children and young people. They'll be conditioned with a great deal of violence from their newspapers. And I would hasten to add, if there's any "mea culpa" business I want it clearly understood I'm including newspapers. But if they're going to meet along the way with a lot of violence and shabby, cheap treatment of sex, we have to ask ourselves—What will the effect be? Each of us, as well as our countries and our regions are a part of our history, and the cultural impacts we've had along the way. I also have a strong feeling that the government has a responsibility to see to it that the children of this country are educated.

I would like to differ just a moment with Dean King, if he will pardon me, because he said the states weren't willing to tax themselves to pay for educating their children.

Now it's not well understood, that in the deep South states where education has been and is at its very lowest ebb, where teachers are paid less, or less is spent per pupil, the paradoxical fact is, that these states are spending more of their tax dollar on education than is Michigan or many of the wealthier states. But there just aren't the tax dollars. And a great many of these states where violence and so forth is going on, I suspect will have even fewer tax dollars in the future. I doubt if industry will be interested in going in.

I'm skipping about, but I do feel very strongly, maybe because I've just finished reading for about the third time, Khrushchev's new "Manifesto." It was interesting that he emphasized an expansion of the use of television in education, and that he announced that in this decade presently entered in, that all children in the Soviet Union were to have a compulsory secondary school education, with emphasis on the polytechnic aspects.

I also am troubled, because I believe in it, about the image of the competitive system. Recently we've had the electrical companies—I was astonished to read the other day that manufacturers of golf clubs and sport equipment had agreed not to fix prices; that national baking chains selling to military installations had agreed not to fix prices on buns, and rolls and bread. Something is wrong here, and I think we must come up with a positive approach.

We in the newspaper field certainly must do so; and I'm an ignorant man about television but I think it too must do this. But I do hope that we can come to an opinion that, if the states can't do it, that the Federal Government, has a responsibility to educate children, or see that they're educated through the states, leaving it to the states to control the money—because I don't like the fact that we lost so much of our talent.

And it's a trite business nowadays to talk vis-à-vis the Russians, but I think the fact that the Russians are getting the use of all of their talented kids regardless of geography is one of their secret weapons.

CONE: It seems to me from all the discussion, that the problem of television is part of the history of the problems of minorities. We don't have any specialized television—we only have specialized times in television.

The results in terms of audience for the more intellectual programs, is as I'm sure you all know, very sad. I took occasion the other day to have checked the audiences of the hundred programs TV Guide listed in defensive reply to your "Wasteland" reference.

Only nine of them managed to beat the competition. Ninety-one of them were snowed under or beat decisively as the case may be. We've heard a great deal in discussions like this about "Macbeth." Well I had a little something to do with Macbeth, having put it on the air for Hallmark. And it got five beautiful Emmys—but it was beaten by all the other programs on the air in its time period. Altogether its audience was less than one-third of the total audience.

I don't think this means that anybody's necessarily wrong—I think it just means that this is the way people's tastes run. I might also say, so that nobody thinks I have long, long hair, that we are one of the participants in "The Untouchables" too. And very happily. But as I say, this is a matter of minorities. There is no *Atlantic Monthly* in the television business, and so, I would like to ask Chairman Minow something that I think gets at this: What *is* the future of UHF?

MINOW: Before I answer, I'll bet that more people saw Macbeth through that television program than could have ever seen it in any other way!

CONE: Well, we're very pleased about that.

MINOW: Right. Somebody was telling me the other day that Walter Lippmann's public affairs show only got 6,000,000 people —only 6,000,000 people!! Where else could Walter Lippmann have reached 6,000,000 people? There are very few magazines in this country that can reach 6,000,000 people.

But I think you're right, the real problem is minorities; and I think the real long term solution is UHF, because it's only through this way that we'll have enough channels to appeal to smaller audiences.

When you have only three networks, and only four channels in Chicago—a city of many millions of people—you cannot appeal to smaller audiences. The only way you can do it is to follow the same thing that's developed in the other media and that is have specialized publications that appeal to a smaller group. You can't do it with the existing scarcity of channels.

The economics of it are going to be difficult. They'll have to feel their way and see if it will pay. One alternative of course is the educational network which will provide a minority with a different kind of programming.

And another alternative that I'm very intrigued with and I hope we'll talk about it at some point during our seminar, is Mr. Cone's suggestion that people who sponsor shows which achieve smaller audiences should pay less for them. This is a matter that I think ought to be discussed during the course of our seminar.

But my basic answer to you is, that UHF is to me the only real solution—providing room for broadcasters who want to reach small audiences.

REINSCH: Then may the Chair exercise prerogative and ask a question—there's been considerable discussion about the UHF-VHF mandatory bill in Congress; would the Chairman like to comment on that?

MINOW: Well, we have proposed, and legislation has been introduced, to require that all sets that are manufactured in the future be equipped to receive both the UHF and the VHF signal. We do this because we feel this is the most painless way, over a period of years, to achieve a conversion. The problem today is that a UHF broadcaster is fighting to find a listener, or a viewer who has a UHF set. It will take time because you cannot very quickly amortize the cost of these many, many millions of sets that are outstanding and also the cost of broadcasters who have equipment, and so on: The only way to do this is over a period of time and we're very hopeful that this legislation will be entertained seriously by Congress and passed.

NATHANSON: I think that maybe we should remember in the interest of a balanced discussion, that Mr. Jaffe made a number of concessions which not everyone would necessarily make, you know. And then everyone else accepted his concessions and jumped on his other points! No one likes to be put in the position of the "long haired" either, and since I'm not really one half as long haired or intellectual as Mr. Jaffe, I'm willing to play that role, for this purpose. It seems to me that it's very debatable at the present time that television fairly represents our culture. And to put it in personal terms, I can't keep up with all the good magazines; I can't keep up with all the good books; I can't even keep up with all the good movies, accepting this for the moment as the minority standard. But I don't think I would have much difficulty keeping up with all the "good" television programs!

And I think that's the problem, irrespective of the solution.

QUAAL: Thank you Leonard! Professor Jaffe in his very cogent observations addressed himself to the alleged "monopoly" in television. Well I disagree with him there very vehemently. I do endorse so wholeheartedly Dean King's observation in this area. I feel, as Chairman Minow has pointed out, there are a handful of markets; and as I look at Messrs. Goldenson and Treyz (of ABC) who are with us today, I appreciate their position regarding communities where there is need for additional competition.

But Mr. Jaffe! and Gentlemen! there is plenty of competition in television. Chairman Minow, here in your home city of Chicago, I assure you there's plenty!

But I should like to go back to the pre-war era in radio. We had 818 radio stations on the air before World War II. Today we have 5,000. And I don't think there's one person in this room, or anyone in or out of broadcasting, who can say that the general program fare on radio has improved through the greatly increased number of stations.

Ours, gentlemen, happens to be one industry that is extremely peculiar in many areas. One primarily is that increased competition does not necessarily mean a better product for the consumer. And I ask you to examine a market like Albuquerque, New Mexico, 201,000 people; 14 radio stations. You listen to those 14 stations Chairman Minow, and you'll find them to be more of a "vast wasteland" than that of which you speak concerning television. I feel very strongly in this area, and I hope that as this discussion goes on, we are not going to take the position that more stations will necessarily mean more quality. I'm afraid the opposite will be true.

MINOW: Well, I think this is the heart of it, Ward. The broadcasting industry in this country is regarded traditionally, historically, as free enterprise. If you're going to have free enterprise, then you're going to subject it to the test of competition. This is our classical theory of economics; the more competition, the better. Otherwise it's not a free enterprise system.

Now the court was faced with this specific question, and faced up to it in the *Sanders* case, where broadcasters said to the Commission: "No! We've got enough stations in this city, don't put in any more." But the court said that broadcasting, unlike common carrier, was a field of open competition.

Now whether in the long run this will improve programming,

I'm not sure myself. I may agree with you that in the long run the competition degrades rather than improves programming, in some respects.

But either you believe in the free enterprise system or you don't! Either you have a free enterprise broadcasting system, or you have some kind of a government regulated monopoly. I don't think you can have it both ways.

JAFFE: Well Mr. Quaal, I agree with nearly everything you said. Of course there is enormous competition for audiences and all that, in broadcasting, and at certain points it's undoubtedly extremely unprofitable. I don't disagree with any of that.

I also do not disagree with you that complete competition in broadcasting may result in a far worse product than we have today. On that we've simply got to take our chances.

I almost think this business of monopoly is an opportunity. It allows us more cultivated people to get our views in and insist on a certain amount of quality programming. But that I don't think is quite the point, which is whether there's competition. The question is: whether in such a market as New York, or Chicago, or in the places in which there is a certain amount of cultivated opinion (and that's very important, as Mr. McGill has said), it's these people who make the important changes in our culture. It may be very small but it's very important. In those places the situation is not that there isn't a great deal of competition; it's that the time is so valuable, it's so expensive (because it's limited) that what compares in TV to the little reviews and the off beat play and the rather exceptional thing like the *Atlantic Monthly*, and *Harper's*, and so on and so on—they can't get into it!

VOICE: Or, discussion of foreign affairs!

JAFFE: Well, I understand there's getting to be good discussion of foreign affairs. But nevertheless, it's at these incredibly important points in our general cultural development and in our general culture that it's difficult to get the time to put that kind of thing on, because it's just too expensive. The time in New York City and the time in Chicago is so extremely valuable, it isn't worth putting those things on.

Now you could start up a little newspaper. You could start up a *Nation* or a *New Republic*. Some rich man can and will do that and we'll support it; that's subsidy. But it's terribly expensive apparently to subsidize that sort of thing in New York City or

Chicago. We're seeing an attempt now to subsidize a New York City station through the purchase of Channel 13 as an educational TV station. This is the point I'm making.

KING: I just wanted to make a remark relative to what Chairman Minow said about the *Sanders* case.

First, there is always some debate I understand as to whether that's exactly what the *Sanders* case held. In any case the Court of Appeals subsequently has held to the contrary, that the Commission should take into consideration the economics of the situation in respect to granting licenses; but the Commission by a gimmick which I'm sure you're familiar with, has refused to do so.

REINSCH: It can be pointed out there too, that the engineering standards over a period of time were tragically degraded in AM as a result of many pressures. The result was other problems that the Commission had to take under consideration and eventually ended up in the Court.

MINOW: I think that's right. I would disagree with you Dean, I think that's an accurate statement of the *Sanders* case.

BARROW: I should like to return to the previous subject for a brief comment. A basic point which Professor Jaffe makes in his paper is that, to the extent that the Government has power to influence programming, it is based upon scarcity of stations.

I would question whether a shift to the UHF, as was suggested by Mr. Taishoff in the discussion, would solve all of our problems. Some of the problems in broadcasting arise because of scarcity of stations. Others do not. We are not in a position to delay our discussion for a few years and see whether the problems are solved by technological developments.

As the chairman has pointed out, this is a unique medium, with unique problems. To point to just one: the high cost of television programming of high quality, which is important to a live and viable television. We must recognize that a shift to the UHF and utilizing all the channels which an advertiser-supported economy can maintain, will not solve this problem. Neither will it solve all of the other problems that we have. Hence, we should preserve the concept that the spectrum is a government owned property, and that those who operate in it are licensed trustees. This concept is necessary to lay the base for solutions of problems which we will have even after there is a viable UHF.

NOVIK: Well, Leonard, I start with even greater disadvantage than Mr. McGill who said he was awed in a university. I'm not only awed in a university I'm scared stiff in a law school! But I am no stranger to broadcasting. I have been in this business a long time.

From 1928 to 1932—before modern radio—I represented Clarence Darrow, Bertrand Russell, Dr. Will Durant and so on, all giants of the lecture platform. I made a fairly good business out of putting them in Carnegie Hall in New York City, Symphony Hall in Boston and at the Auditorium in Washington. We attracted large audiences because we debated issues of the day.

As I think about it now, I wonder how much those issues have changed in their appeal to people of all kinds—not only the intellectuals—the so-called minority groups—the kind of people Mr. Cone referred to in his talk. Our debates, which drew impressive numbers who obviously had a concern about the state of the world we lived in, carried such titles as "Is Democracy a Failure?," "Is Man a Machine?," "Is Education Necessary?."

With the advent of radio, I saw the possibility of enlarging this audience with similar types of programming. I therefore devoted myself to the operation of a New York City radio station, which emerged, after 4 years of broadcasting, as the foremost cultural station of the day in the area. We pioneered the "talk" shows with impressive success in such features as "Forum of the Air" and "University of the Air."

It is unfortunate that programs of this type are a rarity today— almost non-existent. Who is responsible for this state of affairs? What was the intent of Congress when the Communications Act was first written? Well, the record is clear. As has been said before, it was a question of whether we were to adopt a government-controlled system like the BBC or a private enterprise system. The latter was adopted on the premise that the American businessman could be depended upon to operate both for profit and in the public interest. There is abundant literature on this fact.

And whatever I forgot I was reminded of last night when I read Commissioner Ford's speech, delivered in Seattle a couple of weeks ago. He recalled then that there was voluminous testimony by Congressman White. I recall now a Commission Hearing where Mayor LaGuardia appeared with 18 volumes of Congressional debate on the subject!

In 1932 during the debates on broadcasting that were held in Congress, various concepts were presented. There was the question of what percentage of time should be allocated for "the general good." This concept was initiated by Secretary of Commerce Herbert Hoover, later President Hoover. He advocated 25 per cent, morning; 25 per cent, afternoon and 25 per cent, evening; but the proposal lost by one vote in the committee.

Professor Jaffe said earlier today he was mystified why restrictions of equal time were placed on political discussion. Review of the Congressional debate shows that the present system of broadcasting could never have been adopted otherwise. The Congress wanted to be assured that the owner of a radio station would not use the facility for political advantage.

Similarly, blocs in Congress, like the "Dry Belt" influenced restrictions on liquor; others restricted lotteries; still others, indecency. And in a spirit of compromise Congress deliberately injected the phrase, "public interest, convenience and necessity." Then every radio station owner realized that he had to do something for public service in order to hold his license. In the early days he looked on network affiliation as the best way of discharging his public service obligation. Since the advent of television, standards were dropped.

Then, dependence on networks became obsolete. The networks in turn stopped programming public service because their affiliates refused to take the shows. And nobody could force them to do so.

I am happy, therefore, that Commissioner King, and everyone else in the room, agree that we need standards. And I contend, gentlemen, that the answer is not merely in increasing the number of stations. I agree with Ward that the increase from 850 to 5,000 radio stations has not produced a better program service. As a matter of fact, we have less diversification on the air today than we had 30 years ago. We have inherited a situation where the least important station in terms of public service—the so-called independent, local station—sets the standard for the big fellow in the community.

Ladies and gentlemen, I'm not mincing any words. In New York City the property value of an independent station—small and inconsequential less than 10 years ago—jumped from $350,-000 to $11,000,000 within eight years—operating as a juke-box! In the absence of "standards" that operator had a perfect right to program as he did.

If we agree now that "standards" are necessary, we ought at

least to say that it doesn't depend on how many stations are on the air.

When you consider that despite the increase in the number of radio stations, the American people today are less informed on public issues than ever before; that there is less diversification of programming than ever before; then you will understand why I share Dean Barrow's concern of 2,000 television stations existing only because of what Professor Jaffe calls "their competitive legal right." To me that is not living up to the original intent of the Congress, even though Congress perhaps did not sufficiently spell out "intent" in terms of the responsibility of the broadcasters.

So I should like to get away a little bit from what we had this morning of just talking theory. You professors and practitioners of law have agreed that "standards" is a responsibility. So I would like you to try to spell out how the average broadcaster can meet that responsibility.

I do not think that the present system of providing an interview spot in the evening national TV news program, or an occasional public service feature, gives the American people the basic things they need to know to survive in our present world. And without giving the people that knowledge, the broadcaster is not serving his responsibility as a licensee. This holds as true on a national level as it does on a local level.

REINSCH: The Chair would like to make one point, however, that size does not necessarily tie in with guilt, because you have some mighty fine large station operations including WGN and with undue modesty I'll include WSB.

NOVIK: I agree with you, but I don't think it's fair to expect WGN and WSB and the few other such stations to carry the full load by being the only ones in their community to program public service.

I can spell it out further. The WNBC's and the WABC's, and other great clear-channel stations, in the interest of competitive programming have been forced by their local independent competitors to give up their in-depth public service and news programs and to carry only the sketchy spot shows in order to get away from any "talk" because, in the words of the commercial fellows, "It louses up the air."

GOELET: I think I'm one of the few people in this room who has had the privilege of operating on both sides of the, shall I say, radio spectrum, in that I operated a radio station for some eight years. I think things haven't changed so very much; I know what it is to go out and try to sell a spot announcement for $2.50!

And also, to try to set up the National Audience Board as an organization which will, in a sense, be a clearing house or agency through which the people can express their opinions about programming on a representational basis. Since that obviously cannot be done by any one group we have tried as much as possible to align ourselves and work with large groups such as the General Federation of Women's Clubs, and so forth, so we would get a larger representation.

I've heard some references to our own Newsletter that I was very pleased to note, such as Professor Jaffe's. I've heard some remarks about Cadillacs from Sol Taishoff which possibly might have been inspired from the same source.

If I may, since this is such a very complex situation, I would like today to try to set up some of the areas in which I think we have to operate; and then later on, if I should have the opportunity, make some recommendations as to how perhaps we can most effectively operate within that area.

I mentioned in an editorial that it seemed to me television was unique, in that it was a franchise operation which involved both functional and qualitative elements. It's the proportion of the qualitative elements to the functional elements that I think presents a great deal of the difficulty.

As an instance, if a man gets a franchise for a bus (and I'm talking now of a franchise operation because broadcasting is a franchise operation) he only has to supply transportation.

But the great problem we have here is that, in serving the community, the television operator has to put on his "bread-and-butter" programs—which you might call part of his functional element.

Then people criticize him for not supplying qualitative elements. I think it is very difficult to know how we should determine the percentage of the qualitative vis-à-vis the functional.

And I think this all stems from the question which I put to Commissioner Ford. I said to him: "Will you try to spell out for me the 'No Man's Land' which is bounded on one side by the prohibition—the imposition against censorship—and, on the other by this vague standard of 'serving the public interest, convenience and necessity'?"

I think these are some of the areas in which we have to operate; and I also note that the question came up here as to the
problem of putting on public affairs programs more cheaply. I
was very concerned at the time and we ran an article on this
subject in our Newsletter.

I wanted to show those people with whom we deal—the government, the press and the segments of the public we contact—
that there was this great problem of public service programs getting very low ratings. (I would like at this point to thank Sol
Taishoff, of *Broadcasting Magazine,* who made that material
available to us for our Newsletter.)

One other subject I would like to touch upon: the question was,
as to whether "publicity" was a valuable medium or not, whether
it would be helpful.

I think I can express that most cogently by giving you a one
word "test" as to whether it is or not. And the word that I will
throw at you is: "Wasteland."

So, I think there's no question that publicity can be a most effective medium. If I have the chance later on within this broad
area I have defined, I would like to make some recommendations
as to how I think programs can be improved (allowing some reasonable supposition that public interest, convenience and necessity is a criterion) without unduly inhibiting the rights of the station owners.

AGEE: Well Mr. Chairman, I've been a little reticent about
speaking out here because my own background is primarily in
the newspaper field, and in education.

I would like to make a point however in reference to this monopoly matter that was brought up earlier. All of us of course
hate to see the dissolution of fine newspapers throughout the
country. But the monopoly situations that have been developed
in respect to newspapers—at least in the one-newspaper city—
generally have led to higher quality and devotion to public responsibility on the part of those newspapers. You can cite the
Louisville *Courier-Journal* and the Minneapolis *Star* and *Tribune,*
and many others. Conversely there are a number of cities in
which there is great competition where that same high quality
doesn't exist, unfortunately. It seems to me that this same thing
should apply in television broadcasting, with the public being the
arbiter, deciding which stations shall remain and which shall

die. The public is voting every day of course. This then imposes a greater responsibility on those which remain.

In my opinion, the ability of the broadcast industry to meet challenges has been very great for an industry that's been with us such a short length of time, and I'm confident that ways will be found to solve this problem of better programming and minority ownership, in the light of this continuing vigorous public discussion of the goals that are to be desired by our society.

REINSCH: On another tack Fax Cone has talked considerably about the magazine concept. This of course affects the revenue and the program approach. Would you like to amplify that particular point, Fax, at this time?

CONE: Could I say something else first?

REINSCH: Certainly!

CONE: The assumption is made in meetings like this and in so many things I read, that "there isn't *any* good programming." I think this is a terrible mistake. There's a lot of good programming. The trouble with it is that it doesn't come at times when certain people would like to see it and listen to it.

I suppose they don't want to listen on Saturday afternoon or Sunday during the day, or in the early evening hours. Well I think this is too bad. Mention has been made here of the *Atlantic Monthly* and *Harper's*—they don't come out every day. They come out once a month.

The features that are in the big Sunday newspapers that are so thoughtful so many times and so good, they're only once a week; I don't hear anybody screaming because these things aren't more constant.

I don't have a list of programs but there's been a great effort made here in Chicago, particularly by our local station, WGN; and the ABC and NBC and CBS stations carry all kinds of good things!

Now what happens to these is that there don't seem to be enough of them at any given moment to satisfy everyone concerned. And I think this is something that I'm sure you've paid attention to but I don't think a great many critics pay enough attention to it.

It's been mentioned also that some very good programs have poor audiences. Well I think this is too bad, but it is true that the stations continue to carry them; the networks continue to provide them, but it's a pretty difficult thing if I, as an advertising agent, were to try to get a manufacturer in a competitive field, let's say package soap, to sponsor a program with a 300,000 audience in Chicago against a competitive product with a 700,000 audience.

Somebody's going to be out of business in a hurry. I'm going to be first, and the manufacturer's going to be next. So I don't think this is a reasonable proposition.

Let me repeat: I think there's a great deal of good programming on the air; I worry when good programs are not carried by certain stations.

I have a rather amazing list of stations, for example, that didn't carry the much discussed Macbeth. This is too bad. This probably happened in most cases in two-station cities—but anyway they didn't carry it and I'm sorry. But generally speaking I think the networks and the stations do do a pretty good job. Now if I may, to the point that you mentioned.

I may be an idealist in this area, but some months ago, in fact, several years ago I wondered—out loud—whether there were enough—and I think there are—responsible advertisers, thoughtful people, who wouldn't be perfectly willing to underwrite some of the kind of programming that I think we're all talking about when we talk about "better programming"; I'm not talking about "education" now, this is another area. I think they would be willing to underwrite some of these things and indeed I think they are, right now, provided these are made available at lower costs, lower prices, so their costs work out somewhat the same way.

It can't be any secret that some of the big specials, let's take "CBS Reports" are not always sold finally at the original hoped-for price. They are frequently the subject of negotiation, and not a proposal on the part of anybody that "We will sell you a smaller audience program at a smaller price." I think something like the latter could be very helpful. It would relate costs to programming in a much more realistic way.

Then there's another thing that has been suggested, to reclaim the "wasteland." This is the averaging concept of advertising in a variety of programs. And I'm not at all sure that a good many advertisers—I think I know some—would not be perfectly willing to buy "so many" programs of a series high rated, and also "so many" of a series of programs lower rated. The thing here is to adjust the prices; to base these on circulation.

Finally, to go a step further, I'm not at all sure that there aren't a good many advertisers sensing this whole thing who wouldn't be willing to see their commercials "revolved" through a week's programming. This is the way they buy newspapers; this is the way they buy magazines—you cannot buy page 1 of *Life* magazine. You cannot buy page 17 of *Life* magazine. You cannot buy every time in conjunction with "The Movie of the Week," if you please; you cannot buy every time, let's say, in *Look* magazine in the midst of the editorial feature having to do with food. Your advertising is revolved through the publication, issue by issue.

And I'd put it as a question: "Would this be impossible in television?"

Because it would help to pay for, help to support the programs that are tuned out by large numbers of people. There hasn't been a finer series in years than the "Winston Churchill Series," on ABC—and look at the audience. Now to ask somebody in the competitive business area to go into that against a similar product with a high rating program is simply out of the question!

GUIDER: I do think that what Mr. Cone just said is terribly important; that somehow within our end of the industry—and we are the ones that want to settle these problems—we don't want it done through Washington; we're going to have to do some hard thinking about how we could handle our income, perhaps with changed concepts of distribution of where that income lands in programs, as you've just suggested; in a way that will give us the economic means of complying with what is expected of us.

We can't do the impossible. And just before lunch something was said about impressing on our industry the requirements of what are called "monopolies." Now monopolies have certain obligations; they also have certain privileges. The government could do certain things we can't do. But always we've got to do it within the framework of meeting that payroll next Friday afternoon. And not all of us, not all 450 of us are equally capable of doing that.

And the networks themselves in their competitive fights with each other I'm sure are often handicapped.

A third network has now come in and has sometimes been criticized for the character of its programs. Nobody takes the trouble to point out that that third network took what was a two-network monopoly and made a 3-network monopoly out of it, and that, as I understand, is 50 percent less monopoly! It gave three choices of programs in a good many cities instead of two, and many of these are good programs by any standard.

But if we can, over on our side of the fence, if we in our own industry can try to find a distribution of the advertising dollars—of which there is a limit—so that we can spread it over more programs, and have a little more control over things like the Winston Churchill Series being given a good or continued play; or so that we'll come back and support it again another year instead of feeling that it was a show that couldn't carry itself—there I think perhaps there will be some room within our industry for us to do the job, and I think we'll do a better job of it if we do it that way than if the government tells us what we must do or risk a failure of license renewal.

REINSCH: Clair McCollough, as an affiliate, would you like to comment on these points?

McCOLLOUGH: It has been said, "If you wait long enough to talk, somebody will have said almost everything that should be said." I agree with some of the statements that have been made this morning and I disagree with others. Governor Collins, President of NAB, is scheduled to speak this afternoon, basically for the NAB. With this in mind, it would be unwise for me, as Chairman of the Board of Directors of the NAB, to delve too deeply into the major points that have been covered thus far.

However, regarding the discussion concerning the possibility of adopting the "magazine" concept for television with the cost per thousand theory included, many affiliates would be willing to try anything that responsible parties believe would be beneficial to the television industry.

And, while I am on the subject of affiliates, it should be said that the average network affiliate is not afraid of too much government regulation; they are not afraid to show what they are broadcasting; how they are doing it and when they are doing it.

I know of my own knowledge from surveys made for the Television Information Office in New York, that a great many knowledgeable people, including some around this table for whom I have a very high regard, simply do not and will not take enough time to look at many excellent programs that are on television. If they would view these features regularly some opinions might be changed.

Anyone willing to sit down and analyze a week's program, or a month's program, 19 hours a day, day after day, week after week, is bound to reach the conclusion that TV programs are good some of the time regardless of how individual tastes and opinions differ.

There are a great many excellent productions on television that critics would be well advised to see before becoming too critical of the medium.

There is one factor that should be understood about affiliate reaction to network public service programs. This factor is extremely important to affiliates since some claims have been made that affiliates do not accept enough network public service programs.

Very frequently network public service programs are offered in station time which is used for *local* programming. Perhaps a higher proportion of this type of program should be broadcast during time previously optioned to the network by the station. In other words, telecast a greater number of public service programs during *network* time.

Concerning another point that has been raised this morning about requests from the FCC to stations for program information. Many broadcasters, including myself, have been signing license applications for years. No one at the FCC or elsewhere has ever done anything to censor programs on any of our stations and we doubt if they ever will.

If at any time, however, the FCC, or Congress, or anybody else, should attempt to legislate what goes on the air and what doesn't, then I think you would find the broadcasting industry completely consolidated in their efforts to resist censorship or dictated programming.

QUAAL: Well Leonard, with further reference to some of Clair's points, and above all, Fax Cone's reference to the magazine concept, I should like to go back to the early days of the NAB Television Board when Clair McCollough, Cam Arnoux of WTAR in Norfolk, and I were serving together. We said at that time, having watched the errors made in overemphasis on ratings in the radio industry, that in the early days of television we should do everything to avoid repeating that same error. We've fallen into the identical trap, however.

The very excellent solution to which Fax speaks I think can be attained when ratings cease to take on the major importance that they enjoy today. Bear in mind, I am not questioning the integrity of A. C. Nielsen, ARB, Pulse, or any other reputable service. I think they're operated by very responsible people. But in our industry, unlike print media, there is this great overemphasis on per quarter hour audience measurement. Newspapers and the magazines were intelligent enough years ago early in their history to go to the audit bureau of circulation routine. They were far more prudent than we have been.

We tried, going back to 1952, on the Television Board, to establish for television an Audit Bureau of Circulation. We hired the Nielsen Company; we hired Simmons; we used Pollitz and several others. We thought we had something. We took four years to finalize what we thought was a very adequate "pilot." Some of us spoke at several sessions of the NAB on this, and we had representatives of the ten top advertising agencies on hand and we could not "sell" these agencies on the idea of "day part" circulation studies, because they said their advertisers demanded the "per quarter hour" study.

Now, if we can get to a situation where we can take a station circulation from "Sign-on till Noon; from Noon until 6:00; and Six until Sign-off," and if we rotate spots in there, I think we can implement the very sound suggestion of Mr. Cone.

This is a problem that is not going to be resolved overnight, but I think our industry now should address itself to a circulation approach in lieu of ratings.

PIERSON: I'd like to comment on Mr. Cone's statement primarily because I think of the solutions that it may offer in what has been a very difficult legal problem both in radio and in television. I think the Act as presently interpreted and I believe properly interpreted, imposes upon a licensee the job of choosing his own programs. And it says that it cannot be delegated to— the Act doesn't say that but it's been interpreted as preventing his delegation to any other person including a network.

The real fact of the case is that it is impossible for television to function in a national market as an advertising medium and leave the selection of programs and times to every individual station licensee. No matter how many reservations you put in contracts it's impossible to have a national system of program origination or a national system of sales, without delegating in practical effect a very substantial amount of the program choice and selection to networks.

Now a part of this problem is that the programs are not at any given time established for a substantial enough period that the stations can be informed fully and completely.

It seems to me that the magazine concept may offer this possibility, that if the idea means that a network would get together a fixed series that were capable of description to be carried over a substantial period of time, this would offer the possibility of fairly well explaining to all of the stations in much greater detail than now is the case. The composition of the thing and what it proposed to do would be clear, and I should assume this true for a substantial number of hours in the week.

If this is not true, I think we're still left with the problem of trying to adjust to what is a lack of reality in terms of our present regulations. If the magazine is going to be originated by the network, and it's impossible under this circumstance to give stations a full disclosure of what's going to be carried and let them make their decision—then it seems to me that we ought to recognize the reality and put the burden upon the networks to choose and select, and take it away from the station, which has no power to do it in any event; and this I think would require conforming the law to that reality. I believe we're in an unreal situation today.

MINOW: I would agree to that, very much. The theory of the Act, as Mr. Pierson says, is to put the responsibility on each individual licensee. Very often, if he's a network affiliate, he sees the programs at the same time as his viewers. He has no more to say about it than the person in the audience. And I've often thought that our present concept is unreal.

If the magazine concept were adopted by the industry—and I don't think this is a thing that the government can decide—I'm sure the government would entertain any suggestions to amend the law or regulatory process to conform with it, provided it was thought to be an improvement in the quality and balance of broadcasting. But I would agree very emphatically, that our present system is unrealistic; it is not really reaching the problem.

MICKELSON: There is another point that came up a little earlier. And that was the question of gearing the price structure of the informational program to the ratings. And this, it seems to me, would lead us into the worst sort of trap, and it's something that should be exposed to some light of publicity right now and here.

If that were to happen; and if the public affairs program or the informational program were to be based on the costs, or the price on that were to be based solely on the ratings, it seems to me that one of two things would happen: Either, there would be a great reluctance on the part of the network or the local station to schedule such programs because of the lower prices they would receive; or, secondly, and perhaps even worse, the producers of the program would be under the most terrible pressures to give these informational programs the maximum possible audience impact in order to get a high enough rating to justify a higher price, and, consequently it seems to me it would cause a degrading of the program.

In many cases it seems to me the influence of the informational program is not at all in direct proportion to the size of audience it obtains, but it's something like the ripple in the pond that frequently exercises a leadership function; and even though the rating is small, the influence of it and the advertising values of it may be far greater than the rating schedule may show. I hope that somehow or other we can forget this proposal completely and for all time.

COLLINS: I would like to offer a few thoughts about education television. That subject is not embraced in the scope of my remarks this afternoon, and much of what has been said here this morning in some degree is.

I really think, gentlemen, that education through television is the hope of the world. I don't think we can minimize at all the great challenge and the great opportunity there is for the utilization of this medium for educating people. The greatest hindrance we have now to the spread of democratic concepts and ideals is illiteracy, and the extent of illiteracy throughout this whole world is appalling. And our nation is going to have to accept considerable responsibility for much of it. We should have been doing much more than we have for many, many years. And I think we must quicken our pace in that field in the years immediately ahead or the results will really be disastrous to the whole future of our institutions.

Now I did not concur with Mr. King's rather narrow concept about this matter of aiding the states, and leaving the matter of developing its education television potential up entirely to the states. I think frankly that the people of America are all in the same boat in many respects. And one of the most important respects we're all in the same boat is in respect to education. And we are going to have to recognize that the poorly educated child, no matter where he may live, in his adolescence can easily be the problem and the concern of some other state far removed in a very short while, with the great advances in mobility of our people that has occurred, especially in recent years.

The poorly educated child in Mississippi or any other state, can very quickly become a delinquent hoodlum right here in Chicago! And then in a very short time he can become the welfare patient of Florida, or California or some other state. Our people are moving around, and so the education of people in America is everybody-in-America's business! And I think the sooner we recognize that the better off we're going to be in meeting the long range internal challenges which are facing us. Also we must develop our potentials to the best we possibly can, if this nation is to meet the challenges which are external and which are becoming more and more alarming with the passage of time.

Now I think in encouraging and in helping the development of educational television, there is an important relationship with the progress of commercial television. And I want to speak about that very briefly. One of the nation's leading commercial broadcasters was talking to me the other day and we were talking about the enormous cost involved and the risk taken in the development of new creative material for telecasting. And he pointed out that the development of programming was an enormous undertaking now, and involved great cost, and the people who were responsible for developing it had to be as assured as they possibly could be, that it would be successful once projected. And of course that makes good, reasonable common sense.

Now, Broadway productions, the big ones, involve a great amount of effort; a great amount of talent; a great amount of cost. But there is a corollary to the big Broadway productions now— the "off-Broadway" opportunity where people with new ideas can go and produce plays, and drama of one kind or another at reasonable costs.

If it fails, why, not a great deal has been lost; if it succeeds, of course it graduates to a position of greater ability to reach more people, and it may wind up in the big theater on Broadway.

I think the moving picture industry has experienced a similar matter. The production of motion pictures in America now is a tremendously expensive proposition and as people invest their funds in such they've got to be as assured as they can be that what they produce will prove successful. So they have to hire the same stars, and follow pretty much the same pattern that has been proved to be effective, and profitable.

Well this has left out a large opportunity for experimentation that is essential for creativity, and as a result the foreign motion picture producer who can produce a picture say for $100,000, which would cost a million dollars to produce in America—the foreign producer has been stimulated and encouraged to be more creative, and as a result the newest concepts in motion picture production and some of the most successful new trends in motion picture production recently have not come from Hollywood, but have come from the foreign areas where they didn't cost as much and more experimentation could be resorted to.

Now can't we foresee in the development of educational television a good area for experimentation and creativity at relatively low cost that could provide a fine feeder of quality programming, for broader distribution through regular network and syndicated distribution for regular commercial use throughout the United States?

I think that's a very significant opportunity that is embraced within the sound development of an educational television program. There was a time when commercial broadcasters looked with considerable skepticism and much actual antagonism toward education television, but that's not true of this day. I haven't found it anywhere.

To the contrary, I have found commercial broadcasters throughout this land who have been willing and have actually invested enormous funds and invested their own talent and extended their fullest cooperation to help the development of educational television, and I think that's one of the most significant things that's happened in broadcasting. And I think it portends considerable progress.

TAYLOR: I wanted to say one word on the point that was raised concerning the ETV Bill that is before the House.

I think you could even be on the side of that bill if you were against Federal aid education, because, the Bill provides about half a million dollars per state, and it's really nothing more than a "pump priming" measure.

It's a way in which some states will get the capital equipment to start using this medium, and so without getting into the argument as to whether the South has too many children to educate, we progress in one way or another!

The other thing I want to say has to do with the UHF channels. I hope we don't find a solution here too quickly that's going to dry those channels up and get them channeled into the reduction of competition as Mr. Jaffe put it. Because I can see the need for those channels, all of them, for educational purposes, and I mean instructional purposes, not education in the broad sense of the word, because I certainly would not want a U channel here in Chicago to try to spread the general cultural and informational programming.

But Mr. McGill may remember having read a report that four or five educators prepared in his town, and was published this spring for your Local Education Commission. About five of us studied the situation in the metropolitan area of Atlanta for a year and a half, and to make a long story short, we recommended that the Atlanta School System, plus the environs which could be reached by one television channel, needed not one UHF outlet—the City system has a UHF there now—but will need six as we see it in the next decade. And I think as a matter of fact, they've gone so far as to implement the first step of the report; they have set up the Metropolitan Educational Research Council, they've taken a step toward establishing a Metropolitan Educational Television Commission; and they have asked Chairman Minow's organization to allocate a second channel, and they've put him on notice that they're going to ask for four more in the not too distant future.

Another thing that we've been doing in this same connection is working on this Airborne project in northern Indiana. It was first planned that the plane would carry six UHF transmitters. We actually have two, due to weight limitations and what not, but if this thing goes over as I think it will, you'll eventually see a different type of plane, carrying the six transmitters because the education systems need them.

One other thing, the commercial channels can do a great deal toward helping solve the educational problem. In a lot of places they are doing it now. The manpower shortage that we are faced with in education, in the next decade particularly—and it's not going to stop there—is insoluble by the schools, including the higher institutions.

Our American Council on Education comes out with a report

that represents the thinking of the spokesmen for about 1,500 colleges and universities in the country. They said, among other things, that: "All we need is three times as much money; twice as many classrooms; twice as many teachers, and we can handle the doubled enrollment that's going to hit the higher institutions in ten years."

Well I think that's true. But they couldn't do it if they had the money! They couldn't get the people! So they're going to be forced, it seems to me, to make use of what television and other technological aids can do toward getting the educational job done, because if they don't make use of these things, the very least that will happen is that the quality of education will suffer.

You can argue all of the other points that have to do with saving money, and this, that and the other—but the basic thing that we're concerned with is keeping the educational quality from deteriorating; you have to do that before you can take the step that Mr. McGill has talked about in connection with certain challenges facing us from the East. We're going to need every channel you can dig up.

And the engineers can find the way to split the channels from 6 megacycles to 3; we're going to need those too, and we're going to need all the morning time, and the "D" time that the commercial stations can give us as well!

COONS: I'm wondering with regard to the upgrading of commercial programs, were we to make our best efforts to program in the way that some here suggest? Do we have the people that can do it? Are the people who are producing "The Untouchables" capable of anything else? Could these people do anything better? If not, and if they are our sole resource, then I suppose we're in a hopeless situation. If they can't do it, are there others who are really excluded from the market, other talented people who could produce good programs who are excluded from the market because of our present policies in programming? I just don't know.

McCOLLOUGH: The discussion on educational television and Jack Coons' remarks bring me to one of the main reasons why I agreed to participate in this symposium. All broadcasters, particularly telecasters, have been searching for the past 12 years for a definition for one particular thing. Almost every man around this table, has at some time or other this morning, used the terms: "Good Television" and "Bad Television." If anyone here will describe or define each—tell us which is which—then we may get somewhere.

"What is *good* television; and what is *bad* television?" Take "The Untouchables," since we seem to be on that subject. If this program gets a rating of 55, and Macbeth gets a rating of 8, which is *good* television and which is *bad* television? Who decides? Under present circumstances, the majority of viewers like to see westerns, thrillers and adventure type programs. Are they, therefore, looking at good television or bad television when they get what they want to see. I wish those around this table would endeavor to define one item between now and tomorrow's closing: What is good television? What is bad television? Which type of viewer is to be considered a minority for program purposes?

VOICE: I'd like to ask Mr. Cone something that bears on this same question. I'd judge from what Mr. Hall said at the Emmy ceremony, that he felt that he sold more greeting cards with Macbeth than he would have sold with Untouchables. Now is that the truth? Just to what extent can a sponsor expect to get credit with the rank and file of his potential customers for sponsoring quality programming as distinguished from just a spot announcement that appears anywhere—in a magazine or connected with any other type program?

VOICE: Depends on what he's selling!

CONE: Well I think the answer to that is that in the case of Mr. Hall, of Hallmark, this is really an institutional proposition; and I think this is quite different from selling soap or cigarettes or other specific items. Mr. Hall is selling Hallmark cards for Hallmark quality. And the buyer makes the specific card choice.

VOICE: Don't you think he sold more cards with Macbeth than he would have sold if he'd had a spot with Untouchables or some other program that would have had a larger number in its audience?

CONE: This is a very special case. Hallmark has done very well with the kind of programming they've done because it's been possible to extend the effectiveness into the schools as well as into the family, with the feeling that Hallmark is an exceptional manufacturer in a field where artistry and good taste are all important. Not a particular, competitive product advantage. But an over-all quality. And assurance of impeccable taste.

CONE: Before I stop may I say one thing to the previous gentleman: I'd like to know too, what's good and what's bad? I would also like to know what we mean by "Public Service"?

COONS: Well could I ask one more question? If you're not sure what the standard should be—could you tell me if the people who do "Lassie" could do anything else? Could they do something different from "Lassie" whether it's better or worse?

McCOLLOUGH: Jack, you never can tell! It's like, How long is a piece of string? How high is up? What's good and what's bad? You don't know until you try! Maybe you'll make it!

McGILL: Doesn't it come down finally to something that probably a competitive industry can't do? The first time you go to a museum, an art museum, you probably don't like it, you're bored with it. But when you're interested in an artist, or painter, or sculptor or something and you learn a little about it, and you go back, and after you've seen a museum or art gallery, then you like it very much. So that if plays like Macbeth could be produced with some regularity, of this quality, I assume in time this rating would climb.

But then again, I've common sense enough to know that the cost of this makes such a learning process prohibitive, which probably brings us back to the educational television chain which could do these things.

You mentioned sir, the Atlanta station. This has been an interesting thing, bearing on Mr. Minow's point about getting the sets made with the ability to tune in on these channels.

The Atlanta teaching operation by television happens to have been a very successful one, because they were lucky enough to get good television teachers. And we've had a growing demand from parents who say: "I would like to look at what my child is looking at. They come home and talk about it, and they're interested in what they've learned on television," and then they go down and the dealer says it will cost $35.00 to convert your set, and this discourages quite a number of people.

It seemed to me that we could, all of us could get behind this move, to work out the necessary transition time to have all sets supplied with this; which would then seem to me to be the great opening up of the other type stations.

JAFFE: I want to take very strong objection to the way in which Mr. McCollough has put this question, or what he says "Is the question." And Mr. Cone says he "associates himself with the question," but I don't quite believe it!

I think it's a false question. It isn't the question we're really talking about at all! The question isn't what's good, and what's bad, the question is whether there is to be a balance, whether there is to be an opportunity for satisfying a variety of tastes. Now, if you say, "Well what are these tastes?" that is I think a complete "red herring." I don't think there's any question that our whole culture, our whole education, our ideals tell us that there's a difference between Abraham Lincoln's Gettysburg Address and some demagogic speech which may have its purposes. I think everybody admits that there's a difference between Macbeth and "The Untouchables." I don't have to say what the difference is between Macbeth and "The Untouchables." Our culture states that there is a difference between them, that Shakespeare is different!

McCollough: If you had to sign an application for a license renewal you'd have to say!

Jaffe: No you wouldn't have to say at all! The question is, "Are there to be a certain number of Macbeths and a certain number of 'Untouchables'?"

McCollough: Well, I've signed them and you haven't; and I tell you, you do!

Minow: Clair, we never ask any licensee, "How many good programs did you put on; and how many bad programs did you put on?"

McCollough: No, no—that's right. And that could be the trouble!

I don't know whether to go home and say: "From now on we're going to put on 75 per cent bad and 25 per cent good," or "75 per cent good and 25 per cent bad."

Minow: The most we've ever done was to take a set of categories which were developed originally by the industry—not by the government—and to put them on an application form breaking down certain categories.

Now never, that I know of—and I pray never will it happen in the future—has the government ever said "That was a poor program; that was a good program, you've got to make a change." We've never dreamed of anything like that. I think we might as well just see a free society disappear if we ever got into that kind of an atmosphere.

What we're talking about is what Professor Jaffe said is a "balance" which the industry itself recognizes; it is the networks' term, and the broadcasters' term when they say "balanced programming." We're in complete agreement.

PIERSON: I think I must agree with the historical development of the standards cited by Mr. Minow; and I think the broadcasters were primarily responsible for developing even the definitions of them—and then found that the definitions meant nothing! And then complained that the Commission adopted them! I think he is wrong, that the Commission has never condemned an individual program. "Mae West" was one, and "War of the Worlds," was one.

I think on the problem of definition of "Good or Bad," I agree with Professor Jaffe. It seems to me to be irrelevant, because that has not been the Commission's approach. If you're talking about "program content," the Commission has, however, condemned whole categories of programs by implication. Now I don't know whether it's good, if you condemn whole categories of programs and remove a hundred of them, but bad if you remove one.

The other problem of definition seems to me to be particularly in the area of education. As we've had this discussion today, it seems to me that we've been talking about a certain type of educational program; and I would like for us not to leave the subject without suggesting with some support, by dictum in the Supreme Court, that it isn't only the teachers who educate; it's not only the direct approach to instruction that educates—as a matter of fact, artistic expressions subtly educate perhaps far more, in many instances, than the direct approach to education. And I'd like to give you some examples; and I'm doing this because I think we're wrong to say that "entertainment doesn't educate." Even if it's good, or bad, entertainment programming—it frequently educates.

But let's assume we consider only movies and present television fare. Who can say that a talk by a local teacher or professor should be a favored category and movies and television such as the following be disfavored as teaching vehicles: "Advise and Consent," "The Alamo," "Cimarron," "Drums Along the Mohawk," "Northwest Passage," all the movies about Alexander Graham Bell, Curies, Pasteur, Edison, "Sunrise at Campobello," "Diary of Anne Frank," "Exodus," and "The Last Hurrah"— you can go on to endless numbers of purely entertainment pieces that I insist "teach," and the broadcast industry has carried those and continues to carry them. And some of them are in the un-favored categories, many of them old movies.

You find many things that are broadcast as entertainment pieces that deal very definitely with controversial issues: Integration, the labor problem, narcotics problem, alcoholism, all of which are very important subjects of the day.

And it's not difficult to find many movies and much broadcast programming that are entertaining in their thrust, but cover a very wide host of religious subjects, and that teach religious principles and morals.

I'm not saying that they're a substitute for this other, but I don't believe that education necessarily excludes entertainment programs or movies.

GOELET: I would like to exclude myself from Mr. McCollough's blanket indictment that people spoke "categorically" in terms of what is good programming. I went to some pains to say that it seemed to me that one of the most difficult problems to be decided is how one should determine the "balance" between functional elements and qualitative elements.

As to Professor Coons, I'd just like to make this one observation: I think that if there's a demand for Cadillacs, there will be Cadillacs and people to build Cadillacs.

TAISHOFF: Just a few loose ends: First, a footnote on Commissioner King's comment earlier on the British system, and what he called "Government Ownership." The British will deny that; they'll challenge it. They say they have a "State Corporation" which is not a government operation. In effect, it is a licensed operation by the government; their revenue does come not only from license fees on receivers, but also from advertising in commercial publications which the British Broadcasting Company produces, and which are very successful.

Now, I think in 1955, the British set up a parallel system of broadcasting which was, and is, commercially operated, and is highly successful. It gets no revenue from receiving sets, or from publications. It gets its revenue through commercial sponsorship. Now that commercial sponsorship is the first phase of the "magazine concept" it seems to me, but for a different reason.

In Britain they have two parallel systems, there are two networks, and that's essentially all there is, it's a small area geographically, and they operate on the basis of rotating spots which are sold at premium rates. This same system to some degree has been adopted almost everywhere in the world except Russia and the Satellite countries. They're all adopting what was originally the American plan of commercial sponsorship. Not so much free enterprise, but commercial sponsorship.

I'd like to get to Mr. Novik's comment about no worth-while programming on radio—that there's no forum, no platform. I think there are hundreds of platforms. I know that in Washington, for example, practically all members of Congress make tapes, video tapes, commentaries for the people back home, and some on a local or a regional basis rather than on a network basis. Whenever the President of the United States appears on television he also appears on all radio networks. So I think there is considerable public service programming.

Now on the political broadcast Section 315. I'm given to understand that this is the background, or the origin of 315. Back in 1927, when the Radio Act was under consideration, the Chairman of the Senate Interstate Commerce Committee was Senator Big Jim Watson, Republican, Indiana, and there was a Senator Smith Brookhart, of Iowa. Both had tremendous interest in radio.

But they wanted to do something about time for political broadcasting, and political campaigning. So they asked the old Federal Radio Commission which had just been created to give them some idea. The result was what is now Section 315. It was the Federal Radio Commission's recommendation.

Now just one other little observation here. I'd like to read a little quote: "In the 66 Years, from 1895 to now, the top 15 'Best Sellers' included: 3 inspirational books; 2 cookbooks; 1 book on baby care; and 9 novels. The baby book of course is one that you know, Dr. Spock; you're familiar with two of the inspirational books, Dale Carnegie's *How To Win Friends*, and Charles Sheldon's *In His Steps*. Of the novels, *God's Little Acre* by Erskine Caldwell was a dirty book, *Peyton Place* was a dirty book. Those are two of the nine. The remaining seven novels among the best sellers of the past 66 years were all written by the same man, and his name—Mickey Spillane." And that's a quote from Max Wally, the author.

MICKELSON: I think we would have to take into consideration the more rapid and cheap transportation of products, and also the great growth in population.

VOICE: Well we're back to the same question: What's a good program and what's a bad one?

MINOW: I would also add that books aren't published under licenses from the government. Anyone who wants to publish a book can do it; I would also add probably that if you'd put stag movies on television they would get an excessively high rating.

ANOTHER VOICE: Is that a good program or a bad program?

NOVIK: I'd hate to leave Professor Coons hanging up in the air; I think there is absolutely all the evidence that is necessary to prove to him, in the recent testimony in New York of some of the craftsmen that there is an overabundance of talented craftsmen that are able to turn out the kind of programs that you're talking about. I think the Nash group are now doing a lot of programs that they would consider just programs to make a living; that there are enough people available to do the kind of programs that we refer to.

MICKELSON: Leonard made the point I wanted to make which relates to the question that Clair McCollough raised a little while ago, the question of "good" or "bad." It seems to me that whenever a group of persons sits down to a discussion of this sort, you naturally run into a great number of undefined terms. Another one was referred to, "balanced programs." What is a "public service program"? I have no idea what one is. I would prefer to think in terms of informational programs on the one hand; and educational on the other.

We talked about the needs of the community. Nobody really knows what the needs of the community are; we haven't defined the needs of the community. We've been talking about "public responsibility" of broadcasters; nobody really knows what public responsibility is. We've been talking in terms of another—I think cliche—or unproved assertion at least, concerning the failure of the licensees to accept public affairs programs.

I expect before tomorrow is over we'll have some discussion about the "golden era," and nobody will really know what the "golden era" is, and we really won't know whether the "golden era" was really very good or very bad. It probably actually would look pretty bad in terms of 1961 standards.

But out of this I think there are some important conclusions. We started this meeting I believe with a discussion concerning the improvement of broadcasting; and I believe there was at least a strong suggestion in Professor Jaffe's speech that the government needs stronger powers of program control, in order to accomplish some of what we have since been wrapping up within these cliches and bromides and generalizations.

It seems to me that when this effort is made to improve these programs, whether they do or do not need improvement—and I'm not going to argue that there isn't a lot of mediocrity in programming—that somebody then is going to have to define these terms, and going to have to define them quite precisely.

At the point when that definition comes about, then, somebody is going to have to make up his mind what is good and bad; somebody is going to have to make up his mind what is balanced and what is unbalanced; somebody is going to have to make up his mind what is public responsibility and what is not public responsibility; somebody is going to have to make up his mind what is public service and what is not public service.

At this point, it seems to me, some single individual, or some commission of government, is going to have to step in and exercise a good deal of control over the tastes of the public—which is made up of some nearly 200,000,000 persons.

It seems to me to that extent, it is quite important that we do consider here the meanings of some of these terms; what are we talking about is imposition at some time or other, in the future of controls based upon these very vaguely defined terms.

VOICE: I would think it would be a great tragedy sir, if we tried to define what is "good," because the minute you define something as "good" then you limit it to that definition, and you would prevent any expansion. I prefer to keep them vague.

MICKELSON: In fact that's precisely what I meant. The moment that we commence regulation based upon these terms, then we here are discussing what's good and what's bad for the public and we're starting to impose our will upon the tastes of the great masses of the people. Are we in a position to do it, or, is a government agency in position to do it? Are not these terms essentially undefinable?

VOICE: Then I misunderstood; I thought you said we must do it, "We must define."

REINSCH: Well, somebody's going to have to do it some time in the future. If in fact our standards are going to be based upon these cliches that we're setting here; I think we'd be getting into a dangerous position, of somebody determining content for the whole public upon terribly vague standards.

VOICE: It's the broadcasters' responsibility to make those decisions—it's the broadcaster's. It's not the government's. The only place the government can come into this thing is the question of some supervision to assure a good faith effort on the part of the broadcaster to perform. And I don't think many broadcasters would say that they have a responsibility that's less than a good faith effort to do a good job.

MINOW: If a broadcaster for a period of a 3-year license, put on only Mickey Spillane dramatizations, day in and day out, seven days a week, would you say the government was helpless to do anything about the use of that frequency?

MICKELSON: Yes sir, I do!

NOVIK: Mr. Mickelson, on that point I'd like to ask you a practical question: Is a broadcaster, who broadcasts only news and music—and it doesn't make any difference as far as I'm concerned whether it's classical music or rock 'n roll—is such a broadcaster—who does absolutely nothing else—living up to his responsibility as a licensee? Has not the FCC an obligation to Congress to enforce the Communications Act? And while you are at it, Sig, here is another practical question: Is the operator of a TV station in a major city like New York or Los Angeles, who received his license after a competitive hearing, living up to his responsibility by putting on old movies and an occasional news broadcast? This is not a theoretical question. It is being done.

CONE: I just don't want Mr. Novik's to be the only answer to Professor Coons. I don't believe there are enough people alive to write good dramas for American television. And I just got through going through 1,500 manuscripts submitted to the Hallmark people, original ones, and I'm afraid that only two will ever go on the air.

KING: Mr. Minow mentions this fellow that puts on three years of Mickey Spillane. Of course, we're talking about something that doesn't happen. When I was on the Commission, one of the things that always concerned me in connection with programming, was simply the practicality of how you are going to determine that a licensee has discharged whatever responsibility there is in the public interest.

Bear in mind that a licensee's performance is reviewed by the

Commission over a three-year period. Now let's assume again, for the sake of argument, that "The Untouchables" was a poor show. But the same station that puts on "The Untouchables" also put on Winston Churchill, and there will be many instances of the same sort of thing over the 3-year period. How is anybody in the government, or incidentally in the NAB, going to determine that a station did or did not serve the public interest, on the basis of their overall programming for a three-year period? That's the problem that always worried me.

> [*The conversations in this section of Appendix II followed the delivery of the paper by Dean Barrow and the comment thereon by Mr. Pierson, both of which appear earlier in this book.*]

MINOW: I think every human being is imperfect, and I think I'm far less perfect than most. But I must take very vigorous exception to Mr. Pierson's violently imperfect rewriting or restating of what are supposed to be my views. I have never advocated or suggested or thought of centralized control of communications.

It is not for nothing that I have been a member of the American Civil Liberties Union concerned about liberty and free speech for a long time. This was precisely to encourage diversity and to discourage conformity. I would also note that the Federal Communication Commission study of network practices and programming practices was undertaken by Dean Barrow in 1955, long before I ever arrived on the scene.

Now I respect Mr. Pierson's views, but I think his anger is with the law, and with the role the courts and the Congress have given the Commission, rather than anything else. His views, as he indicated at the end of his remarks, are conspicuously lacking in legal authority. The law is the other way, so his quarrel really is with the system that Congress and the courts have established.

The worst thing we could ever do in this country, it seems to me, is to centralize broadcasting into one place to require conformity. The facts of the matter are, however, that today broadcasting is centralized. It's centralized in the hands of very, very few people. Very few people today decide what a hundred and eighty million people are going to see on television, what they're going to spend their time with. It is precisely to break these centers of control that the Commission, and the country, I think, should be, and I think are deeply concerned. If the argument is that the law is wrong, the place to make that argument is in the halls of Congress and in the courts. But as long as the law and the duty has been trusted to me and my colleagues, I believe we will faithfully follow it.

The unfortunate fact of life which I tried to emphasize yesterday, and which Mr. Pierson does not accept, is that broadcasting is unique. As the Supreme Court said in the *NBC* case, unfortunately not every one who wants to broadcast can do so. Would that it were otherwise. If it were, I don't think we'd be here today. Would that it were possible for everyone who wanted a frequency to have one. But as long as we are dealing with a scarce commodity, Congress decided long ago that these precious resources must be used in the public interest. It's painful and tortuous to decide on a case by case basis what it means to serve the public interest, but this is a fact we must face rather than quarrel about the law or talk in terms of getting a second class mail privilege for other media of communication—for newspapers, or talk about using the highways. Access to the highways and to the second class mail privilege are unlimited. Anyone who wants one, who is qualified, can have one. There is not just a matter of three that are available for magazines or two that are available for newspapers. So this is the central fact of life in broadcasting. We have to face up to that as Congress did, as the courts have done many times, and turn our heads to the future, rather than quarrel with the past.

JAFFE: Well, I admire tremendously Mr. Pierson's statement, its intensity and its passion, its sincerity and true feeling. I also agree with some of his arguments, though they're more or less subsidiary arguments, not central.

I, too, react against the notion that I hear so much stated that the broadcaster is using some kind of a public property and, therefore, he is a trustee, and he has to account. I think his analogies to the Post Office and the roads, and the fact that none of us can operate without all kinds of uses of public property, is absolutely sound, as a matter of law. I tried to put it myself, and I didn't succeed in convincing my wife that I put it very well, so I dropped it out. But I think Mr. Pierson really put it excellently; the kind of statement that's being made to the effect that a public property is being used and, therefore, you can demand this or that, and that the First Amendment doesn't apply, is the sort of thing that Mr. Justice Brandeis dissented from in the famous *Burleson* case, when a majority seemed to use the same argument with respect to the second class mailing privilege; that since it was a privilege, you could make all kinds of restrictions on free speech. I deplore this use of privilege. I deplore this argument that in some way or other, because you first set up this abstraction about the air waves being a public property, you thereby get your hooks in, and you can begin to do all sorts of things you couldn't otherwise do. But I don't think that's very central.

I would like to see Mr. Minow recede to, and stake his flag simply on the notion that this is a scarce thing, that it is an absolutely basic and vital method of communication and that it's of a limited character and, therefore, there must be some control of access to it. I can't agree with Mr. Pierson on a number of grounds.

First, as Mr. Minow says, and as he, himself, admits, the law doesn't sustain him. We've accepted, as I suggested yesterday, the notion that we can control political discussion by requiring equal time. This to my mind, as I said yesterday, is a far, far more significant and vital control of the business of speaking, not the content, but of the whole mechanics of speaking, than anything remotely suggested in the notion of the balanced program. I think, I feel that Mr. Pierson has kind of glorified this word, the notion of freedom and the notion of censorship somewhat in the way Mr. Justice Black has done where he sets it up as a sort of glowing ideal and then you can't make, from that point on, any distinctions whatever, because as soon as you make a distinction, why then everything is gone. You can't, for example, say to a broadcaster, "Why haven't you got a news program?" Because if he hasn't got a news program, and then you make him put the news program on, you're coercing him. Well, I agree, of course you're coercing him. But I think one has to go back to the function of free speech. The function of free speech is to promote discussion by the general public so that they can, over the course of years, make the proper adjustments to changes and also express themselves. It's very important just to be able to talk and express yourself. Now, how does telling a broadcaster to put on some news programs or to have a little agriculture, or to make some weather reports contravene this function of free speech? Quite honestly, I don't see it!

Of course you can eventually—like Mr. Pierson, who is a brilliant lawyer, and like all brilliant lawyers—begin pushing the thing and pushing the thing and point out that if it comes down to

one program, and if there were only one program available, only
one news program in the whole United States, so that he would
have to put on that one, you would actually be compelling him to
put on a specific thing. This is what they call a parade of horribles.
That doesn't seem to me to be what is involved. Of course you can
put it any way you want: you can say, "All right, it is censorship,
but a certain amount of censorship is involved in our society." Or
you can say it isn't censorship. I'd rather go back, not to whether
it is or it isn't, but to what the function of free speech is, and I
don't think that the requirement of balance in any way impairs
the function of free speech. I agree with Chairman Minow, I
don't think free speech is impaired by what he has suggested.
What precisely it will amount to we can only tell in the future by
the way Mr. Minow performs.

Nor do I think it is going to result in a greater and greater conformity. My idea would be that it would involve some diversity.
Concerning conformity Mr. Pierson introduced an important particular about which we disagreed yesterday and concerning which
Mr. Minow said he didn't quite know and Mr. Novik said he did.
And that is, whether, as we get more and more channels we might
think of diversity of balance in terms of the whole market rather
than in terms of particular stations.

Indeed, I'm sure that very few of us would disagree. This is by
far the better approach. It's just precisely what we are heading
for. But that I think is an administrative problem. It's partly
whether we are going to get enough channels, and partly to what
extent you can administer this whole concept or idea in terms of
a market rather than in terms of particular licensees. And, as Mr.
Minow said, and as we all know, "It's a baffling problem!"

Now, I just want to make one other comment. Maybe we're not
going to get on to the question of control by the chains of the local
broadcaster and what not; it was a little bit suggested by Mr. Barrow. I feel that there is a tremendously unresolved conflict here.
I think it's going to be one of the important things before the Commission. I thought there was going to be considerable discussion
of this difficult and rather technical problem. And Mr. Barrow
presents us with what is known to be the case; namely, that programming, particularly in prime time of a licensee, is pretty much
controlled by the chains. At one point, he seems to suggest that
that's more or less necessarily so because of the cost of programs. But then, in a rather unresolved way, he sets over it this

notion, that well this is somehow against the responsibility of the licensee to make his own choices, and I suppose it is, but in terms of what we're trying to get—good television—it doesn't seem to me to help very much to simply present this unresolved dilemma. Which is it we're most concerned about at this point, from the point of view of government policy? Encouraging a mechanism that will improve programs or emphasizing the responsibility of particular licensees? This seems to me what is involved and just possibly it comes ultimately down to a matter of ways and means as to how the Commission is going to face the chain broadcasting problem. I listened to Mr. Minow's feeling about the matter yesterday, and he expressed the idea he seemed to respond to the suggestion of the magazine concept by advancing the notion that as a matter of law it might be better to give up local responsibility in order to encourage this magazine concept. But he said that would require a change in the law. Well, I'm not much of a believer in the likelihood of changes of this sort in the law, and so I think that a response in such terms is an evasion. I think the Commission has probably got to face this kind of a problem on the basis of the present law. In other words I rather doubt you're going to get a change in the statute saying the local licensee doesn't have any responsibility—that it all depends on chains— I don't think we're ever going to get a statute like that. But on the other hand, I don't think that we can keep talking out of the two sides of our mouth at the same time—I don't think we can keep pointing out that this is a very expensive thing to get good programs, that we'll probably have to have them somewhat organized on a national basis and then turn around very quickly and say, "but of course a licensee has to be absolutely free." I have the feeling that there's an awful lot of double talk. It seems to me that that is a very important and difficult, I call technical, problem. It probably doesn't go to roots of our great question of freedom and responsibility.

KING: I'm extremely pleased to hear Professor Jaffe talk about this proposition that the public own the air waves and when the right to use one is granted to a licensee, he is therefore using public property and must act in the public interest. That has always impressed me as being a myth. In the first place, the air waves—I'm speaking now as a lawyer—are incapable of ownership. They are absolutely worthless unless somebody uses them.

I have a vague recollection back in my early years in law school that something had to be capable of being reduced to possession before it could be owned.

Moreover you can disprove the proposition historically. The regulatory scheme as we know it today came into existence in 1927, when the government assumed the power to regulate the use of the air waves. But there was a good deal of broadcasting going on before that time. I think KDKA was organized back in 1920 or thereabouts. WWJ, in my home town, purports to be even older. In any event there was lots of broadcasting prior to 1927 and those who were doing it certainly weren't stealing something. So this public property concept simply isn't true and I'm pleased that Professor Jaffe has some misgivings about it.

Another point he made was that it is not a violation of free speech to require a broadcaster to put on a news program. If you look at it that way, it's true, but if you look at the other side of the coin, any time you require a broadcaster to put on a news program you are requiring him to put something else off. . . .

VOICE: Well? So!

JAFFE: Well, it still goes back to the question, what is the function of free speech? You're just juggling, it seems to me! What you do, is you start with a great concept, but then you reduce it to a word, censorship, then you come down and say more about restraint—this would be a restraint, that would be a restraint. I say go back to the function of free speech, which is to promote political, social, and artistic discourse among our people. Furthermore, I'm not the kind that believes with the Supreme Court that you've always got to do down to the last ditch and cross every *t*, dot every *i*, and every time you interfere with anything a little bit, in this interchange, the Constitution is gone, as Mr. Justice Black would say! I'm very hostile to that whole point of view.

PIERSON: I have no better than and probably worse than an even break in present legal authorities. It seems to me that you have just conceded that I might get the break the other way in the one that decides the final law.

JAFFE: I think you might well get the break, for example, if the FCC were to say: (here you begin, to my mind, to get a close case) "We don't like all these violence programs that this licensee has been putting on. They're in very bad taste, they're excessive, and as someone expressed to me last night, the violence has just been put in, it isn't necessary to the story." But if you argued that to the Supreme Court, I think probably you'd lose.

PIERSON: Do you think you could win *Schuler* in the Supreme Court today?

JAFFE: I think they might win *Schuler* on the ground that he was using the thing to commit a crime.

PIERSON: That's the point I'm making!

JAFFE: But you're making the point you can't use that form of sanction at all.

PIERSON: No, I think *Schuler* could have been denied without placing it on the basis that it was, and so could *Brinkley*. The Commission has long had a rule, and I think quite a proper one, that a broadcast frequency cannot be used for private communication and as an adjunct to your business. But in cases of both *Brinkley* and *Schuler*, this is precisely what they were doing. Now, the Commission has been given the power to classify frequencies according to uses. This is the only way it could be done. You couldn't have private people using broadcast channels, fire and state police and enforcement agencies using the same channels, so the Commission said we'll set aside this number of channels for broadcasting, and then for a host of other purposes, many of them purely private, which is the kind of thing Brinkley and Schuler were doing, and they could have said you can't use it.

JAFFE: You couldn't tell a newspaper that it couldn't use its facilities for private enterprises of any sort it wants.

PIERSON: No, no, the Commission is not telling them they can't use radio for the purposes they have stated. The Commission is telling them that you can't use this band for that purpose.

KING: Well, it seems to me also in connection with the newspaper, here we have a specific statute which says that licensing must be done in the public interest; and where the licensee is using the airways for the purpose of promoting purely a private interest such as Brinkley and Schuler were, I think you've got an entirely different problem from the newspaper situation.

And then we get to this matter of examining overall programming which Mr. Minow spoke about yesterday. These cases are old, and they tend to get stretched a little bit; and I think it's considerably in doubt whether or not *Brinkley* and the other cases give to the Commission the authority to review overall programming except for obvious abuses such as the *Brinkley* case, and the type of thing that I mentioned yesterday, when I said that I conceded to the government the power to impose minimum standards of program content that would be obviously offensive to the public health, safety and morals.

One other point and then I'll quit. During the course of Dean Barrow's remarks, particularly on this Advisory Committee, I couldn't help but think, if this group sitting around here today, that are intimately concerned with television and that sort of thing, could not get a concensus as to the proper way to improve television, I have some question about the desirability or the efficiency of a council such as Dean Barrow suggested.

MINOW: Professor Jaffe, before we leave the "law"—because I think for the benefit of both the lawyers and non-lawyers we are now thoroughly confused—I understood yesterday that you were in substantial agreement with the legal conclusion that the Commission did have authority to review a licensee's overall programming. Now is that correct, or incorrect?

JAFFE: Yes.

MINOW: But you've left the impression that the Commission should not have anything to do with programming, so I'd like you to explain that more clearly.

JAFFE: It ends up that I agree with the main position of Chairman Minow that they can take into account the whole program. And if that isn't censorship! I do have a problem when you get down to the point of saying: "Well, there are an awful lot of violence programs on this; and an awful lot of sex." I have a problem there, both from the constitutional point of view, and, from the point of view of whether that's practical.

The thing that seems clearly to me within the power of the Commission is to say, "Why hasn't there been any time devoted to public service programs; why don't you have adequate news programs; why don't you have agriculture?" I think that an approach along this line is legal particularly when as I suggested yesterday it's done on a fairly minimum basis, and not in strict percentages, and that sort of thing.

This seems to me to be the kind of thing that the Court has indicated from your citations yesterday, from your brief, as appropriate, and I take it, appropriate under the statute, and not violating the First Amendment, and also more or less administrable. I recognize it's difficult.

MINOW: Well the reason I asked was just to have the record clear, because I'm confident otherwise there would have been a great deal of confusion. Thank you.

COONS: I was going to ask Professor Jaffe a question, prefacing it by saying that I agree that it's impossible to talk in terms of abstractions about free speech and censorship and make too much good sense. We have to talk in terms of—I think you called it—"the function of free speech." Walter Lippmann talks about this a lot. He says that after all, you've got to preserve the medium as an arena where you can debate.

The trouble is that if you look at it that way, it's hard to know what programs perform this function. Traditionally I suppose you'd say, "Well it's the discussion programs and the news programs," what we would call public service, and so forth.

But as Mr. Pierson pointed out yesterday, education comes from all kinds of sources on the air, and you never know what kind of program is going to perform best the free speech function.

I don't want to overemphasize that because I personally have the feeling that some programs are more valuable in this respect than others—but the minute you've said that you've started to set some kind of standard in motion that you have to implement with words and it becomes very, very difficult for the Commission to say which kinds of programs will best preserve free speech. And I wondered, do you see some standard for distinction?

JAFFE: I wasn't addressing myself at all to that point. I was not addressing myself to the question of how TV would serve free speech; I wasn't remotely addressing myself to that question.

I was addressing myself to the question whether telling a person to put some news programs on would violate the right of free speech. I wasn't addressing myself to the thing you say Walter Lippmann was addressing himself to, "How can TV be made a good medium of free speech?"

PIERSON: You agree that that would be unconstitutional for the government to attempt, do you not?

JAFFE: No. I don't think I do. I think that I regard all the media as media of free speech, and that since this is a limited media. . . .

PIERSON: It's not any more limited than the newspapers.

JAFFE: Yes it is. I think it is more.

PIERSON: Well there are about three times as many broadcast

stations as there are daily newspapers. Now it doesn't seem to me to make any difference, whether the limitations in terms of numbers arises from scarcity because of a limited natural resource, or arises from scarcity because of the inability of our economic system to support more; or, arises from scarcity from any number of other reasons. It seems to me the limitation is the important fact. And if the limitation exists in terms of numbers, in any medium, it seems that you can justify equally invading one or the other.

VOICE: It is always possible for a paper to be published about agriculture, or a little magazine. . . .

PIERSON: Well now this is where I disagree! Unless you define what you mean by "possibility."

If "possibility" includes the economic possibility of any person doing that, it's much more limited at this time than the broadcasting is.

VOICE: You cannot make a statement about agriculture unless you get a license to use a frequency. Nothing can go out about agriculture unless somebody's licensed to use a frequency. Now if all the people who have frequencies say "No agriculture!"— then no agriculture goes out!

PIERSON: If this were a possibility, then I think he may have some argument. But that hasn't happened and it will not happen. There's no basis to conclude that it will happen. And as a matter of fact, it isn't true, that the small specialized magazines or the large newspapers can really operate effectively without a government permit from the Postmaster General. They use the public domain; they have a license; and if there is a limitation imposed upon the number that there can be, it doesn't seem to me to be important from what source this limitation comes.

CONE: I would like to get back to something that came up in Dean Barrow's discussion. Although I didn't have a copy of all of his remarks, I was struck by something that I think is unfortunate, and I hope we can get at it somewhere, perhaps not today but some day soon, and away from some of the generalities with which this whole business is strewn.

I'll just take one line. No, I'll take two. One I can quote, that somewhere in the national, what was it, the President's Committee on National Purpose, that you quoted from, stated that "television has the lowest standard of any art form." This is just one of these wonderful things that I'd like to have somebody explain a little bit to me some day. If this is a lower art form than the paper backs that are for sale in every drug store and bus and railroad station in the country—I want to have it explained "How come?" I don't believe it!

And another thing that's typical of some of these generalities; I've got one "pip" that didn't come out of this meeting, that I want to refer to.

But one that was in Dean Barrow's remarks again was that "Advertiser and agency participation in program production is a very important part, and a questionable part of the operation of television in the U. S." I think this was absolutely true ten years ago; absolutely untrue today. Somebody has to tell me who the advertisers are; who the agencies are—that are doing it! I work for a fairly large advertising agency; for our clients we buy something in excess of $50,000,000 worth of television a year, and nobody lets us tell them anything! I was asking Mr. Goldenson and Mr. Treyz yesterday afternoon if we helped them in any way with the seven or eight programs in which we participate on their network. And they only laughed, because they won't let anybody help them! They certainly don't let us.

I think we have eight million for one client, don't we? Eight million ought to give you by these rules something to say! But it doesn't give us anything to say.

And the point is: Nobody, today, is letting advertiser or agent do it. I want to read you a little thing so you don't think this is just something that I dreamed up for rebuttal. Let me read you a few lines from a published statement by Mr. William S. Paley, Chairman of the Board of Columbia Broadcasting System, that was made to the CBS affiliates on May 5th of this year, and subsequently published and sent around to everybody in the business. And I quote: "The price of freedom is always sooner or later resolute action, often in the face of alternatives that are easier, more immediately possible.

"This circumstance has no novelty for CBS. In 1946 for example it seemed clear to me that broadcasting stood at the crossroads. We have been jogging comfortably along the road providing time for advertising agencies to fill the programs—chosen by them; controlled by them; and produced by them or by outside packagers answerable to them.

"Except for news and public affairs we had little creative role in what went on the air. Audiences went up and down as a result of someone else's decision.

"At CBS we made up our minds to take another road, to assume a direct role in programming; to create programs; to enlist talent; to plan the use of our time. Despite threats and warnings we took action. Even though many of our programs were at first unsponsored we eventually led the radio industry to new heights of prosperity and achievement."

And please listen: "By 1953, following the same pattern we attained the same position in TV." End of the quote. Now that's Mr. Paley! So I just hope that somewhere along the line the programming which has been so much a part of our discussion can be and will be tagged, where it ought to be tagged!

May I repeat to you that ten years ago this was not true. I'm talking about now.

BARROW: May I just say that I'm not referring to ten years ago, when of course the participation of the advertiser and agency was much greater than today; I appreciate that the participation by advertiser and agency in creative control of programming is less now than it was ten years ago. But I was quoting in this paper from statements made by representatives of the networks themselves, in the Commission's recent hearings on programming, regarding the participation of advertisers and advertising agencies. And it was Dr. Stanton who testified for CBS in this instance, and he stated that "in the creative aspects of production the sponsor and advertiser might well participate with them at each and every step of the way." Those are his words. Incidentally, I did not . . .

CONE: Mr. Stanton and Mr. Paley had better get together! Mr. Stanton is president of CBS.

BARROW: Well, it might be. I don't know who's supposed to know; one statement was made at one time and for one purpose; and another was stated at another time for another purpose.

Incidentally Mr. Cone, I was not indicating that it was necessarily bad that this distribution took place! Whether the network controls, in the interest of the advertiser, or the network divides control with the advertiser and agency, the result may be about the same.

CONE: Well I think it would be bad.

BARROW: Well I wasn't saying so. I was really writing here in a reportorial way, to describe the participation by advertiser and advertising agencies and networks in the control of programming.

I appreciate that the networks today have a much greater weight in this function than they did ten years ago, at the time that you are quoting from Mr. Paley's statement.

CONE: This is just to the point of these generalities. Let me quote *Time* magazine, which had the following to say about the recent FCC hearings, and this is a direct quotation from Mr. George Jessel. I'd put him up as a fine expert, too:

"During the recent tour to raise funds for the Israeli Government, the speaker offered a box of candy or cigars to anyone in his audience who had ever had a phone call from the TV Rating Service. I took a gamble," said Jessel, "but no one came forward."

"Now this testimonial to the absurdity of TV rating," says *Time*, "was given at a special FCC hearing in Manhattan." And so the notion was broadcast that television audience research is pure humbug.

Now I know that people in this audience don't believe it, but this is what goes to the public. Another man who was at this hearing and who was quoted by *Time* was Mr. Worthington Miner, sometime Studio One, as you know, and Play of the Week producer. And he had a fantastic accusation to help things along and he said—and I quote—to the FCC Committee:

"Sponsors often insist on contracts specifying a *minimum* number of killings or shootings per program."

Well this is just plain untrue! Just plain untrue. It's no more true than for Mr. Robert L. Aurthur, the playwright, to describe:

"The cold slitted eyes of advertising men." Can't you see it? But this kind of thing is really upsetting to the public.

QUAAL: Well I know better, Leonard, than to challenge my very good friend of many years, Ted Pierson. Having great respect for him personally and professionally, I do not intend to question his greater knowledge of the constitution. I think he made a very fine statement.

I should like as a broadcaster, however, to address myself briefly to the matter of balanced programming. After all, there's only one thing inherent in the Communications Act that counts program-wise, and it's the underlying statutory philosophy set forth in Section 303, namely, "the public interest, convenience and necessity." How can you satisfy that without balanced programming?

Now as we visited here yesterday I couldn't help but think of the Chairman's comments in regard to the balance that has developed, relatively speaking; and I still say, basically the industry is good, and has done a great deal during its first twelve young years. And I was glad that Mr. Cone spoke for the record as one of our great advertising leaders on that subject yesterday. But I feel that every station does have an obligation to produce balanced programming as set forth in the categories: Education, Religion, Discussion, Agriculture, etc.

I do not agree with Governor Collins on specialized stations. Who is to go to Washington, D. C., or Albuquerque, or to Duluth, Minnesota and say: "Mr. Cone, you run a classical music station; Mr. Cottone, you operate a rock 'n roll station"?

And I say, gentlemen, it is unfair to the licensee who is trying to fulfill his obligations, with a franchise, who is programming on a well-rounded over all basis, to compete with a man who has a stack of 40–50 rock 'n roll platters, or, for that matter, an endless library of classical recordings!

That is one point where I disagree with Governor Collins in what was in every other respect I think a truly great speech!

I think that all Mr. Minow needs to get his job done, and I know he's very sincere and extremely dedicated, is the continuance of emphasis on balanced programming and rededication of all licensees to the greatly strengthened NAB code! I think the Code has done a tremendous job!

Beyond this point, I think we have a renewed enlightenment of our industry to improve its programming. I'd say we're "under way" after these first twelve years and much betterment is going to be forthcoming.

But I did want to speak, and I'm afraid at too much length on the matter of program balance; I say we must have it, and it's the licensee's obligation to deliver.

McCOLLOUGH: Well I sit here with two hats on! One as Chairman of the NAB Board of Directors, and the other as a broadcaster. It has been difficult for me to remain as quiet as I have during the past two days because broadcasters are being kicked back and forth here more than the football will be kicked back and forth tonight in the All Star Game. And I think this situation will continue during any symposium where there is a lack of knowledge of the everyday problems of broadcasting.

One day, what should be done in a conference of this type is to get together: Three members of the FCC, headed by the Chairman; three broadcasters; three lawyers; three educators; perhaps a few others, put them in a room like this; close the door and lock it; then throw the key away—and really have it out!

Everyone has a right to their own opinion. However, when you are speaking for the record, which is the case here, there are some areas in which more privacy is needed in order to assure full discussion.

Along the same line, the NAB has under consideration a sizeable research project; and the Television Information Office in New York is considering the possibility of an Arden House symposium. If undertaken, these projects should develop a number of answers along the lines we have been discussing.

For example, what is a "balanced program"? What is a "good program," and what is a "bad program"? Questions that, at times, defy definition thereby leaving the average broadcaster considerably "up in the air" at times.

The NAB Code activities are being stepped up. One group of people will say the NAB should have stiff Codes, and enforce them. Another group of people will say the NAB hasn't any right to enforce Codes. Both sides of the argument arise constantly.

I have been trying to decide in my own mind what useful opinions have been expressed here during the last day or so. Some good questions have been asked and some good answers have been made. But—have we considered the viewing public fully? Everyone has been talking about their own viewpoint but hardly anyone has talked very much about what the public thinks and wants.

It might not have been a bad idea to invite three people from Michigan Avenue and have them present. They could be given "equal time." You might be surprised at some of the practical and useful answers you would get.

Perhaps it would be a good idea one day to take a group such as we find here and go to a local television station for a symposium of broadcasters, the public, churchmen, political figures, etc., from that particular area. The same questions could be asked. Perhaps we might come a bit nearer to some of the real answers from the public's viewpoint.

NATHANSON: I just wanted to ask Mr. Cone a question, mostly to keep him talking. That is, I don't think he really finished the subject that he started on. I don't want this to sound personal, but I think that you just referred to your own experience here in this connection; you also referred to it yesterday and I had a little trouble putting together the two things you said.

Yesterday, in answer to Jack Coons' question, "Is there real talent available?" to fill the vacuum if there were one you said you doubted it because you'd just been reading—I don't know how many manuscripts—to find a couple of good ones.

And you know, I assumed that this was a good thing—that you were trying to really get the best kind of program. And then today, you say you have practically no influence on the program. You see, it makes it sound as if you were wasting your time, which I'm sure you're not—so I wondered if you would reconcile these for us?

CONE: Well, let me say first of all, I didn't read any 1,500 manuscripts. Fifteen hundred were read by a competent group of judges. This was a contest put on by Hallmark.

This is the one of the few programs on the air, and the only exception in the case of my company, where it is an independently produced program which is not on a regular schedule which has put on Shakespeare and Shaw and Barry and so on, as well as some hopeful originals. There are five or six programs a year. It's a clear exception. Other than this we don't have anything to say.

NATHANSON: I'd like to follow up on what Mr. Cone said earlier, about whether in your opinion it's desirable or not to have advertisers involved in the programming.

CONE: I can answer you very fast. I think advertisers should be involved in no way, any more than we're involved with the Chicago *Tribune* when we place an advertising schedule with them. I've almost always felt this way.

NATHANSON: But why?

CONE: Why I just don't think advertisers should have anything to do with media.

NATHANSON: And are you also suggesting that it isn't necessary as a governmental matter to try to carry out that policy because it's coming about anyway? In other words, this is the sort of policy which is naturally growing up?

CONE: I think so. I think Mr. Paley was right in the statement I read.

NATHANSON: But I suppose that the main thrust of Mr. Barrow's remarks on this subject was not so much what person, or even what organization necessarily, exercised the judgment, but that the judgment was being made with respect to certain kinds of interests, and that the main interest, that still would dominate would be the sponsor's interest, the sponsor's interest in getting what he thought, or what he would be induced to believe, would be the best audience for his product. And that whether he, the sponsor himself does it; whether he does it through his agent; or whether the network does it for him—it's still the same process taking place.

BARROW: That's precisely what I intended to convey!

VOICE: Then I think what we're talking about except for the limited number of channels, is the very same thing that goes on every week in *Life* magazine and every two weeks in *Look* and every month in *Harper's*. I see no difference.

NATHANSON: And it really gets us back to Mr. Pierson's point doesn't it, as to whether there is a substantial difference here between the media, that is, whether you need something else beside the market mechanism. And I don't want to get back to the lawyers' discussion here, but it just seems to me that in a way it comes back to the choice that Mr. Pierson was giving us.

He said: "Well, we'll get this—we'll achieve our objectives eventually through the market; as more stations come on the mass audience will be fragmented, so that even the minority taste will become a substantial factor in the picture." And I think that probably almost all of us would agree that would be wonderful, that would be much better, than the artificial way of doing it; that the real disagreement is whether or not we can wait that long, whether it will come about really, just that way; or whether it's appropriate to do something in the meanwhile, to help it along; whether it's something that the government does either somewhat directly in this program balance idea, or, something indirectly in more complicated difficult ways which apparently we all shy away from. I think that's what Jaffe was kind of pressing us towards; what really particular kinds of interference with the industry operation as it now exists, might be appropriate in the public interest, so that the industry itself, would tend to accomplish these objectives; so that the decisions would all be made within the industry, but, nevertheless, there would be some kind of governing rules which would tend towards the kind of ideal situation which Mr. Pierson himself postulates, as the thing that we'd all love to have if we could have it.

JAFFE: I think Professor Nathanson's right, that Mr. Cone is not the kind of person who on his own speaks his whole mind, and he has a very good one. I talked with him yesterday just about this same thing, and he said a good deal more along this line than he's yet expressed, and he suggested to me that the advertisers themselves possibly were moving in the direction of circulation rather than specific rated programs, and somewhat moving along the line of having the chains possibly sell a group of programs, and thus place their responsibility for circulation on the chain and by the same token increase the responsibility of the chain for the character of the programming, and make it somewhat more possible to put into the whole mix some of these programs that if you had to sell them alone would not possibly be able to pay their way.

It's that kind of statement by him that makes me so interested, and concerned in an intellectual way with what the thinking is going to be by the FCC about the function of the chain. Are they going to emphasize local responsibility, or, are they going to recognize that the chain, as presently set up or as it's moving, is an invaluable vehicle for getting precisely the thing they want to get? That's really why I have my eyes more looking out in the future to these questions than all these we've been talking about, and what their thinking is going to be about the chain.

Is the problem about the chain going to be thought about in old-fashioned anti-trust terms, or, is it going to be looked at from the point of view of this problem of programming, and what is the most likely way in which the industry can organize and get our programming. And I think that's going to become the most important issue before the FCC in the near future.

MINOW: It seems to me one of the great values of this kind of a meeting is to germinate ideas like that. I would welcome guidance and suggestions from a group as distinguished as this on what the government should be doing in this area. It seems to me a very fruitful area of discussion.

PIERSON: I couldn't agree more with what both Chairman Minow and Professor Jaffe have said, and may surprise a lot of people. I think that the idea of the magazine concept is not new; I'm sure it was considered back in the days of radio; my best recollection is that certain difficulties arose between the stations and the network with respect to the split of the revenue, evoked by the networks proceeding on a spot announcement basis and thereby taking away the bread and butter that Mr. Guider referred to.

But it seems to me from what I've understood from people in the industry here, that the magazine concept ought to solve a tremendous number of problems of placing responsibility for programming where it must really be, if the medium is going to be effective.

And I suggested earlier that this would probably involve a modification of the statute which Professor Jaffe believed—somehow or other he doesn't believe that those things will be done.

I disagree with him. The statute has been amended many times since 1934; I think that, if the Commission and the industry agreed upon an elimination of the concept, derived from the statute as now written, that there's a non-delegable control in the broadcaster; and that this control can be legally split so that the responsibility is where the control must and should lie—if the industry were reasonably well united with the Commission on that —I don't think the difficulty in obtaining a modification of the statute presents insurmountable problems at all! Not nearly as much as the modifications they got in Section 315.

I'd like also to go back to the balanced programming concept. I appreciate the comments of Mr. Quaal. That's why I was careful to say at the end of my remarks, that it should be apparent to everybody that I do not represent the industry; and the reasons that I do not is because there's a substantial view in the industry that is precisely the same as Mr. Quaal's. You will find that view, generally, with any station that has a good strong position in the market; and that has itself decided to present a balanced program format. You will not find it among those who diversify—I mean, who have specialized.

Now it always has seemed a little bit presumptuous to me for Mr. Quaal, for example, at WGN, to voluntarily select the kind of format that he wants to do business on—and then insist that the Commission impose his format upon all others who might reach different decisions! I think that Mr. Quaal might even be a better competitor by having to confront people with different ideas, and therefore put him in the position, or give him at least the incentive of improving his own.

Now I didn't say, as Mr. Quaal suggested, that the public was not entitled to balanced programming. My only argument was the way balanced programming should be achieved; whether we get balanced programming out of the market as a result of wide specialization and diversification of station program formats, or, whether we have to get it by imposing stereotyped formats from the top.

Now getting back further into the balanced programming concept, I'm very interested in the views of Professor Jaffe, I respect them very highly. I used to entertain those same views myself.

I have changed them however, perhaps by a little myopia in Washington trying cases, and trying to represent to the Commission what you actually proposed—that I wouldn't have if I were at Cambridge.

But the real problem, after you get away from the generalities in which Professor Jaffe speaks, is to then sit down, and set down first, your public interest goals, in general terms, and then to use the English language or Latin or Greek or anything that the scholars might choose to employ in expressing a human idea, and capturing this in words, so that you can say uniformly, or substantially uniformly: "A station that does this will be serving the public interest."

I submit that this is an impossible task, based on the attempts by the Commission and the industry to date. I could go on and give many examples where the statistical breakdown of one applicant's program would lead you to believe, on any standard that you could generalize on, it was serving the public interest; and another, that on the basis of those standards, you would decide was not.

But, then, if you go out into the field and look at their actual performance; what you've decided on a statistical and summary basis in Washington will only accidentally have any relationship to the reality of the situation in the market. And this is where the tremendous arbitrariness arises in the specification of program types; the Commission has never specified percentages; the Commission has never said that "so much education," is required; or that "so much entertainment is too much."

And they haven't done it because they've shirked their duty, they haven't done it because it's an impossible thing to generalize on for 5,000 stations.

Now I'd like one more personal remark. I had an intimation from Chairman Minow, at the recess, that he thought that I was somewhat personal in my handling of the problem. I apologized to him then; I want to apologize on the record for it. I suppose it's the zest for advocacy which I, as a matter of constant practice in earning a living, am cursed; I really intended to refer to Mr. Minow as exemplifying, most recently, the thing that I think is wrong. I think that he is correct, as I have agreed before, that he didn't start this; he's only using the tools that have been previously built, and provided at the Commission; he's doing it with a great deal more vigor than has occurred since Mr. Fly; but I certainly do not think that Mr. Minow does anything more than exemplify the problem.

MCCOLLOUGH: Professor Jaffe said this morning, "What we are trying to get is good television." Now I wonder if he would say, for the record—and this is not a facetious remark, this is a very serious remark from a broadcaster, and I think it would be of interest to all 5,000 operating broadcasters in this country—I just wondered if for, just about two minutes, you could say what you think would be "good television." Mr. Jaffe could do a real service for the broadcasting industry and a lot of other people if he did express, from his innermost mind what he thinks would be good television—because we'd all be apt to take it pretty seriously and listen to him.

JAFFE: Well I'm afraid I'll have to decline the invitation. Because, as has been pointed out, it's impossible to define what would be good television. And if I made that statement, all I meant was that I would like to see "good television."

Yesterday you said that you had yet to hear a definition of a "good program" and a "bad program." And I'm sure you're going to go through the rest of your life without getting a definition; except that I've kind of "flirted" with the notion of putting it this way:

"All programs are good." That ought to help you. All television and all programs are good programs. I've tried to speak only insofar as government regulations are concerned, as opposed to my feeling as a person, what I want to look at, what's good for me, or what's good for somebody else, or what's good to the critic! I think the more critics we have the better. But as far as government regulation went, I tried to put my thought in terms of the notion of providing certain services: News; Agriculture; Entertainment; Education; highbrow shows; lowbrow shows—and by those categories I refer to well received categories. It's every so often said that "Nobody has the remotest idea as to whether there's any distinction between Shakespeare and Mickey Spillane." I just don't believe there's a person around the table who doesn't believe that our culture has established a difference between Shakespeare and Mickey Spillane. Certainly in our schools we have an idea that some things are great. As I said yesterday, we teach the Gettysburg Address, we regard it as great. We accept this, that Lincoln was a great man; and he spoke great things. And all that I suggested was that I would like to see a television in which all of these different things were represented; all of them are good, even Mickey Spillane. I'm prepared to go that far. They're all good. But I think that the objective is for balance.

McCOLLOUGH: It depends on a person's viewpoint, a little bit like the man who was walking down the street and another man asked him: "How's your wife?" And he said: "Compared to what?"

JAFFE: Well there is important difference of opinion; I don't want to pontificate; Mr. Quaal thinks that there is some such notion, that he can run a radio station on the basis of some such notion—and you apparently don't think so.

McCOLLOUGH: Oh, I think we can; I'm willing to buy your concept, actually, and Chairman Minow's.

PIERSON: Well I think as long as comparative cases have come up—we analyzed in our office in 1950, thirty-six of them, and the volume and the record of program evidence was tremendous—tens of thousands of pages. And if you take those thirty-six decisions where the Commission was attempting to determine the differences between applicants with respect to program proposals, you will have a hard time finding a significant difference. You will find that the Commission held that they were all substantially equal in by far the largest number of cases.

And in the cases where they did find a difference that difference was not generally controlling in the final decision. In only two cases that I recall it was controlling, and in those cases the reasons given for the choice of one over the other was based upon about 30 minutes of programming in each case. If you could justify this as a highly significant thing in the public interest, I'd like to have it explained.

The fact is, that in comparative cases, the program comparisons have been of practically no value to the Commission; and moreover, they have cost the Commission and the government and the applicants thousands and hundreds of thousands of dollars to prepare, even the storage of this thing alone must run the Government into the hundreds of thousands of dollars.

REINSCH: At this point the Chair must get arbitrary; there are several members who have not participated this morning; we have sixteen minutes to go; I'll start to my left—and unfortunately there has to be a time limitation of about two minutes for each one, and we'll start with Peter Goelet!

GOELET: I will have to omit some of the remarks I had prepared, and so admitting for some oversimplification I will start with an opinion that I would like to express. As a layman, I think that the requirements the FCC is making of licensees, as stated by Chairman Minow, are valid and in the public interest. I'd also like to make the following recommendations: That programs be divorced from individual sponsorship; that ratings be qualitative as well as quantitative. This qualitative approach is a service we have been rendering and that many other companies and firms render.

I may not have time to develop this, but I also wanted to suggest—as a corollary measure—that newspaper columnists give more attention to serious discussion, rather than trivial gossip. I would like to call on Messrs. Agee and McGill to use their very great stature in their journalistic profession to at least give consideration to advancing that idea.

I would like to make just one final remark. There has been much talk about publicity, and the value of it, and so on; and also some feeling on the part of the industry that they have not been well treated.

Now the organization I happen to head, which taps the opinions of people numbering nearly fifty million, has just issued a report which was rather unfavorable to the industry.

I would like to go on record that this has been given the widest publication; that at no time have we had the slightest resentment on the part of the industry; that Mr. Taishoff and everyone else concerned have given us most wonderful consideration.

I think as long as public opinion is given that much exposure, there's bound to drain off some of the resentment that exists. And I would like to go on record as thanking everyone concerned for the very fine treatment we've had.

McGILL: I hesitate to speak at all, because I can't speak from the legal viewpoint or the technical. It occurs to me as a dealer

in words, that one of the vital problems of the industry is one—
and I hate to use the phrase, "public relations."

For example, I think it would be very bad, if a very pragmatic
and inescapable fact which has been talked about here, were just
boldly presented to the public, namely that we must make a profit,
and therefore we haven't got time, or we haven't got the ability, to
really go at the business of programming. Now this is true, and I
see it. But it would be very bad public relations–wise if we said,
only a profit making business we must be—and I have every
admiration for the profit making system, don't misunderstand
me—but the point is, we don't want to get the image of saying we
can't do things because we must make a profit. We must make a
profit, but I don't think we ought to let that get in.

And then I would like to comment quickly: We've had a race
riot here in this city, just a week or two ago. This is explosion of
long-enduring and I think continually aggravated conditions. This
is going to be true in all of our cities large and small. And I think
that newspapers and the broadcasting media, have a real obligation, a real responsibility to try to deal with these things before
they become riots. In other words, if as you get into these particularly dangerous slum areas, you could find some sort of leadership which could be organized. These people have an enormous
frustration. They can't go talk to the mayor; they can't really approach their aldermen, or their councilmen; they develop a feeling that they are cut off from life; cut off from the life of this
country. Now what do they want? What are their lacks? If we
could get more and more programs of a social nature, I think it
would have enormous audience appeal. Don't wait till they become riots to put them on television and radio.

This fellow Martin Luther King, whatever you may think of
him, is a very valuable leader for the Negro people—the way he
has gone at it, the passive resistance idea, playing down the
violent approach.

This city had a very interesting election, I am told, in its taxicab business where they threw out a racketeer of the Hoffa type
so-called, so explained to me. And their explanation was, that
there were so many taxicab drivers, Negro taxicab drivers who
had a college education or part of one—who knew what they
were doing.

Well, here's a resource that could be tapped to help develop leadership in panel shows or discussions. I don't know if this makes any sense or not, but I think that all of our cities are growing; the social problems are aggravated by slums and unemployment of people with no skills, in a time when you must have skills. I think we have an obligation, the newspapers perhaps more than anybody else, or as much certainly, to work in this field of programming. And I don't know how to do it, but I think here's a real opportunity for leadership and public social service.

NOVIK: Yesterday everything was about TV. Radio was brought in by Governor Collins; it was brought in by the Chairman, so I want to go back. I tried to put it down on paper, and then the learned counsel to the left injected a couple of points on balanced programming. For the best statement of balanced programming, I bow to Ward.

I am scared, and I was worried; maybe I didn't understand Professor Jaffe about going back to free speech, until he explained to Clair what he thought "free speech" meant in terms of programming—and I buy that in whole.

Ted was worried about the Supreme Court, and then the learned Dean kind of agreed with him; and finally they solved it by saying: "Maybe you'll get a better break in the Supreme Courts," or "it will go back to the Supreme Court."

I am going to be 58. I have been in this business thirty years. I can no longer wait thirty years for a Supreme Court to decide how you solve in New York City the problem that you've just referred to? Not only on the race riot, but the riot of the population; the riot of ignorance; the riot of uninformed—or not-informed America.

So I say, I must start. The Chairman is right in terms of the law. And until he's challenged in courts, this is the law. Therefore I say, my concern is:

"What has happened to radio?"

A TV explosion occurs and radio operators who made a great deal of money and got their licenses by a competitive hearing, they ran for cover. The best brains were converted from the radio part of the shop over to the TV shop; the best brains; the best money to TV—and radio went down the sewer!

And what do we find: The little 250-Watters, I tried to suggest yesterday, set the patterns about the program. Record companies have actually made more money in recent years than radio and television put together; they've turned out 40 popular records.

And with that went the whole swing of radio programming.

And I say to Ted, what bothers me is the future of America; what bothers me, what scares me, is what is happening at the present time when talk is art. Gentlemen, I repeat again, on 90 per cent of the radio stations—don't hold Novik to figures, I haven't got the Commission staff—on 72 per cent of the radio stations in the United States no one can go on if he speaks more than five minutes, and the five minutes is pretty much limited to an announcer that is trying to speak as rapidly as Novik is at this present moment. But he has a different purpose—because the jingle that follows with Coca-Cola is in the same speed and therefore he can't compete.

I say: Ward gave you the answer. Let us go back to where we started at the beginning. We had greater diversification; we had diversification, years ago. We had better program service. It isn't a mystery "What do we mean by program service?"

I submit Clair McCollough's radio program schedule of 1932, of 1941, of 1961 as against the 78 per cent of the radio stations that are not carrying that program service.

I offer—and really I must apologize, and you keep it out of your paper. For Novik to defend WGN owned by the Chicago *Tribune* is really great. This only happens in America. But here are the facts: We're not talking about mystery; we know what we mean by a "program service in radio." Either that or all of us, all of you gentlemen, were crazy for 30 years when you gave that program service. It wasn't challenged in court; no one said it was unconstitutional for the FCC to grant licenses, to review licenses—and gentlemen, may I remind the elder statesmen and Professor Jaffe especially, originally licenses were given only for six months.

It was only because some budgetary-minded committee of the Congress tried to save a couple of thousand dollars and then they decided to save a thousand dollars by bringing the license up to one year first, and then three years.

Well let me close, let me skip all of this. I was going to give a very great quote; I submit *Broadcasting* magazine, when it said: "The purpose, the struggle is minds in conflict between the advertiser and the service." When it said: "We ought to compare this with the 24-sheet *Billboard* and the New York *Times*. Both serve useful purposes, but it hardly need to be said that their natures are dissimilar."

Gentlemen, I spent a great deal of time worrying about this.

We came up with the suggestion at the last conference in Ohio that we ought to hold a Radio Conference. I don't want to know who suggested the agenda.

All I say to the Chairman is, please don't commit yourself until you've heard the whole case as to why this conference should be called by the FCC; it should be called by the Federal Communications Commission, not by the NAB, or by any group, or by Ohio State or Northwestern—because I think you can give it meaning, you can give guidance, and you can let the broadcasters know, who want to take this job of theirs seriously, whether they are doing the right thing or they're doing the wrong thing.

And I wind up, if we have a better informed America, if talk is not barred just because it isn't good profit or it isn't what they think to be "good business"—then we will have a better America.

But as we are going today, the American people via radio are not informed as to what's happening in the world; and they're not informed as to what's happening in the Congress, and they are not better citizens, and therefore they are subject to the race riot mentality and psychology that comes.

I too want to fight Communism, but I want to fight it with a better informed America, rather than the America that will run 5,000 radio stations against 800, but with exactly the same format. There is no choice for the majority except to give us the tastes of the minority.

AGEE: I'm in the position of the commentator following the jingle, so I'll really abridge. Sigma Delta Chi throughout its 52-year history always has opposed censorship in any form in the realm of the printed and spoken word—the realm of news, opinions, ideas, creativity.

Our professional journalistic society, composed of 16,000 newsmen and students representing newspapers, magazines, radio and television, repeatedly has warned that governmental regulation in this realm of ideas so vital in a democracy can be exceedingly dangerous.

History bears tragic testimony to the fallacy that a people can surrender a portion of its freedom without surrendering it all. Once the camel gets his nose under the tent, his neck and body soon follow.

Sigma Delta Chi is dedicated to the highest ideals of journalism. It is constantly endeavoring to raise the standards of our profession. So it is that we look with pleasure at the giant strides made by the television industry during its fledgling years, and we too share the hope of all that the quality of programming will continue to improve.

But censorship by threat is as insidious as censorship by prior restraint; both are alien to our democratic form of government. When government interposes itself in the free market place of ideas—even, admittedly, with the very best of motives—we lose far, far more than we can possibly gain.

As the National President of our society, E. W. Scripps II, declared before the Federal Communications Commission in December, 1959:

"We all know the people of this country are intelligent and responsible. If they were not our free democratic society would have floundered long ago.

"Our society is built on the concept that its free people can guide it best.

"Every time the government steps in to take away from the people another function which rightly belongs to them, the democratic system and its ability to govern itself is further crippled.

"The danger of such intervention, which could put in the hands of a governmental agency unwarranted power, is a constant threat to our society.

"It is not entirely unreasonable to assume that hasty action . . . could put in the hands of a future administration a dangerous weapon which could seriously strangle the people's free access to information so essential to the healthy continuation of a truly free society."

Those words of Ted Scripps are as applicable today as then, and I speak today both personally and in his behalf as National President of Sigma Delta Chi.

The men and women who manage and conduct our radio and television industry are responsible and intelligent people, willing to cooperate with the public in improving its broadcast fare. May we all work together for this worthy aim without forfeiting even a small portion of our heritage as a free people.

GUIDER: All I want to say, Mr. Chairman, is that I wish every other TV licensee could have sat at this table and heard what's happened in the last three sessions of the last three half days. I think it's been a wonderful thing; I think there is an answer to Clair McCollough, "What did we do?" I think we've cleared the air of a lot of misconceptions as to what was in each other's minds.

I think it's been a wonderful meeting and I hope there'll be more like it, whenever they're possible.

MICKELSON: Well I'm glad that I have the opportunity before we close to deny the ugly rumor that's been spreading around the halls—that my trip here was subsidized by Mickey Spillane. There is one thing that I would like to have an opportunity to say. It seems to me that through this discussion this morning perhaps the one central issue that we've been returning to constantly, one way or another, is the question of balanced programming. But the principal frame of reference toward balanced programming this morning, I believe, has been through the question of advertiser control.

Now having sat in the spot for a number of years where I think I've been squarely up against those pressures—and I believe the only one here who has been through it on a network basis—I do have some credentials, I believe, to say a couple of words about it as it applies to this whole question of balanced programming and the relationship of the FCC to broadcasting in the country.

Unfortunately at a meeting of this sort we always get all tangled up in generalizations, and we're generalizing I think frequently from far too little evidence. Now for example, the generalization has gone in the last two days, because Chrysler objected to the mention of the name "Lincoln" in the Andersonville program, that Chrysler was exercising advertising control on the program which was finally named, "The Trial of Captain Wirtz"; or, because the American Gas Association in one program, I think rather stupidly, objected to the word "gas" in "gas chamber" in the Nuremberg trials, all you heard was a "beep" at that point.

But it seems to me this is really not very significant. These are rather external and superficial aspects of this whole thing and don't really have much influence on the real question of balanced programming and advertiser control.

Now if I could have just about 60 seconds, I'd like to say that this question really takes some analysis and takes a breaking out into its various parts. With respect to advertiser control I think we can safely generalize that there is virtually no positive advertiser control on informational programs. I suppose there is some negative control, at least a control which is exercised on the part of the producer who is afraid he might offend a sponsor if he slips in something that the sponsor might take offense to and he might lose the commercial sponsorship. But I honestly believe that that's a very negligible factor.

I would guess also that the direct advertiser control on the program is also relatively limited. I do however believe, and I'm quite certain that there is an indirect advertiser control which takes two forms: The first of these forms of course relates to the selection of the program schedule itself. The network has to be able to sell out its programs scheduled in order to be able to live economically in a healthy economic environment and be able to get the money to support the other activities that it does. And in the selection I believe the advertiser does exercise some control in the selection of the program.

Secondly, I would think that the advertiser exercises a certain amount of control in the nature of the program and I would be willing to concede has a tendency to make programs blander than they otherwise might be if there weren't these negative controls being exercised by the advertiser through his influence.

Now it seems to me this is the crucial element when we're talking about balanced programming. If this has a tendency to slightly upset the program balance, then this is the issue toward which we ought to direct ourselves in trying to come up with some solution for this problem of achieving program balance.

It seems to me we've discussed here a possible solution of this program, a solution which would give the broadcaster the opportunity to work his way out of it rather than to ask the imposition of government control in an effort to work the broadcaster's way out. And this is through this magazine concept. Now I realize that there are financial problems involved, that this bumps up into some economic problems; it bumps up into some legal problems. It works very well I think in England where the ITA operates on this basis. But this at least gives the broadcaster the opportunity to develop his own program schedule; to present his own program schedule as he wants to, and rotate the commercials within that schedule so that the advertiser never knows what program he's going to be running adjacent to. This gives the broadcaster the real program control, it seems to me.

Now the reason I make quite a point out of this whole thing is the fact that the alternative to that as it's been outlined here during the course of these two days, has been the imposition of government control and it seems to me that one is infinitely better than the other.

The trouble is, with a little government control, you can never hold it to a "little" government control, and you get this creeping control that eventually would extend up to the point, in all probability, where it might even be imposed over the expression of opinion. And that I'm sure is something we want to stay out of.

Appendix III

WARREN K. AGEE

Former Dean of the School of Journalism at West Virginia University, Warren K. Agee became National Executive Officer of Sigma Delta Chi in November, 1960. He has also headed the American Society of Journalism School Administrators and the Association for Education in Journalism.

ROSCOE L. BARROW

Roscoe L. Barrow, consultant to the Federal Communications Commission, has been Dean of the University of Cincinnati Law School since 1953. In the period 1955–57 he conducted a comprehensive study of the television industry as Director of the Network Study Staff of a House of Representatives Committee. The findings of this study are published in *Network Broadcasting*.

LEROY COLLINS

President of the National Association of Broadcasters, LeRoy Collins has been Governor of Florida, Chairman of the Southern and National Governors' Conference, and Permanent Chairman of the 1960 Democratic National Convention. He also serves as Chairman of the National Advisory Council of the Area Redevelopment Administration and as a member of the Peace Corps Advisory Council.

FAIRFAX M. CONE

Chairman of the Executive Committee of Foote, Cone and Belding, Fairfax M. Cone is a past Chairman of both the American Association of Advertising Agencies and The Advertising Council. His other

249

duties include being a Trustee of the University of Chicago, a member of the Chicago Board of Education, and a Trustee of Channel 11, Chicago's educational television outlet.

JOHN E. COONS

Mr. Coons is Associate Professor of Law at Northwestern University. He acted as Director of the Conference on Freedom and Responsibility in Broadcasting.

PETER GOELET

Founder and President of the National Audience Board, Inc., Peter Goelet also has worked on the National Board of Review and is a member of the Academy of TV Arts and Sciences and the Radio and Television Executives Society. In 1932 he established and operated Station WGNY in Newburgh, New York.

JOHN W. GUIDER

Presently President and General Manager of Mt. Washington TV-FM, John W. Guider has been a professor of radio law and is a member of the Bars of the District of Columbia, New Hampshire, the Supreme Court of the United States, and the Federal Communications Commission.

LOUIS L. JAFFE

A specialist in administrative law, Louis L. Jaffe conducts a seminar on the Federal Communications Commission as an example of the administrative process. Mr. Jaffe is a faculty member of the Law School of Harvard University and is writing a treatise on administrative action.

CHARLES H. KING

Charles H. King has been on the faculty of Detroit College of Law since 1937 and the Dean since 1944. He was Republican nominee for the Michigan Supreme Court in 1952 and served as a Commissioner of the Federal Communications Commission, 1960–61.

CLAIR R. MCCOLLOUGH

Actively associated with broadcasting projects for over thirty years, Clair R. McCollough is now Chairman of the Joint Radio and TV Boards of the National Association of Broadcasters, Chairman of Television Information Office and Member of the Board of Directors, Television Bureau of Advertising.

RALPH MCGILL

Ralph McGill, 1958 recipient of the Pulitzer Prize for Outstanding Editorial Writing, has been on the staff of the *Atlanta Constitution* since 1929 and is now Editor-Publisher. His daily columns—mostly on national and southern politics—have been collected into four volumes.

SIG MICKELSON

As Vice-President of TIME-LIFE BROADCAST, Inc., Mr. Mickelson is charged with the responsibility for the international broadcasting interests of TIME, Inc. He was previously President of the CBS News Division of the Columbia Broadcasting System, Inc., and Vice-President of the parent corporation. Prior to joining CBS, he taught journalism at Louisiana State University, the University of Kansas, and the University of Minnesota.

NEWTON N. MINOW

Chairman of the Federal Communications Commission, Newton N. Minow has varied experience in both law and broadcasting. He served as Administrative Assistant to Adlai Stevenson when the latter was Governor of Illinois and was an active participant in the campaigns of the last three national elections. Chairman Minow was also a law clerk to Chief Justice Vinson.

NATHANIEL NATHANSON

Professor of Law at Northwestern University, Mr. Nathanson is an author and specialist in the field of administrative law and a member of the Executive Committee of the Administrative Conference of the United States.

MORRIS NOVIK

Mr. Novik is a radio consultant in New York City. He has been active in the industry for many years as a broadcaster and labor expert.

W. THEODORE PIERSON

Senior partner of the law firm of Pierson, Ball and Dowd in Washington, D. C., W. Theodore Pierson is a member of the District of Columbia Bar, the Federal Communications Bar Association, and the American Bar Association.

WARD L. QUAAL

Executive Vice-President and General Manager of WGN, Inc., Ward L. Quaal is also President of KDAL, Inc., Duluth. He was previously Director of Crosley Broadcasting Corporation, Director of Mt. Olympus Films, and Director of Clear Channel Broadcasting Service.

J. LEONARD REINSCH

Communications Consultant to President Kennedy, J. Leonard Reinsch handled arrangements for the "Great Debates" in the 1960 presidential campaign. He is Executive Director of Stations WSB, WHIO, and WSOC in the southeastern United States.

SOL TAISHOFF

Sol Taishoff, winner of the Distinguished Service Journalism Award and the Wells Key, is President, Editor, and Publisher of *Broadcasting* magazine and *Television* magazine. He has also served as National President of Sigma Delta Chi and this past year was President of Broadcast Pioneers.

JOHN W. TAYLOR

The pioneer of educational television, Dr. John W. Taylor inaugurated the first radio correspondence course for college credit and the first TV college course while President of the University of Louisville. He is now Executive Director of the Chicago Educational Television Association and of WTTW-TV, Chicago.

DUE